CHAUCER STUDIES XXI

CHAUCER ON LOVE, KNOWLEDGE AND SIGHT

In this study Norman Klassen shows how Chaucer explores the complexity of the relationship between love and knowledge through recourse to the motif of sight. The convention of love at first sight involves love, knowledge and sight, but insists that the claims of love and the realm of the rational are in strict opposition. In the metaphysical tradition, however, the relationship between love, knowledge and sight is more complex and subtly nuanced, manifesting qualities both of opposition and of symbiosis. The situation is similar in late medieval natural philosophy, heavily indebted to the importance of sight and light in metaphysics, in which visual concepts represent the confidence to understand the natural order and are central to discussions of how the mind acquires knowledge, while being invoked to explain, and in some instances to express, what happens in love at first sight.

The author argues that Chaucer is unorthodox in exploiting the possibilities for using sight both to express emotional experience and to accentuate rationality at the same time. The conventional opposition of love and knowledge in the phenomenon of love at first sight gives way in Chaucer's development of love, knowledge, and sight to a symbiosis in his love poetry. The complexity of this relationship draws attention to his own role as artificer, as one who in the process of articulating the effects of love at first sight cannot help but bring together love and knowledge in ways not anticipated by the conventions of love poetry.

NORMAN KLASSEN is a Social Sciences and Humanities Research Council of Canada postdoctoral fellow at the Centre for Medieval Studies and the Department of English Language and Literature at the University of Minnesota.

CHAUCER STUDIES
ISSN 0261–9822

CHAUCER ON
LOVE, KNOWLEDGE
AND SIGHT

NORMAN KLASSEN

D. S. BREWER

First published 1995
D. S. Brewer, Cambridge

ISBN 0 85991 464 X

D. S. Brewer is an imprint of Boydell & Brewer Ltd
PO Box 9, Woodbridge, Suffolk IP12 3DF, UK
and of Boydell & Brewer Inc.
PO Box 41026, Rochester, NY 14604–4126, USA

British Library Cataloguing-in-Publication Data

Klassen, Norman
    Chaucer on Love, Knowledge and Sight. –
    (Chaucer Studies, ISSN 0261–9822; Vol. 21)
    I.Title   II. Series
    821.1
    ISBN 0–85991–464–X

Library of Congress Cataloging-in-Publication Data

Klassen, Norman, 1962–
    Chaucer on love, knowledge, and sight / Norman Klassen.
        p.   cm. – (Chaucer studies, ISSN 0261–9822 ; 21)
    Includes bibliographical references and index.
    ISBN 0–85991–464–X (hardback)
    1. Chaucer, Geoffrey, d.1400 – Philosophy.   2. Knowledge,
Theory of, in literature.   3. Philosophy, Medieval, in literature.
4. Vision in literature.   5. Love in literature.   I. Title.
II. Series.
P R1933.K6K58   1995
821'. – 1dc20   94–47959

The paper used in this publication meets the minimum requirements
of American National Standard for Information Sciences –
Permanence of Paper for Printed Library Materials, ANSI Z39.48–1984

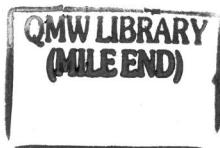

Printed in Great Britain by
Boydell & Brewer Ltd, Woodbridge, Suffolk

Contents

To Anne

Acknowledgements

I am grateful for the guidance I have received on this project from Helen Cooper at University College, Oxford. She has been a constant source of support, insights, and instruction, and she has been extremely generous with her time. I would also like to thank Douglas Gray and Peter Brown for their careful examination of my work, and Eric Stanley for the opportunity to present work-in-progress in the seminar on medieval literature at Oxford University.

I am grateful too for the support and encouragement of many friends. I would particularly like to thank Peter Erb for reading my work with such interest, and for his incisive comments. Thanks also to Tony Cummins for his meticulous reading of an early draft.

I would also like to thank the Social Sciences and Humanities Research Council of Canada for partially funding this study.

My wife, Anne, has provided abundant encouragement throughout this project. It gives me a great deal of pleasure to dedicate this book to her.

Abbreviations

ACW   Ancient Christian Writers: The Works of the Fathers in Translation. Ed. Johannes Quasten et al. Westminster, Maryland, 1946–.

CHLMP   *The Cambridge History of Later Medieval Philosophy.* Ed. N. Kretzmann et al. Cambridge, 1982.

EETS   Early English Text Society

MED   *Middle English Dictionary.* Ed. Hans Kurath, Sherman M. Kuhn, et al. Ann Arbor, 1956–.

PL   Patrologia Latina. Ed. J.-P. Migne. Paris, 1844–65.

Introduction

Let us begin with an example from Chaucer's poetry that is more complicated than it at first appears. In the Knight's Tale, the conflict between Palamon and Arcite begins with the very familiar introduction of Emily. The description draws on a number of motifs that are immediately familiar to the reader of medieval romance: the temporal setting is that of May, the month of lovers; we meet Emily in a garden very much like the garden which Amans from *Le Roman de la Rose* entered, and both recall the comparison of the beloved with an enclosed garden in the biblical Song of Songs; the beautiful Emily is compared to flowers, especially the rose; and, most importantly, when Palamon and then Arcite see her, her beauty instantly pierces them to the heart, inflicting on them the intense and overriding pain of love. What specifically has been overridden is the faculty of reason in the lovers, and what ensues is a long conflict between the claims of love and the realm of the rational.

This is the convention of love at first sight, and Chaucer, like Boccaccio before him in *Il Teseida*, expresses it beautifully. From the first exchange between Palamon and Arcite onward, however, elements of the tale suggest that Chaucer has more sophisticated plans than a straightforward restatement of the opposition of love and rational knowledge. While what has happened to both knights typically entails the overthrow of reason, the exchange between Palamon and Arcite on what this event means is markedly rational. Both protagonists articulate long defences of their positions, Arcite even buttressing his with a quotation that appears in *The Consolation of Philosophy*. When the knights are separated, Chaucer has both victims wax philosophical on the role of Fortune and the question of governance. He then pauses to ask another question, a *demande d'amour* on which of the two lovers is worse off. This succession of teasing intellectual problems is striking in the context of a convention in which knowledge is supposedly banished. Coexistent with the dramatic struggle that results from love at first sight are hallmarks of a rationalism that the convention strictly forbids.

The Knight's Tale unfolds several philosophical observations in the context of love. The manner in which Chaucer maintains audience interest in the love story while adding a serious intellectual component indicates that for him the concepts of love and knowledge function together. They do so even as their proximity to one another highlights the difference between them and fulfils the expectation of opposition. The motif of sight is integral to both discourses and contributes both to the sharpened sense of opposition and the symbiosis: if vision impels the love conflict, it also impels the understanding towards which

Theseus is working. The importance of sight is underscored by its potency in love; it is folded back into the Knight's Tale in ways that connect the potentiality of sight with various strains of loving and knowing.

Chaucer explores this duality of opposition and mutuality with reference to love, knowledge, and sight throughout his *oeuvre*. Other poets such as Jean de Meun, Dante, and the *Pearl*-poet also develop their poetic works to create a more complex system of love and knowledge, one in which they themselves are implicated as rational and rationalizing artificers. Far from lamenting his weakness as an artist or the awkwardness of his presence, Chaucer depicts and affirms the place of the poet in the telling 'of loveris up and doun.' The conventional opposition of love and reason, so prevalent in love poetry of all periods, gives way in the poetry of Chaucer and certain other medieval poets to a degree of complexity, paradox, and fruitful possibility; it will do so again in the poetry of Donne.

The investigation of how Chaucer effects this analysis of the relationship between love and knowledge in terms of sight requires a solid understanding of the ubiquitous presence of visual motifs in metaphysics and natural philosophy. The complex relationship between love, knowledge, and sight is revealed in metaphysics, and subsequently in natural philosophy, as one of parasitic hostility and symbiosis. Metaphysics provides the impetus for an appeal to visual concepts throughout the Middle Ages with reference to love and knowledge. From analogies based on sight as the most important of the five senses to expressions of sheer delight about visual phenomena, from sermons against lechery, which begins with sight, to a vision of Christ that leads to love, ideas of Beauty and Truth find expression through appeal to the eye. In thirteenth- and fourteenth-century natural philosophy, the physics of sight gains fresh currency through the metaphysical tradition and a fusion of Western and Arabic naturalistic thought. Many medieval thinkers hold a proper understanding of the principles of light to be the foundation for developing an inquiry into the processes of nature. The concepts of this area of thought and confidence in the centrality of sight spill over into philosophy as sight becomes strongly associated with varieties of knowledge. Sight as a science also figures prominently in naturalistic efforts to explain rationally the processes of love.

The development of such concepts in the poetry of Dante, Jean de Meun, the *Pearl*-poet, and Chaucer is most easily traced by beginning with the convention of love at first sight. Such an approach is somewhat arbitrary given the complexity of the interrelationships between love, knowledge, and sight. This convention, however, brings these three terms together in a very simple way (at least on the surface of it); it accentuates the importance of vision as the basis of a relationship of hostility between love and knowledge. Furthermore, the convention is central to medieval love poetry. Where the language of metaphysics overlaps with that of erotic love hostility gives way to symbiosis. Poets build on the complexity of the relationship between love, knowledge, and sight to explore the erotic discourse of love at first sight. Appreciating the symbiosis that results from the shared language of spiritual and erotic love enhances our awareness of the symbiosis of love and knowledge that derives from naturalistic concepts. Complicating the story of *Le Roman de la Rose*, Jean de Meun develops a number of naturalistic ideas of sight that together serve as an interpretive crux for the poem. Following his example, Chaucer uses a range of concepts related to physical vision to extend the interplay of love and rationality. This system of hostility and symbiosis points to and helps explain Chaucer's deep interest in the poetic yet rational handling of the subject of love, putting into context his sense of limitation, interest in the observer, and awareness of his own recurring presence.

This is an interdisciplinary study. It benefits considerably from the recent work done in the late medieval period that recognizes the complexity of late medieval intellectual trends. Metaphysical assumptions and questions, humanistic confidence, a profound interest in nature, and epistemology all interpenetrate in this period, especially in terms of vision. More and more modern scholarly efforts in understanding fourteenth-century thought are being devoted to the borderlands between the discourses of philosophy, theology, psychology, and literature.[1] Such explorations often begin and end with observations – presented with due caution – on the strange but apparent overlaps in this border area.

This study seeks to participate in the enterprise that can make these areas more mutually accessible and it seeks to do so from the quadrant of Chaucer's poetry. The categories of love and knowledge in particular are as relevant to this fourteenth-century poet as they are to the philosopher or psychologist, but Chaucer approaches them with a different agenda, one formed by literary convention and authorial self-interest as well as by his metaphysical and scientific interests. Points of solid contact therefore exist but the rigour is defined differently. Chaucer's poetry, particularly his handling of visual motifs, reveals a conscious bringing together of various strands of inquiry. Through vision he appeals to the doctrine of illumination, physical representation in aesthetics, revived interest in optical theory, and the widespread fourteenth-century discourse of epistemology. He does so for reasons that involve his central concerns as a love poet.

---

1   Good examples of this interest in the potential interpenetration of areas are Arthur Stephen McGrade, 'Enjoyment at Oxford after Ockham: Philosophy, Psychology, and the Love of God,' in *From Ockham to Wyclif: Studies in Church History* Subsidia 5, ed. Anne Hudson and Michael Wilks, Oxford, 1987, 63–88; William J. Courtenay, 'Between Despair and Love. Some Late Medieval Modifications of Augustine's Teaching on Fruition and Psychic States,' in *Augustine, the Harvest, and Theology (1300–1650)*, ed. Kenneth Hagen, Leiden, 1990, 5–20. Early in his paper, McGrade explains his exemplary approach: 'For these two purposes, then – to add to our ways of interpreting the rest of medieval culture and to discover intrinsically valuable, disciplined psychological thought – we may do well to look into scholastic discussions of such topics as enjoyment' (65).

1

An Eye For Truth and Beauty
A Metaphysical Preface to Middle English Literature of Love and Knowledge

> No caress is sweeter than your charity and no love is more rewarding than the love of your truth, which shines in beauty above all else.[1]　　　　　(Augustine)

> The parasite always plugs into the system; the parasite is always there; it is inevitable. The parasite is the third in a trivial model, the three-branched star. Here now is the relation that cannot be analyzed; that is to say, there is none simpler. Here then is the beginning of intersubjectivity. The third is always there, god or demon, reason or noise.[2]
> 　　　　　(Michel Serres)

In the *Confessions* and throughout his writings Augustine persistently attempts to articulate, often with beautiful results, the ineffable relationship between love and knowledge. He recognizes, as the passage quoted above attests, the difficulty of ordering these categories, the sublime relationship between them which, with reference to the mystical union of the soul with God, verges on complete fusion of emotional and intellectual experience. And he intuitively understands the value of metaphors of seeing and light when attempting to grapple with these concepts. Vision provides a sense of immediacy; it can connote apprehension of truth and beauty; and it can be made to apply to the realm of the senses as well as to the realm of the numinous.

The relationship between love and knowledge is, throughout medieval

---

[1]   Augustine, *Confessions*, trans. R.S. Pine-Coffin, London, 1961, 2.6. 'Sed neque blandius est aliquid tua caritate nec amatur quicquam salubrius quam illa prae cunctis formosa et luminosa veritas tua.' Augustine, *Confessiones*, ed. Martin Skutella with corrections by H. Juergens and W. Schaub, Stuttgart, 1981.

[2]   Michel Serres, *The Parasite*, trans. Lawrence R. Schehr, Baltimore, 1982, 63. 'Toujours vient se brancher le parasite. Le parasite est toujours là, il est inévitable. Il est en tiers sur le schéma trivial, sur l'étoile à trois branches. Voici la relation inanalysable, j'entends par là qu'il n'en est aucune plus simple. Voici comment commence l'intersubjectivité. Le tiers est toujours là, dieu ou démon, raison, rumeur.' Michel Serres, *Le Parasite*, Paris, 1980, 85.

metaphysics, a parasitic one, bearing the features both of hostility and symbiosis. There is hostility in this relationship, marked by the urge to distinguish and prioritize between love and knowledge that always persists. But parasitism can also describe a relationship of symbiosis: hostility gives way to hospitality. There is hospitality, or symbiosis, between love and knowledge in the recognition that the relationship in some ways defies expression, and that the principle of paradox is integral to the discourse. Love and knowledge operate together as a system, to use Michel Serres' term, one that extends well beyond medieval metaphysics into the realm of natural philosophy and ultimately that of literature. In this system vision functions as the representation of the parasite, the third in a three-branched star. It gives the system, when applied either to an eschatological vision or to the effects of a beautiful woman's piercing glance, the aspect of utter simplicity. But such simplicity is, as Serres suggests, just the beginning. We find in the medieval formulations of love, knowledge, and vision something like gods or demons, reason or noise. Vision becomes a key concept to signal the interpenetration of ideas, which when traced through to Chaucer's poetic reveals his complex attitude towards love and knowledge, and the poet's task.

Sight in Tradition

The imagery of vision and light dominates the Christian scriptures from the first verses of Genesis to the last of the Apocalypse, and normally invokes at least one and usually both of the concepts of love and knowledge. It is the language of choice for describing an encounter with God, as in the vision of Paul on the road to Damascus and John's vision of Christ at the beginning of the Apocalypse. In an aphorism that obviously deeply impressed Bonaventure, the writer of the Epistle of James describes God as 'the Father of lights, with whom there is no change nor shadow of alteration.'[3] The New Testament often uses this language to describe a saint's growing understanding of spiritual truths. The Epistle to the Ephesians contains the prayer that 'the eyes of your heart [be] enlightened, that you may know what the hope is of his calling' (Eph.1:18).[4] Easily one of the best known passages from the Bible in medieval Christianity is, for numerous reasons, the *In principio* of John 1:1–14. One reason is its resonance of the Genesis creation myth; in both passages the concept of light plays a pivotal role. Genesis opens with an account of the creation of the world, a world which becomes known in the Middle Ages as the book of Nature. Through diligent reading of this book, one can know God better and comprehend something of the meaning of life. A poem by Alain de Lille

3   All translations of biblical quotations are from *The Holy Bible* Douay Version, London, 1956, here Jms 1:17. 'Patre luminum apud quem non est transmutatio nec vicissitudinis obumbratio.' All references to the Bible in Latin are from the *Biblia sacra iuxta vulgatam*, ed. Robert Weber, Stuttgart, 1969.
4   'Inluminatos oculos cordis vestri ut sciatis quae sit spes vocationis eius.'

expresses the hope commonly brought to a consideration of the works of creation:

> Omnis mundi creatura
> Quasi liber et pictura
> Nobis est in speculum;
> Nostrae vitae, nostrae mortis,
> Nostri status, nostrae sortis
> Fidele signaculum.[5]

> (All creation is to us a mirror, like a book, a picture: a faithful signal of our life, our death, our place, our fate.)[6]

The representation is a faithful one, so that careful study will produce reliable results. The natural world, a world suffused with light, will reward with knowledge the person who studies it closely. Perhaps no single thinker would take this principle more seriously than Robert Grosseteste. The *In principio* of the Gospel of John also begins with references to signs, initially to the sign of the word: 'In the beginning was the Word, and the Word was with God, and the Word was God' (Jn 1:1).[7] The passage in John makes knowledge its central feature. *Logos*, a rich concept signifying not only word but also the idea of a message, a conversation, the settlement of an account, a book, or Divine Reason, not to mention Christ, has come down to earth but humanity has not understood it. The idea collocated with *logos* is light: 'And the light shineth in darkness, and the darkness did not comprehend it' (Jn 1:5).[8] In the process of creation as described in Genesis, God creates light first as he broods over the waters, an act for which I can think of no better sensory interpretation than the opening of Haydn's *Creation*. The importance of light in the act of creation contributes incalculably to medieval thought and the subject often receives special attention in commentaries on this book.

The prolegomenon in John explicitly links knowledge and light, and implicitly includes the idea of God's love. God seeks that which is his own, and the Word is full of grace and truth. The relationship between these elements becomes explicit in John 3 as the author sounds the opening theme again. First he refers to the divine love that impelled God to send the Word to humanity: 'For God so loved the world, as to give his only begotten Son' (Jn 3:16).[9] Three verses later he summarizes the argument thus far:

5   Alain de Lille, 'Omnis mundi creatura,' *The Oxford Book of Medieval Latin Verse*, ed. F.J.E. Raby, Oxford, 1959, 369, 1–6.
6   My translation.
7   'In principio erat Verbum et Verbum erat apud Deum et Deus erat Verbum.'
8   'Et lux in tenebris lucet et tenebrae eam non comprehenderunt.'
9   'Sic enim dilexit Deus mundum ut Filium suum unigenitum daret.'

And this is the judgment; because the light is come into the world and men loved darkness rather than the light; for their works were evil. For every one that doth evil hateth the light and cometh not to the light, that his works may not be reproved. But he that doth truth cometh to the light, that his works may be made manifest; because they are done in God.

(Jn 3:19–21)[10]

This statement recapitulates the essential argument of the introduction. The opening, an important and popular source of doctrine, brings together the concepts of love and knowledge and makes the idea of light integral to the description. Its resonances with the opening of Genesis and the creation myth reinforce the ubiquity of interest in vision and light as well as the ways in which this imagery is collocated with knowledge and love.

Although the Bible informs medieval culture more than any other single text, individual thinkers also contribute enormously to the status of vision. Their discussions of the nature of light, the relationship between vision and degrees of knowing, and the relevance of light and sight for the apprehension of beauty, transform medieval perceptions. The following observation by the great intellectual historian Jaroslav Pelikan will serve to organize my consideration of some of the more important of these thinkers:

The most fascinating aspect of the westward odyssey of Dionysian spirituality is the interaction between the Neoplatonism of Dionysius and the Neoplatonism of Augustine (with perhaps the Neoplatonism of Boethius as a third partner). Each had a distinctive metaphysics; but more importantly, each was the fountainhead for a distinctive piety and devotion. And when they came together, as for example in both Bonaventure and Thomas Aquinas, the result was a spirituality in which intellectuality and fervor were fused.[11]

Pelikan strikes a provocative tone with the metaphor of an odyssey; fascination with vision plays an important part in this odyssey for all the thinkers mentioned here as well as for others.

The writings of Augustine (354–430), which so profoundly shape medieval Christian thought in many different ways, provide the basis for the influence of vision in the theme of illumination.[12] In its pervasiveness, if not in its sys-

---

10 'Hoc est autem iudicium quia lux venit in mundum et dilexerunt homines magis tenebras quam lucem erant enim eorum mala opera omnis enim qui mala agit odit lucem et non venit ad lucem ut non arguantur opera eius qui autem facit veritatem venit ad lucem ut manifestentur eius opera quia in Deo sunt facta.'
11 Jaroslav Pelikan, 'The Odyssey of Dionysian Spirituality,' in Pseudo-Dionysius, *The Complete Works*, trans. Colm Luibheid, London, 1987, 24.
12 This is so in spite of the fact that, as Athanase Sage has observed, 'Le thème de l'illumination, dont on discerne d'une manière plus ou moins accentuée la présence dans la

tematic presentation, this theme accompanies Augustine's presentation of what he considers to be the goal of the Christian's spiritual experience and growth in understanding; it divides into three kinds of vision.[13] Augustine explains these three kinds in the twelfth book of *De Genesi ad litteram* in a discussion arising out of his conjectures on the nature of Paul's vision of the 'third heaven' (2 Cor.12:2–4). The first vision consists of what the eye of the body sees; the second of the sensible representation of such objects by the imagination; and the third of immaterial realities directly perceived by the intelligence:

> When we read this one commandment, You shall love your neighbor as yourself, we experience three kinds of vision: one through the eyes, by which we see the letters; a second through the spirit, by which we think of our neighbor even when he is absent; and a third through an intuition of the mind, by which we see and understand love itself.[14]

Augustine tackles the ambiguity surrounding Paul's statement regarding *how* he saw Paradise and this raises an important point regarding his discussion of these categories of vision: in this life[15] there is some overlap between them and

---

plupart des écrits de saint Augustin, n'est jamais exposé et développé pour lui-même.' Athanase Sage, 'La dialectique de l'illumination,' *Recherches Augustiniennes* 2 (1962), 111.

[13] The idea of illumination relies on the two virtually inseparable concepts of light and vision. François-Joseph Thonnard has identified no fewer than ten degrees of light in Augustine's writings, which divide into three categories roughly corresponding to three kinds of vision:

1. La lumière physique, celle du soleil et de nos lampes.
2. La lumière vitale, de l'oeil vivant et du rayon «émis par la pupille».
3. La lumière psychologique, de la connaissance sensible, soit externe, soit dans la vie intérieure des images.
4. La lumière intellectuelle, de la pensée spirituelle.
5. La lumière substantielle, par laquelle sont créés les esprits.
6. La lumière surnaturelle de la foi.
7. La lumière théologique, où la raison collabore avec la foi.
8. La lumière mystique, celle des dons du Saint-Esprit.
9. La lumière incréée de Dieu-Vérité.
10. La lumière du Verbe dans le mystère de la Sainte Trinité: «Lumen de Lumine».

François-Joseph Thonnard, 'La notion de lumière en philosophie augustinienne,' *Recherches Augustiniennes* 2 (1962), 129.

[14] Augustine, *The Literal Meaning of Genesis*, trans. John Hammond Taylor, ACW 41–42, New York, 1982, 12.6.15. 'Ecce in hoc uno praecepto cum legitur, "Diliges proximum tuum tanquam teipsum," tria genera visionum occurrunt: unum per oculos, quibus ipsae litterae videntur; alterum per spiritum hominis quo proximus et absens cogitatur; tertium per contuitum mentis, quo ipsa dilectio intellecta conspicitur.' Augustine, *De Genesi ad litteram*, PL 34.

[15] These three will be maintained after the resurrection but will be perfectly distinguished: 'Then, indeed, there will be the three kinds of vision . . . but no error will induce us to mistake one thing for another, either in regard to corporeal objects or in regard to spiritual objects, or especially in regard to intellectual objects' (12.36.69). 'Nimirum enim erunt et

this absence of absolute distinctiveness creeps into Augustine's handling of sight. He appeals to the three categories to make both comparisions and contrasts.[16]

There are two further interesting points about this choice of illustrations. First of all, Augustine has chosen an example from reading even though his topic does not immediately suggest this choice. Reading, however, takes us very much into the realm of cognitive processes; it also is directly relevant to the correspondence in John between Truth, the Light, and the Word. Furthermore, the choice of verses here highlights love as the Platonic category to be understood. For Augustine, love is the ultimate goal of intelligent sight. The passage from physical sight to Platonic love takes only a few steps, easily recognized in the lucidity of his paradigm of illumination. That paradigm's simplicity and breadth of potential application render it compelling.

Augustine makes the superiority of the third kind of vision clear; this level of sight involves both an increased capacity to know and, ultimately, an increased capacity to love. In *De videndo Deo*, a letter to the Christian Pauline who has asked whether it is possible to see God with the eyes of the flesh, Augustine weighs various scriptures but ultimately distinguishes between sensible knowledge and intellectual knowledge, and the superiority of the latter.[17] The importance that Augustine ascribes to intelligible light underscores the priority of Platonic categories in his thinking. For him, and for the medieval tradition of spirituality after him up to Aquinas, spiritual light and vision have

---

tunc ista tria genera visionum, sed nulla falsitate aliud pro alio approbabitur, nec in corporalibus, nec in spiritualibus visis; multo minus in intellectualibus.'

16   Paul's vision of the third heaven provokes discussion of dreaming as well, which goes along with an analysis of various kinds of vision but which becomes a specialized topic. We need only note here that for Augustine and later commentators the phenomenon of dreaming also has its physiological and psychological components, so that the overlap between the sensible and the spiritual realms persists and the threefold theory of vision remains intact. For the late medieval interest in the realism of dreams, this aspect of the commentary upon vision will acquire additional significance. Steven F. Kruger discusses the importance of Augustine's interpretation for dream theory in *Dreaming in the Middle Ages*, Cambridge, 1992, 36–39.

17   'But if we cannot yet prefer the light which judges to the light which is judged, or prefer the life of the mind to the life of sense-experience only, or prefer the nature which is not different in different places, but which has everything which it possesses in unity – such as our intellect is – to that nature which is made up of parts, so that the half is less than the whole – such as our bodies are – then it is useless for us to discuss such great and high topics.' Augustine, *Letters*, trans. Wilfrid Parsons, FC 20, New York, 1953, 147.45. 'Quod si nondum possumus praeferre lucem judicantem ei luci de qua judicatur, praeferre vitam intelligentem vitae tantummodo sentienti, praeferre naturam non alibi hoc et alibi aliud, sed omnia quae habet in uno simul habentem, sicuti est nostra ipsa intelligentia, ei naturae quae ita partibus constat, ut minor sit dimidia quam tota, sicuti est omne corpus; superfluo de rebus tantis ac talibus disputamus.' Augustine, *Epistolae*, PL 33:147.18.45.

real being. The language is not merely metaphorical; it concerns Platonic verities.[18]

The concepts of light and illumination help Augustine to clarify his understanding of internal processes. In his explication of John 4, where Jesus explains his identity to the Samaritan woman at the well, Augustine interprets the woman's understanding as being absent from her soul, even though it is part of the soul and ought to rule it. He draws a comparison with the relationship between the eye and light to explain this state of affairs:

> But although the eye is something of the flesh, nevertheless it alone fully enjoys the light; but the remaining members of the flesh can be flooded with light; they cannot perceive the light. The eye alone is both flooded by it and enjoys it fully. So in our souls there is something which is called understanding. This very part of the soul, which is called understanding and the mind, is enlightened by a higher light. Now that higher light by which the human mind is enlightened is God. For 'there was the true light which enlightens every man who comes into this world.'[19]

The fully operative soul benefits from a vision of God himself as well as from the effects of having the light which is God enlighten the understanding. Physical light and physical sight have a unique relationship to one another that serves as the basis for Augustine's understanding of the processes of the mind. These concepts allow him to develop a complex if somewhat arcane understanding of the relationship between God, faith, understanding, and the soul.

Although for Augustine to know is normally to see, this correspondence involves certain distinctions; the superiority of faith over sight can be demonstrated by the presence of the former when the latter is absent. At the outset of *De videndo Deo* Augustine clarifies the various ways in which sight can be used, and he distinguishes between them by using authority as a touchstone. He differentiates between seeing and believing as two ways of coming to knowledge:[20]

---

18   In describing the philosophical idea of light in Augustine's works, Thonnard argues that 'il ne faut pas commencer par une théorie du phénomène sensible, mais par la *lumière intelligible*. C'est le monde intelligible qui seul possède l'infaillible vérité: le monde sensible n'a qu'une réalité moindre' (Thonnard, 127–8).

19   Augustine, *Tractates on the Gospel of John 11–27*, trans. John W. Rettig, FC 79, Washington, 1988, 15.19. 'Cum autem carnis aliquid sit oculus, solus tamen luce perfruitur: caetera autem membra carnalia luce perfundi possunt, lucem sentire non possunt; solus ea oculus et perfunditur et perfruitur. Sic in anima nostra quiddam est quod intellectus vocatur. Hoc ipsum animae quod intellectus et mens dicitur, illuminatur luce superiore. Jam superior illa lux, qua mens humana illuminatur, Deus est; "Erat" enim "verum lumen, quod illuminat omnem hominem venientem in hunc mundum." ' Augustine, *In Joannis evangelium (Tractatus CXXIV)*, PL 35.

20   He makes this distinction when expounding upon *vitium curiositatis* as well. Augustine's handling of the sin of curiosity provides an instructive example of his concern

The things which are not present to our faculties are believed if the authority on which they are offered seems trustworthy; things which are before us are seen, hence they are said to be present to our mental or bodily faculties. (147.7)[21]

This creates a breach between sight and belief, which Augustine recognizes; but he quickly asserts that belief is a kind of sight superior to physical sight:

Moreover, if it is not inappropriate to say that we also know what we firmly believe, this arises from the fact that we are correctly said to see mentally what we believe, even though it is not present to our senses. It is true that knowledge is attributed to the mind, whether the object of its perception and recognition has come to it through the bodily senses or through the mind itself, and faith itself is certainly seen by the mind, although what is believed by faith is not seen. For this reason the Apostle Peter says: 'In whom also now, though you see him not, you believe,' and the Lord Himself said: 'Blessed are they that have not seen and have believed'. (147.8)[22]

This is not just disingenuousness on Augustine's part; it does reveal an aspect of the complexity of appealing to sight. This contrast will develop in medieval preaching into a standard opposition between outer and inner vision, one which Chaucer applies to the Merchant's and Second Nun's tales. In the hands of Chaucer, of course, the fissures between the various kinds of sight create the opportunity for confusion, ambiguity, and moral uncertainty; the sometime credibility and sometime weakness of physical sight afford him the opportunity to deconstruct the system built upon the theme of illumination.

If the language of sight in Augustine is the language of cognition, it is also

---

about the relationship between faith, learning, and various kinds of sight. Richard Newhauser, 'Augustinian *vitium curiositatis* and its reception,' in *St Augustine and His Influence in the Middle Ages*, ed. Edward B. King and J.T. Schaefer, Sewanee, 1988, 99–124.

21 'Creduntur ergo illa quae absunt a sensibus nostris, si videtur idoneum quod eis testimonium perhibetur. Videntur autem quae praesto sunt, unde et praesentia nominantur vel animi vel corporis sensibus' (147.2.7). In this passage Augustine goes on to indicate the way sight stands in for all of the senses and is most relevant for the notions of spiritual and intellectual sight: 'Not only do we say "See, how bright it is," but also "See, what a noise," "See, what a smell," "See, what a taste," "See, how hot it is" ' (147.7). 'Non enim tantum dicimus, Vide quid luceat; sed etiam, Vide quid sonet, Vide quid oleat, Vide quid sapiat, Vide quid caleat' (147.2.7).

22 'Porro si scire non incongruenter dicimur etiam illud quod certissimum credimus, hinc factum est ut etiam recte credita, etsi non adsint sensibus nostris, videre mente dicamur. Scientia quippe menti tribuitur; sive per corporis sensus, sive per ipsum animum aliquid perceptum cognitumque retineat: et fides ipsa mente utique videtur, quamvis hoc fide credatur quod non videtur. Unde et apostolus Petrus dicit, "In quem modo non videntes creditis": et ipse Dominus, "Beati qui non viderunt, et crediderunt" ' (147.3.8).

the language of the heart. The knowledge to which Augustine gives priority requires vision with the eyes of the heart. He returns to this concept insistently in his letter to Pauline by quoting Matthew 5:8:

> Since, therefore, we do not see God in this life either with bodily eyes . . . or with the gaze of the mind . . . why do we believe that He is seen, except that we rest our faith upon the Scripture, where we read: 'Blessed are the clean in heart, for they shall see God'. (147.3)[23]

Augustine treats this matter quite carefully, conscious of the overlap between sight, knowledge, and belief; ultimately this strengthens their connectedness in his mind, ratified by the authority of Scripture.[24] The more transcendent the experience, the more potent the fusion between love and knowledge. This beatitude, as Augustine interprets it, suggests the imperative of faith that remains an important component of the spiritual experience of sight in medieval writings. At the same time, the language of the heart will become increasingly important in its own right and the discourse of sight becomes a discourse of love. By comparing these various types of vision, Augustine stresses the condition of the heart and for him this language reconfirms the difference between sight and belief.[25] Although the condition of the heart is a qualifying concern, basically it is his emphasis on the heart – rather than sight, touch, or hearing – that is interesting. The role of the heart shifts the discourse in the direction of love and Augustine increasingly uses the language of love. God, who is Light, becomes the desired one.[26]

This emphasis on love comes to the fore when Augustine analyzes the experience of rapture in Paul's vision. Here too he stresses how an intellectual vision, the highest kind, can involve the peeling away of all virtues (and their corresponding vices) except love. Love consumes everything else, and the

---

[23] 'Cum igitur, nec corporis oculis . . . nec mentis aspectu . . . nunc videamus Deum; cur credimus eum videri, nisi quia Scripturae accommodamus fidem, ubi legitur, "Beati mundo corde; quoniam ipsi Deum videbunt" ' (147.3). Cf. also chs 12, 13, 15, 18, 28, 37, 39, 46.
[24] 'Therefore we were right in saying: "We know that God can be seen," although we have not seen Him, but we have put our faith in the divine authority which is contained in the holy books' (147.12). 'Recte itaque diximus, Scimus Deum posse videri; quamvis eum non viderimus, sed divinae auctoritati quae sanctis Libris continetur, crediderimus' (147.5.12).
[25] 'Thus, He will be seen by the clean of heart, who is not seen in any locality, is not sought by bodily eyes, nor limited by our sight, nor held by touch, nor heard by His utterance' (147.28). 'Quoniam mundo corde videbitur qui nec in loco videtur, nec oculis corporalibus quaeritur, nec circumscribitur visu, nec tactu tenetur, nec auditur affatu' (147.11.28).
[26] 'Since, then, we have chosen that light in preference to any corporeal light, not only by the judgment of our reason, but also by the longing of our love, we shall make better progress in that love the stronger we become in it' (147.44). 'Cum igitur lucem istam omni corporali luci, non solum judicio rationis, sed amoris quoque appetitu praeposuerimus; quanto id magis valebimus, tanto melius valebimus' (147.17.44).

vision produces an ardent desire to possess what you love. In fact, this virtue is the goal of all the others:

> The one virtue and the whole of virtue there is to love what you see, and the supreme happiness is to possess what you love. . . . It is surely in pursuit of this end, where there will be secure peace and the unutterable vision of truth, that man undertakes the labor of restraining his desires, of bearing adversities, of relieving the poor, of opposing deceivers. There the brightness of the Lord is seen. (*De Gen.* 12.26.54)[27]

The concepts of virtue (*virtus*) and possession (*habere*) suggest the power of ravishment associated with the convention of love at first sight. Augustine also quotes Matt. 5:8 in this context. This is the 'third heaven,' which is also Paradise (cf. 12.28). The experience of this kind of vision entails an experience of love, of complete desire and paradisal fulfilment, all of which happens on the highest level of sight: vision, knowledge, and love become inextricably interwoven. As we shall see, medieval poets of erotic love draw on the same semantic range of vision, desire, and paradise, though, crucially, negating knowledge.

In one of the many remarkable passages of the *Confessions*, he uses the image of light to describe his growing awareness of God, a growth in terms of both knowledge and love.[28] Ultimately, God is the source of all knowledge and love, and in a moment of ecstatic insight Augustine sees the unity between them. Often, he refers to the light of knowledge, then moves on to the related idea of love; here, however, he applies Light to both truth and charity, and makes a connection between light and love.

Augustine gives absolute priority to intelligent vision and the related ideas of knowing and loving in his theory of illumination. At the same time, however, he develops this theme by taking advantage of physical light and sight as

---

27 'Una ibi et tota virtus est amare quod videas, et summa felicitas habere quod amas. . . . Propter illud quippe adipiscendum, ubi secura quies erit et ineffabilis visio veritatis, labor suscipitur, et continendi a voluptate, et sustinendi adversitates, et subveniendi indigentibus, et resistendi decipientibus. Ibi videtur claritas Domini.'

28 'I entered [the depths of my soul], and with the eye of my soul, such as it was, I saw the Light that never changes casting its rays over the same eye of my soul, over my mind. . . . What I saw was something quite, quite different from any light we know on earth. It shone above my mind, but not in the way that oil floats above water or the sky hangs over the earth. It was above me because it was itself the Light that made me, and I was below because I was made by it. All who know the truth know this Light, and all who know this Light know eternity. It is the Light that charity knows. Eternal Truth, true Love, beloved Eternity' (*Conf.* 7.10). 'Intravi et vidi qualicumque oculo animae meae supra eundem oculum animae meae, supra mentem meam lucem inconmutabilem. . . . non hoc illa erat, sed aliud, aliud valde ab istis omnibus. nec ita erat supra mentem meam, sicut oleum super aquam nec sicut caelum super terram, sed superior, quia ipsa fecit me, et ego inferior, quia factus ab ea. qui novit veritatem, novit eam, et qui novit eam, novit aeternitatem. caritas novit eam. o aeterna veritas et vera caritas et cara aeternitas!'

analogies and this increases their own value; he contributes to fascination with the physical properties of sight and light. In book eleven of *De Trinitate* Augustine begins by reestablishing this dialectic: 'No one doubts that, as the inner man is endowed with understanding, so the outer man is endowed with the sense of the body.'[29] Casting about for an analogy by which to relate the mystery of the Trinity, he seizes upon the body or 'outer man.'[30] At once interested in lines of continuity between spiritual and physical concepts, and adjusting himself to the weakness of carnality, which more easily understands the visible and external, Augustine picks on the chief of the body's five senses as the vehicle for this analogy.[31] The phenomenon of physical sight is very impressive to the Church Father; when he finds it necessary or desirable to allude to the ordinary world of sense experience, he naturally appeals to the sense of sight. Not only is it chief among the physical senses but by being constantly employed for the purposes of analogy it accrues additional prestige. In that physical sight here bears a profound spiritual truth regarding the Trinity, the distinction between the levels of vision becomes blurred. Elsewhere, in his exegesis of the first verses of John, Augustine ostensibly dismisses all of the physical senses but his emphasis on ways of seeing has implications for medieval appreciation of reading and the pleasure of the text, where the intellectual and the physical meet. He insists that the Son declares himself inasmuch as he is the Word, not a sound echoing in our ears but an image giving knowledge.[32] Although he distinguishes between the senses and intelligible vision, the distinction between hearing and sight as fleshly abilities and the relevance of the latter to 'reading' Christ is also apparent. It is only a small step from here to the medieval enthusiasm for the beauty of the written word.

Augustine's language of love describes primarily the quest for divine love and eternal truth but again his terms have sensory applications. He himself uses similar language to describe the lust of the eyes, where he refers to earthly loves rather than the divine one. After describing the process of rediscovering the

[29] Augustine, *The Trinity*, trans. Stephen McKenna, FC 45, Washington, 1963, 11.1.1. 'Nemini dubium est, sicut interiorem hominem intelligentia, sic exteriorem sensu corporis praeditum.' Augustine, *De Trinitate*, PL 42.
[30] 'Let us endeavor, therefore, to discover, if we can, any trace at all of the Trinity even in this outer man. . . . And by the very order of our condition, whereby we are made mortal and carnal, we apply ourselves more easily and, so to speak, more familiarly with visible than with intelligible things, since the former are external and the latter internal, and we perceive the former through the sense of the body, but the latter through the mind' (11.1.1). 'Nitamur igitur, si possumus, in hoc quoque exteriore indagare qualecumque vestigium Trinitatis. . . . Et illo ipso ordine conditionis nostrae quo mortales atque carnales effecti sumus, facilius et quasi familiarius visibilia quam intelligibilia pertractamus: cum ista sint exterius, illa interius, et ista sensu corporis sentiamus, illa mente intelligamus.'
[31] 'Let us, therefore, rely principally on the testimony of the eyes, for this sense of the body far excels the rest, and comes closer to spiritual vision, though it differs from it in kind' (11.1.1). 'Itaque potissimum testimonio utamur oculorum. Is enim sensus corporis maxime excellit, et est visioni mentis pro sui generis diversitate vicinior.'
[32] Ch. 15.37; compare ch. 29.

love of God in his memory, he faces some of his lingering weaknesses. His admission of how he suffers temptation through the eye shows his love of visual stimuli:

> The eyes delight in beautiful shapes of different sorts and bright and attractive colours. . . . For light, the queen of colours, pervades all that I see, wherever I am throughout the day, and by the ever-changing pattern of its rays it entices me even when I am occupied with something else and take no special note of it. (10.34)[33]

This observation reveals an attitude of passiveness before things seen, a quality important to sight in love literature. Light pervades all he sees and entices him even when he is not thinking about it: he is vulnerable. He describes earthly light and the phenomenon of sight with ardour, in spite of the fact that he contrasts such light with true light, which reflects a higher order of love. In both earthly and spiritual senses, Augustine refers to light in terms of pleasure, delight, and love; his interest in both the earthly and the spiritual contribute to the parasitic system of love, knowledge, and sight. Combining these general equations with his descriptions of the love of truth and the discovery of truth as illumination, the notions of light, love, and knowledge become tightly interlocked in his thought.

The close relationship between knowledge and love is part of the bedrock of his philosophy. In *De civitate Dei* he discusses the role played by Plato and expands to itemize what he considers to be the essential components of any philosophical system – physics, logic, and ethics – which he describes as a kind of trinity. God is the author of all being, the giver of intelligence, and the inspirer of that love which makes a good and happy life possible. He asserts that all philosophers direct their full attention to the study of these three important, general questions.[34] As the bases for philosophical inquiry, these three areas are distinct yet united, as the metaphor of a trinity suggests. The strength of these concepts lies also in their proximity to tangible realities, the phenomenon of physical sight and the acquisition of knowledge made possible by it. The vision of beauty similarly spans the gap: it can mean the vision of God or of pleasing sensible objects, such as the scriptures on the page or a beautiful living form. The system includes tension or noise as part of its functioning. The doctrine of illumination focuses attention on vision and assures that interest in this almost archetypal concept will continue to flourish at least as long as Augustine's writings themselves.

Pseudo-Dionysius ranks among the most influential writers for the medieval

---

[33] 'Pulchras formas et varias, nitidos et amoenos colores amant oculi. . . . ipsa enim regina colorum lux ista perfundens cuncta, quae cernimus, ubiubi per diem fuero, multimodo adlapsu blanditur mihi aliud agenti et eam non advertenti.'
[34] Augustine, *De civitate Dei*, PL 41:11.25.

period. Like Augustine, he integrates spiritual love and spiritual knowledge under the rubric of vision. In the famous fourth book of *The Divine Names* he expounds his ideas on love and knowledge in terms of the good. The following lengthy passage conveys the forcefulness and centrality of this language in the mystic's thought:

> Let us move on now to the name 'Good,' which the sacred writers have preeminently set apart for the supra-divine God from all other names. They call the divine subsistence itself 'goodness.' This essential Good, by the very fact of its existence, extends goodness into all things. Think of how it is with our sun. It exercises no rational process, no act of choice, and yet by the very fact of its existence it gives light to whatever is able to partake of its light, in its own way. So it is with the Good. Existing far above the sun, an archetype far superior to its dull image, it sends the rays of its undivided goodness to everything with the capacity, such as this may be, to receive it. These rays are responsible for all intelligible and intelligent beings, for every power and every activity.[35]

This passage, which derives from Plato's analogy of the cave in the *Republic*, shows the ubiquity of light and its reality for pseudo-Dionysius as an ontological category. Goodness exceeds the sun and its light; however it has the same properties as this lower order of light. Goodness, like its dull image light, diffuses itself to everything and is responsible for everything. As in Augustine, these properties engage rational faculties: the 'Good' sends its rays to all 'intelligible and intelligent beings.' The mystic's understanding of the final goal for human participation in God is one of freedom from passion and the fusion of our understanding with the divine light.[36] This goal presupposes the connaturality of the soul and the Good; later in this chapter he expresses this idea directly.[37]

For pseudo-Dionysius, the Good naturally includes the Beautiful and Love, since everything must yearn for the Beautiful and the Good. He develops the correspondence between these three after establishing the similarity between Good and light. First he cautions, 'But do not make a distinction between "beautiful" and "beauty" as applied to the Cause which gathers all into one' (76); and he goes on to assert that 'The Beautiful is therefore the same as the Good, for everything looks to the Beautiful and the Good as the cause of being, and there is nothing in the world without a share of the Beautiful and the Good'

---

35 Pseudo-Dionysius, *The Divine Names*, in *The Complete Works*, trans. Colm Luibheid, London, 1987, 71–2.

36 'And there we shall be, our minds away from passion and the earth, and we shall have a conceptual gift of light from him and . . . our understanding carried away, blessedly happy, we shall be struck by his blazing light' (52–3).

37 The souls 'are able to have a share in the illumination streaming out from that Source. They too, in their own fashion, possess the gift of exemplifying the Good' (73).

(77). This conflation of Goodness and Beauty leads him to consider love in the Platonic sense of an urge: 'And so it is that all things must desire, must yearn for, must love, the Beautiful and the Good' (79).

We will find ourselves returning to this complex of ideas in which light, love, and intellection share common ground. Pseudo-Dionysius becomes an important fount for the mystical tradition, where emphasis remains on divine love; but he influences many medieval thinkers, not only spiritual mystics. His notions of beauty recur in the context of later discussions of aesthetics, where the complex of vision, love, and knowledge has shifted ground but in many ways remains intact. Indeed, the overwhelming presence of this language breeds applications and pseudo-Dionysius, like Augustine, makes occasional remarks that draw metaphysical and phenomenal applications together. In *The Celestial Hierarchy*, for instance, he makes a very positive comparison between the two kinds of light: 'Material lights are images of the outpouring of an immaterial gift of light' (146). In the early Christian church, this relationship manifests itself in the form of symbolism. Elsewhere, he explains that baptismal clothing is bright because light shines through all the life of the person baptized.[38] In the thought of Aquinas the emphasis on metaphor becomes very prominent. In others the metaphysics of vision remains much stronger but also includes phenomenal applications of these Neoplatonic principles.

Before exploring later theological interpretations of the meaning of light and vision, I wish consider the importance of Boethius' Neoplatonism with regards to our central concerns. Like the others, especially Augustine, Boethius collocates knowledge and vision, though his *Consolation of Philosophy* is remarkably free from overt references to the Christian religion.[39] Boethius ascribes to physical sight the place of preeminence among the outer senses; it is the closest of them to the internal processes of the mind. For him vision represents the senses in the hierarchy of the human faculties; it indicates the nature of the higher processes; and it helps explain the nature of divine foreknowledge. As for Augustine, it is not merely an analogy but a Platonic reality. In the climactic book of *The Consolation of Philosophy* Boethius makes two important appeals to sight. The first occurs in the prisoner's complaint to Lady Philosophy that the foresight of Providence entails necessity. To illustrate his point, he uses the example of seeing a sitting man.[40] It is an important passage not least because

---

38   Pseudo-Dionysius, *The Ecclesiastical Hierarchy*, in *The Complete Works*, 208.

39   He makes a second notable contribution to the use of sight in the promulgation of the dream vision. Though technically not the progenitor of this genre, Boethius established the dream vision as a lastingly influential form in medieval European literature however much it evolved in the writings of Alain de Lille, the *Roman de la Rose* poets, Chaucer, and a host of others. Chaucer's appeal to this form is in some important ways of a piece with his other interests in vision.

40   'For certes yif that any wyght sitteth, it byhoveth by necessite that the opynioun be soth of hym that conjecteth that he sitteth; and ayeinward also is it of the contrarie: yif the opinioun be soth of any wyght for that he sitteth, it byhoveth by necessite that he sitte. Thanne is here necessite in the toon and in the tothir; for in the toon is necessite of syttynge,

Troilus will repeat the line of reasoning almost exactly in his philosophical reflections. In the *Consolation*, the reference to physical sight introduces several complex issues and it consolidates the importance of physical sight in the metaphysical discourse. Later, Lady Philosophy elaborates upon the hierarchical nature of various kinds of sight to explain the true nature of the foresight of Providence to her student. Using the example of what happens when one perceives a man, she explains that this comprehension involves four levels of activity, all of which involve some form of vision.[41] Once again, physical sight provides a useful springboard for psychological and metaphysical assertions. The argument reveals the respect given to the sense of sight and its associations with a range of ideas about knowledge, human and divine.

Lady Philosophy clarifies the value of this analogy in terms of the human ability to comprehend divine foreknowledge in the following prose section:

> But certes yif we myghten han the jugement of the devyne thoght, as we ben parsoners of resoun, ryght so as we han demyd that it byhovith that ymaginacioun and wit ben bynethe resoun, ryght so wolde we demen that it were ryghtfull thing that mannys resoun oughte to summytten itself and to ben bynethe the devyne thought. (5.pr5)

One participates in the divine vision by recognizing personal limitations and coming to terms with the human place in the divine scheme of things. This was Lady Philosophy's diagnosis of the prisoner's problem in the first place.[42] His restoration to health in the cosmic sense involves a complete understanding of vision: both its role in the way human reason works; and as the best analogy for the limits of human abilities in comparison with the abilities of God. The metre with which the first book closes incorporates these related concepts by

---

and certes in the tothir is necessite of soth.' All quotations from *The Consolation of Philosophy* are from Chaucer's translation *Boece* in *The Riverside Chaucer*, ed. Larry Benson et al., Boston and Oxford, 1987, here 5.pr3.

[41] 'And the man hymself, ootherweys wit byholdeth hym, and ootherweys ymaginacioun, and otherweyes resoun, and ootherweies intelligence. For the wit comprehendith withouteforth the figure of the body of the man that is establisschid in the matere subgett; but the ymaginacioun comprehendith oonly the figure withoute the matere; resoun surmountith ymaginacioun and comprehendith by an universel lokynge the comune spece that is in the singuler peces. But the eighe of intelligence is heyere, for it surmountith the envyrounynge of the universite, and loketh over that bi pure subtilte of thought thilke same symple forme of man that is perdurablely in the devyne thought. . . . The heyeste strengthe to comprehenden thinges enbraseth and contienith the lowere strengthe; but the lowere strengthe ne ariseth nat in no manere to the heyere strengthe' (5.pr4).

[42] 'For thow ne woost what is the eende of thynges, forthy demestow that felonus and wikkide men ben myghty and weleful; and for thow hast foryeten by whiche governementz the werld is governed, forthy weenestow that thise mutacions of fortunes fleten withouten governour. . . . I have gret noryssynges of thyn hele, and that is, the sothe sentence of governance of the werld, that thou bylevest that the govemynge of it nis nat subgit ne underput to the folye of thise happes aventurous, but to the resoun of God' (1.pr6).

referring to the way dark clouds can hide starlight from the mind, how waves can turn the sea opaque and thick with mud so that the eye cannot pierce the water, and what one must do in order to see the truth. Ultimately, Boethius is far more interested in attaining a cosmic perspective and calling his reader to seek such a perspective. God's governance, which gives comfort to the individual who thinks that 'that thise mutacions of fortunes fleten withouten governour,' is the governance of vision:

> . . . for the devyne sighte renneth toforn and seeth alle futures, and clepith hem ayen and retorneth hem to the presence of his propre knowynge; ne he ne entrechaungith nat, so as thou wenest, the stoundes of foreknowynge, as now this, now that; but he ay duellynge cometh byforn, and enbraseth at o strook alle thi mutaciouns. And this presence to comprehenden and to seen alle thingis – God ne hath nat taken it of the bytidynge of things to come, but of his propre symplicite. (5.pr6)

Lady Philosophy commands the prisoner to strive to see the light of truth; such a vision leads to the recognition of the superiority of God's gaze. This *sentence* further consolidates the relationship between vision and knowledge in Neoplatonic Christian writings. The entire development of the idea in the *Consolation* illustrates the importance of sight in a way that is especially relevant for reading Chaucer.

Many medieval poems belong to the tradition of dream-poetry inspired in part by Boethius: up until Chaucer's time all of them aspire to producing the singular voice of authority. Even the *Roman de la Rose* purports to be a textbook on love, an incontrovertible vision of what happens in the garden of love. The authoritative stature of such visions is bound up with the Neoplatonic commitment to vision and light as hierarchical concepts. For Augustine dreams find their valuation in terms of three ascending kinds of vision; his dream theory engages with his commitment to the doctrine of illumination. The authority of certain dreams depends on the degree to which they cause the dreamer to experience a higher order of light. For Boethius the vision of the *consolatio* has a similar value. When Lady Philosophy gathers her dress into a fold and wipes away the prisoner's tears, the effect upon him is one of coming into the light.[43] The vision form in *The Consolation of Philosophy* embodies a vision of light, which for the Neoplatonic Boethius is everything that Philosophy represents. The twelfth-century poet Alain de Lille will use the powerful symbolism of light in his *De planctu Naturae*: he bases his character Nature on the model of Lady Philosophy, but the first thing the dreamer notices about Nature is her

---

43   'Yif thanne the wynde that hyghte Boreas, isent out of the kaves of the cuntre of Trace, betith this nyght (*that is to seyn, chaseth it awey*) and discovereth the closed day, thanne schyneth Phebus ischaken with sodeyn light and smyteth with his beemes in merveylynge eien' (1.m3).

brilliance, not mentioned in Boethius' account. The vision form, and the fact that the dreamer envisions a scene infused with remarkable light, go hand-in-hand. Obviously the dream-vision clearly develops into a genre all its own with many other characteristics besides this association. The genre attracts medieval poets for many reasons, some of which undoubtedly have little to do with the theme of vision and light. Nonetheless, this simple observation on the relationship between the vision as an authoritative form and a particular interest in light within such literature can easily go unnoticed. It should not, because interest in vision in general and particular ways depends upon the importance of light as a metaphysical category.

The influence of Augustine, pseudo-Dionysius, and Boethius in their use of the language of vision is incalculable. They give priority to sight in ways that assure its lasting attractiveness and applicability. It contributes immensely to the Christian discourse about God, and to that of the soul's involvement with God. Furthermore, it contributes to the discourse of man's being, especially in terms of his intelligence, that part of man that brings him closest to the divine. For a very long time, vision remains relevant simply because of the prevailing interest in ontological categories, among which it is firmly established; and as interest in nature and natural processes increases, vision and light are well-placed to continue to provoke speculation and debate.

Mystical theology makes a crucial contribution to the discourse of the relationship between love and knowledge, especially with the writings of the Cistercians Bernard of Clairvaux and William of St Thierry. They articulate a relationship between these terms in keeping with the heritage of Augustine and pseudo-Dionysius. It is worth noting that there is a resurgence of interest in Bernardine piety in the fourteenth century; the translation *Hid Divinitie* in the same century evinces late medieval interest in pseudo-Dionysius as well. Bernard's mystical theology heightens the tension between love and knowledge. Famous for his debates with the brilliant scholastic Abelard, Bernard argues for a simple faith, against what he considers to be the prideful intellectual excesses of Abelard and the scholastic tradition he represents. He puts this emphasis laconically in one of his sermons on the Song of Songs: 'Instruction makes us learned, experience makes us wise.'[44] He distinguishes between dry instruction and the favourable disposition of the will, which belongs to the concept of *affectio*. Bernard does allow for the roles of both heart and mind. Jean Leclercq captures the essence of Bernard's emphasis on affect (*affectus*) when he describes the goal of Bernardine mysticism as movement from scholastic *quaeritur* to *desideratur*, from *sciendum* to *experiendum*.[45] The Cister-

---

[44]   Bernard of Clairvaux, *On the Song of Songs*, trans. Kilian Walsh and Irene Edmonds, Cistercian Fathers, vols 4, 7, 31, 40, Kalamazoo, 1971–80, here 23.14. 'Instructio doctos reddit, affectio sapientes.' *Sermones super Cantica Canticorum*, in *Opera* vols 1–2, ed. J. Leclercq et al., Rome, 1957.

[45]   Jean Leclercq, *The Love of Learning and the Desire for God: A Study of Monastic Culture*, 2nd ed., trans. Catharine Misrahi, London, 1978, 7.

cian mystic writes of the eradication of one's own will, invoking the prayer of
Christ 'Not as I will, but as you will.' For him, this attitude finds its fulfilment
in affective union with God, who is beyond reason. He describes the union as
'a communion of wills and an agreement in charity' (71.10).[46]

Bernard's sermons on the Song of Songs help us further understand love,
knowledge, and vision as a parasitic system. His explication of many passages
draws together the physical and the spiritual, as in Augustine a tendency important for understanding this system, and compounds the value of metaphors
of vision. He interprets this book with a well-known freshness that acknowledges the erotic nature of the material while adhering to the allegorical method
of interpretation. While giving priority to the reading that the love relationship
described refers to that of the soul with God, Bernard does not shy away from
the natural beauty of the text or the erotic sense of ardent desire being expressed. He pays particular attention to visual stimuli, as in the following am-
plification of the phrase 'Pulchrae sunt genae tuae, sicut turturis':

> Tender and sensitive is the modesty of the Bride, and I think that at the
> reproof of her Bridegroom her whole face was suffused with one blush,
> and its beauty made so strikingly apparent as to draw from Him the
> praise: Thy cheeks are beautiful as turtle-dove's. But nevertheless, that is
> not to be understood in an outward and carnal sense, as if He spoke of the
> flush due to the blood coursing in the veins, mounting into the counte-
> nance, and mingling there swiftly with the pearl-white tints of the com-
> plexion. That causes, indeed, a beauty momentary and perishable,
> varying from one moment to another, as the bright colour now flames
> upon the cheeks, and now sinks into paleness. (40.1)[47]

Bernard may not want to dwell on the carnal sense, but he imagines the physical
beauty of the blushing bride admirably well. His interest in visual appearance
is in keeping with his commitment to the principle of desire; he acknowledges
the irreplacable role of vision in any love relationship. His description of the
final union of the soul with God simply indulges this connection:

> However, what about those souls already loosed from their bodies? We

---

[46] 'Et haec unio ipsis communio voluntatum et consensus in caritate.'

[47] This delightful translation is from *The Life and Works of St Bernard*, vol. 4, trans.
Samuel J. Eales, London, 1896. 'Tenera est sponsae verecundia; et ad increpationem sponsi,
puto, facies eius rubore suffusa est, pulchriorque ex eo apparens, illico audivit: *Pulchrae
sunt genae tuae sicut turturis*. Vide autem ne carnaliter cogites coloratam carnis putredinem,
et purulentiam flavi sanguineive humoris, vitreae cutis superficiem summatim atque
aequaliter suffundentem: e quibus sibi invicem moderate permixtis, ad venustandam
genarum effigiem rubor subpallidus in efficientiam corporeae pulchritudinis temperatur,'

believe they are completely immersed in that immense ocean of eternal light and everlasting brightness.[48]

The principle of vision is ultimately located in light, and for Bernard the achievement of union with God takes one into the very source of vision. Passages such as this one have exercised defenders of Bernard's orthodoxy, who want to point out that the mystic allows maintains a distinction of wills between the soul and God. This passage is less about some depersonalizing fusion than it is about his enthusiasm for love and vision.

Admittedly, the intellect receives little attention in Bernardine mysticism, but the concept of wisdom and intellectual growth pervades his reading of the Song of Songs. This book completes a triad of Salomonic canonical texts, which begins with Proverbs and advances to Ecclesiastes before culminating in the Song of Songs. The *Glossa ordinaria* labels the three as works in moral philosophy, natural philosophy, and contemplation respectively, underlining their increasing difficulty. It refers to the *hiddenness* of the wisdom of Proverbs and describes the challenge of reading the Song of Songs as greatest in that we have superseded the visible to contemplate those things which are of heaven.[49] Bernard writes within this tradition of recognizing the special need for insight when reading any of Solomon's three books, and the accepted distinction between those which concern the visible world and the Song of Songs as that which supersedes the visible.

Bernard's fellow Cistercian William of St Thierry, whose works often circulated as Bernard's, gives beautiful expression to the joint workings of reason and love in mystical experience. Like Bernard, he emphasizes the primacy of love in the soul's quest for union with God, but even as he does so he makes comparisons with the role of reason. Early in the epistle he proffers the following definition of piety:

> For this piety is the perpetual mindfulness of God, the continual striving of the will to the understanding of Him, the unwearied affection to the loving of him.[50]

The goal is always love, and the means is the striving of the will, but the activity of the person in pursuit of God involves mindfulness and understanding. William celebrates reason as a gift, making it integral to spiritual growth, bound

---

[48] Bernard, *On Loving God*, 11.30, my translation. 'Quid autem iam solutas corporibus? Immersas ex toto credimus immenso illi pelago aeterni luminis et luminosae aeternitatis.' *De diligendo Deo*, in *Opera* vol. 3.

[49] *Glossa ordinaria*, PL 113.1079C, 1127B.

[50] William of St Thierry, *The Golden Epistle*, trans. Walter Shewring, London, 1980 (first published 1930), 4.9. 'Pietas enim hec iugis est Dei memoria, continua intentionis actio ad intelligentiam eius, indefessa affectio in amorem eius.' William of St Thierry, *Epistola ad fratres de Monte-Dei*, ed. M.-M. Davy, Paris, 1940, sec.17.

up with desire, which ultimately determines reason's end benefit.[51] Spiritual progression initially follows the route it does for Augustine:

> Let us labour to see, that by seeing we may understand, and by understanding we may love, and by loving we may have. (14.48)[52]

We continue to operate within the parasitic system of love, knowledge, and sight. Sight involves rational processes and it promises the experience of love. William's mysticism closely resembles Bernard's in its final emphasis on love, yet it more actively engages in the paradox of the contribution of reason and the pervasive tension between love and knowledge. William's enthusiasm for sight reflects both his absorption of the Augustinian language of illumination and his thoroughgoing commitment to affective mystical experience.

Cistercian mysticism has a considerable influence upon medieval theology and popular spirituality.[53] Sermonizers drop Bernard's name as an authority which they clearly expect their audience to recognize. A Bernardine prayer to Mary finds its way into Dante's *Paradiso* and from there into Chaucer's Prologue to the Second Nun's Tale. One important line of influence is the place of Cistercian theology in the French *Quest del Saint Graal*. Visions of the grail bring together the concepts we have been considering. After the grail appears initially to the knights on the feast of Pentecost, Arthur comments in lacklustre fashion that they should all give thanks for this sign of God's love. Gawain corrects him and draws attention to their blinded state, then vows to set out on a quest. The king plays a very curious role in this episode. He responds to the vow by expressing anxiety, and when Lancelot tries to reassure him Arthur protests that it is his love for the knights and the fellowship that makes him bitter. Given his status as God's anointed, it is odd that he should in any way be seen to impede worthy spiritual ambition, but he serves as a foil for the unfolding of a lesson. The sequence bears all the hallmarks of Cistercian theology: the vision produces a recognition of the need to see clearly, a hope for mystery to be revealed, and an immediate effort to help the king understand; more significantly, it represents the love of God, with the use of language that recalls the Song of Songs, and it moves the knights to action as a response of desire to the sign of divine love. This pattern repeats itself throughout the fable when the vision of the grail is the immediate subject.

The fourteenth-century French Cistercian Guillaume de Deguileville's *Le Pèlerinage de la Vie Humaine*, translated by John Lydgate as *The Pilgrimage*

[51]   Ch. 6.
[52]   'Ideo nitamur, quantum possumus ut videamus, videndo intelligamus, et intelligendo amemus, ut amando habeamus' (sec. 82).
[53]   Giles Constable, 'The Popularity of Twelfth-Century Spiritual Writers in the Late Middle Ages,' in *Renaissance Studies in Honor of Hans Baron*, ed. Anthony Molho and John A. Tedeschi, De Kalb, Ill., 1971, 3–28

of the Life of Man, also embodies this parasitic system of mystical theology.[54]
As an examination of the whole of life from this theological perspective, the
poem presents many aspects of our central concerns, especially in its heavy
reliance upon ideas of sight. From the outset it implicates various kinds of
vision, including dreaming, remembering, mirrors, signs, and spiritual insight.
The poem offers an almost encyclopedic collection of bits of wisdom, with
illustrations from the natural world; it combines visionary experience with the
enlargement of knowledge and, by virtue of the pilgrimage motif that underlies
the work, acknowledges the impulse of desire that moves the dreamer-pilgrim.

In his dream the narrator sees the city of Jerusalem in a mirror:

> ffor me thouht I hadde a syht
> With-Inne a merour large & bryht
> Off that hevenly ffayr cyte. (317–19)

The description emphasizes sight, especially in its focus upon the mirror. That
reference naturally includes a commonplace metaphorical component but, as
illuminations of this scene take pains to point out, the dreamer sees the city in
a mirror, not merely in the sense of a simile; Guillaume takes pains to locate
what the dreamer sees literally in a mirror, which he describes as large and
bright. This stress establishes a precedent of interest in the medium of sight,
and provides the basis for a broad appeal to visual concepts. As in *Le Roman
de la Rose*, which the prologue to the first version tells us the dreamer has been
reading, the dreamer at the outset observes, as an outsider, many detailed, even
graphic, scenes.[55] When he sees a sword bloodied with Christ's blood he reports that 'I was a-stonyd in my syht' (477): the appeal to vision is meant to be
overpowering.

The dreamer's guide for his pilgrimage is Grace-Dieu, a figure whose beauty
has a clear meaning accompanying it:

> ffor gladly, wher ys most bevte
> Ther ys grettest hym ylyte,
> And that ys verrayly the signe,
> Swych ar most goodly & benygne. (725–8)

The poem celebrates visual beauty and it swiftly provides signification, much

[54] John Lydgate, *The Pilgrimage of the Life of Man*, ed. F.J. Furnivall, EETS es 77, 83,
and 92, London, 1899–1904. Throughout I refer to Lydgate's far more accessible version,
based on Guillaume's expanded version of 1355.
[55] Guillaume de Deguileville, *Le Pèlerinage de la Vie Humaine*, ed. J.J. Stürzinger, Roxburghe Club 124, London, 1893. Susan K. Hagen draws attention to this point in her helpful
book *Allegorical Remembrance: A Study of* The Pilgrimage of the Life of Man *as a Medieval Treatise on Seeing and Remembering*, Athens, Ga., 1990, 9.

as the *Quest del Saint Graal* does. Grace-Dieu extends the meaning of sight associated with herself:

> ffor to pylgrymes, day & nyht,
> I enlumyne, & yive lyht. (787–8)

Though her role as instructor has only begun, 'enlumyne' already conveys the idea of spiritual illumination. Her description also suggests the comfort that physical light, a lamp or fire, would give a pilgrim. It also brings to mind God's guidance of the Israelites as a cloud by day and burning pillar by night, and hints at the mystical possibilities of spiritual pilgrimage.

The poem combines love and learning in terms of vision. Grace-Dieu promises the pilgrim:

> I shal the shewe of gret delyt
> fful many thyng for thy profyt,
> Yff thow ha lust to lerne of me
> Thynges that I shal teche the,
> And vnderstond hem by & by. (1371–5)

Here the guide gives free rein to the concepts of delight and desire; she places learning within that luxurious context, and the metaphor of sight aptly conveys the symmetry of these notions. An earlier vision of the doctors of the Church similarly conveys a Cistercian emphasis upon the affective:

> Yiff they (pilgrims) ther lernyng vnderstood,
> Wych they tauhte hem in ther lyff
> By doctryne contemplatyff,
> Outward schewyng, as by cher,
> Ther love was to hem ful enter,
> ffounded vp-on charyte. (528–33)

This scene illustrates the ideal of combining learning with charity. This proclamation locates the relationship between love and knowledge in a strictly human sphere, though undoubtedly informed by mystical concepts of the soul's union with God. *The Pilgrimage of the Life of Man* consistently reapplies concepts familiar from mystical theology to the daily life of the average pilgrim's experience.

The pervasive theme of vision applies equally well to some of the temptations the pilgrim must endure. One of these potential dangers is Venus, and the dreamer-pilgrim describes his meeting with her in the conventional language of love at first sight:

> And, to me-ward as she gan flare,
> With a sharp dart wych she bar

> She smette me, or I was war,
> (Longe or I koude aduerte,)
> Thorgh the Eye vn-to the herte. (13106–10)

In this poem the assault of a woman's eyes is a passing episode, just another of the sights and incidents along the way. It furthers the motif of vision in two ways: the figure of Venus serves as an icon of love, and the incident of her glance piercing the pilgrim's heart illustrates the power of the eye in action. Similarly, Guillaume presents Envy as a threat that particularly assaults the eyes. The character tells the pilgrim that

> Myn eyen ben off kynde lyk
> The Eyen off a basylyk,
> Wych, with a sodeyn look, men sleyth. (14955–7)

The whole organization of *The Pilgrimage of the Life of Man* serves to draw attention to visually-oriented challenges such as Venus and Envy. Their presence is in keeping with the positive abiding interest in vision, love, and knowledge as well as providing a sense of encountering difficulties to be overcome as part of the pilgrimage. The eye operates on both sides of this spiritual battle: it can contribute to spiritual progress, with the implied goal of mystical union with God; or it can work destructively, in contexts where it subverts any mystical system of love and knowledge.

Metaphysics and Aesthetics
Light, colour, and visual apprehension, for which metaphysical writings often reveal sheer delight, are important components in medieval aesthetics, which itself relies heavily on the terms we have been exploring and extends the system of love, knowledge, and sight. The symbolic value of this world enhances the importance of what it means to see beautiful sights. Signs of medieval love of light and colour, apart from layers of meaning, are also ubiquitous. Dante's description of Beatrice when he first encounters her in *La Vita Nuova* reveals his sheer love of colour and its associations with beauty. In *Le Roman de la Rose*, Guillaume's descriptions of the garden and the rose make the scene brilliant and lavish with contrasting colours; the illuminations of several manuscripts of the poem capture that brilliance in miniaturized form. The medieval art of illumination itself further attests the contribution of colour in making a book a rich and pleasing artefact. *Le Pèlerinage de la Vie Humaine* continues in this vein with its celebration of light and colour. Chaucer shares this fascination with light, and indeed illumination. In his short poem 'An ABC,' which he essentially translates from Guillaume's *Pèlerinage*, he compares those who call on Mary with the illuminated letters of church calendars:

> Kalenderes enlumyned ben thei
> That in this world ben lighted with thi name. (73–4)

Chaucer's allusion nicely draws together the art form with traditional spiritual connotations of enlightenment. Another example from the world of books is the emerging popularity of *speculum* titles and motifs, and a fascination with the properties of mirrors.[56] Stained glass and cathedral windows give most people perhaps their best and most common opportunity to enjoy the mystical effects of light. Nature's explanation of the rainbow in the *Roman* provides yet another glimpse of the medieval love of colour and light in the natural world. Fascination with light and colour pervades the culture, from aristocratic tastes in dress to scientific interest in the sun and rainbows to poetic descriptions of beauty. Light endows created things with nobility and the medieval passion for it is affective.[57]

As interest shifts away from ontological realities as suggested by symbols, phenomenal details such as the relationship between subject and object begin to attract increasing attention. The phenomenon of *seeing* itself, seeing beautiful objects and the conditions necessary for such an experience, also attract attention: behind the affective passion for dazzling sights and bright colours is a growing pleasure in understanding the phenomena as well, and the developing interest in the relationship between perceiving subject and the perceived object under the rubric of vision has implications for both aesthetics and epistemology.[58] On the matter of the relationship between subject and object especially, it is impossible to demarcate clearly the boundary between an epistemological and an aesthetic vision. Aesthetics, we must also bear in mind, deals directly with the question of Beauty: at this point, vision has the power to induce love. If phenomenal vision leads to thoughts about epistemology in the late Middle Ages, it also leads to thoughts about love; in vision, epistemology and love lie side by side, largely due to Neoplatonic Christian thought. Through the medium of physical sight both knowledge and love are considered on a more naturalistic level. The tradition in medieval thought of what it means to see fortifies the relationship between love and knowledge. Chaucer can at once play with these categories as understood in classic Christian terms and limit them in a more naturalistic framework, producing a complicated interpenetration that reveals conflict, ambiguity, and resonance created out of the basic experience of seeing.

---

56   Herbert Grabes has listed 150 mirror-titles in Latin, English, and French in the thirteenth and fourteenth centuries alone. Herbert Grabes, *The Mutable Glass: Mirror imagery in titles and texts of the Middle Ages and English Renaissance*, trans. Gordon Collier, Cambridge, 1982, 240–59.
57   See also Douglas Gray, '*Of Sunne Ne Mone Had Thay No Nede*: Notes on the Imagery of Light in a Middle English Text,' *Essays in Honor of Edward B. King*, ed. R.G. Benson and E.W. Naylor, Sewanee, 1991, 85–108.
58   The latter I will consider in the following chapter.

Almost half a century ago Edgar de Bruyne established the parameters for discussing medieval aesthetics.[59] Here we need only examine some of the fundamental principles to appreciate the basis of medieval aesthetics and the growing place of vision in it. As D.W. Robertson reminds us, we will do well to return briefly to the thought of Augustine who, like others, articulated an aesthetic of order, harmony, and proportion.[60] Augustine's is an aesthetic of the intelligence. Much of his discussion of this topic occurs in *De musica*, which has six books and culminates in a consideration of unchangeable numbers. God himself contains the perfect form of equality, which is the most perfect proportion.[61] The basis for Augustine's investigation into the beauty of proportion and equality is his understanding of the idea of 'number.'[62] The principle of numerate beauty fills the world, applying to all of creation;[63] and this process applies as well to the way an artisan produces a beautiful work.[64] It also applies to the individual's ability to appreciate beauty. Robertson explains: 'Anything that is delightful to the flesh through the corporal senses will be found to be rationally ordered (*numerosus*). However, no one is able to judge the presence of "number" in corporal things unless he has within himself certain laws of beauty to which he can refer the "numbers" that he observes outside of himself.'[65] The numerical beauty of proportions in both sound and sight which Augustine stresses in the climactic book of *De musica* fulfils the goal of focusing attention on the truth of God. The aesthetic of the beauty of proportion implies the fusion of love and knowledge.

Often in the same breath he calls this appreciation an act of love. He speaks both of a love of truth and a delight in the equality of numbers, or beauty:

> For we only thought it ought to be undertaken so adolescents, or men of any age God has endowed with a good natural capacity, might with reason guiding be torn away not quickly but gradually, from the fleshly

---

[59]   Edgar de Bruyne, *Études d'Esthétique Médiévale*, 3 vols, Bruges, 1946; Umberto Eco has distilled these in his introductory *Art and Beauty in the Middle Ages* (1959–61), trans. Hugh Bredin, New Haven, 1986.

[60]   D.W. Robertson, *A Preface to Chaucer*, Princeton, 1962, 52ff.

[61]   'Quae vero superiora sunt, nisi illa in quibus summa, inconcussa, incommutabilis, aeterna manet aequalitas?' Augustine, *De musica*, PL 32:6.11.29.

[62]   Towards the end of *De musica* he develops the theory at some length. Thonnard has noted that Augustine uses the term in four senses: '(1) in the ordinary mathematical sense, (2) in the sense of rhythm, (3) in the sense of harmony among the parts in physical movement, or, in man, harmony among the various sensible, intellectual, or moral activities, (4) the supreme unity of God, which is the source of mathematical law, beauty, rhythm, and the harmonious activities of nature and of man.' Quoted in Robertson, 114.

[63]   6.17.57.

[64]   'Or is it rather the artisan can operate the sensible numbers of his habit by the reasonable numbers of his art?' Augustine, *On Music*, trans. Robert C. Taliaferro, FC 4, New York, 1947, 6.17.57. 'An vero faber potest rationabilibus numeris qui sunt in arte ejus, sensuales numeros qui sunt in consuetudine ejus operari.

[65]   Robertson, 114.

senses and letters it is difficult for them not to stick to, and adhere with the love of unchangeable truth to one God and Master of all things, who with no mean term whatsoever directs human minds. (6.1.1)[66]

As he begins book 6, in which he wants to explain why he has spent so much time on the aesthetics of music, he does so in terms of reason and love. Through reason one tears away from the fleshly senses and with love adheres to God, the source of all Beauty. The appeal, in the first instance, to adolescents (male, by inference), brings to mind the other sources of beauty the fleshly senses of youth stick to, and the potential conflict between reason and love when that source is a woman. Later he develops the conflict between sensory attraction and the love of unchangeable truth further: 'You will easily see, if you notice the things we direct the mind to most, and have the greatest care for. For I think they're those we very much love, isn't that so?' (6.13.38).[67] Augustine's aesthetic promotes reason and the intelligible love of number; at the same time it includes the principle of love. But it distinguishes between the lower love inspired by the fleshly senses and the higher love of Beauty.

Beauty has more to do with proportions and the properties of numbers than with any one sense but Augustine includes the senses in this appreciation that ascends Godward. In *De musica* the art of music serves as a natural point of reference, since the importance of 'number' to medieval theory of proportions entailed a special interest in music theory. Augustine moves easily from sound to sight and acknowledges the naturalness of considering beauty in visual terms:

These beautiful things, then, please by number, where we have shown equality is sought. For this is found not only in that beauty belonging to the ears or in the motion of bodies, but also in the very visible forms where beauty is more usually said to be. (6.13.38)[68]

He speaks elsewhere of the artisan who operates the sensible and advancing numbers of his art from which he can fashion visible forms.[69] The care with which Augustine refers to the 'fleshly senses' recalls his argument as to why it makes sense to appeal to the senses for an analogy for the Trinity. Ultimately

---

[66] 'Quem non ob aliud suscipiendum putavimus, nisi ut adolescentes, vel cujuslibet aetatis homines, quos bono ingenio donavit Deus, non praepropere, sed quibusdam gradibus a sensibus carnis atque a carnalibus litteris, quibus eos non haerere difficile est, duce ratione avellerentur, atque uni Deo et Domino rerum omnio, qui humanis mentibus nulla natura interposita praesidet, incommutabilis veritatis amore adhaerescerent'.
[67] 'Facile id videbis, si animadverteris quibus rebus maxime animum soleamus intendere, et magnam curam exhibere: nam eas opinor esse quas multum amamus?'
[68] 'Haec igitur pulchra numero placent, in quo jam ostendimus aequalitatem appeti. Non enim hoc tantum in ea pulchritudine quae ad aures pertinet, atque in motu corporum est, invenitur, sed in ipsis etiam visibilibus formis, in quibus jam usitatius dicitur pulchritudo.'
[69] 6.17.57.

he is interested here again in the eye of the intelligence with which one beholds the beauty that is God; his aesthetic involves the principle of illumination we have already encountered and the tension with the senses reflects the tension in his doctrine of illumination. However, the analogues for Beauty in the sensible realm include sight.[70]

In the thirteenth century, the metaphysics of sight contributes to a strengthened aesthetic of light and vision; this is primarily due to the revived influence of Neoplatonism. Also increasingly influential is interest in vision and light in natural philosophy, especially in Arabic thought. As de Bruyne has written, 'L'Esthétique du XIIIe siècle se développe dans un climat particulier, celui d'une mystique de la lumière. Certes, nous ne disons pas que l'idée de proportion disparaît: elle ne perd rien de son importance fondamentale. Mais . . . le XIIIe siècle attache une importance considérable à tout ce qui est clarté, lumière, splendeur.'[71] For many important thinkers, including Robert Grosseteste and Bonaventure, the starting point continues to be the essential reality of light. It is a term used more rigorously in the spiritual than in the physical sense but light has something of corporeality in its meaning, especially in its common usage. In his famous little treatise *De luce*, Grosseteste presents light as the beginning of creation, the cause of the multiplication of species or forms that make up the created order:

The first corporeal form which some call corporeity is in my opinion light. For light of its very nature diffuses itself in every direction in such a way that a point of light will produce instantaneously a sphere of light of any size whatsoever, unless some opaque object stands in its way.[72]

---

[70] Boethius exhibits the same tendency towards abstraction in his treatment of the beauty of proportions, attracted as he is to the art by virtue of its roots in mathematics. This interest in a mathematical understanding of proportion has its roots in Platonic habits of mind. Although the idea of harmony and proportion was applied readily to music, for Augustine the aesthetic applied equally well to all of creation. Boethius also makes this broad application. For him, the soul and the body are subject to the same laws that govern music, and proportions appear in all of creation. Eco summarizes: 'Microcosm and macrocosm are tied by the same knot, simultaneously mathematical and aesthetic' (Eco, 31).

[71] De Bruyne, 3.9.

[72] Robert Grosseteste, *On Light*, trans. C. Rield, Milwaukee, 1940, 10. 'Formam primam corporalem, quam quidam corporeitatem vocant, lucem esse arbitror. Lux enim per se in omnem partem se ipsam diffundit, ita ut a puncto lucis sphaera lucis quamvis magna subito generetur, nisi obsistat umbrosum.' Robert Grosseteste, 'De luce seu de inchoatione formarum,' *Die Philosophischen Werke Des Robert Grosseteste, Bischofs von Lincoln*, ed. Ludwig Baur, Münster, 1912, 51. Bonaventure says something very similar to this: 'Nulla substantia per se existens, sive corporalis sive spiritualis, est pure forma nisi solus Deus. . . . Si ergo lux formam dicit, non potest esse lux ipsum corpus, sed aliquid corporis. Si enim lux esset ipsum corpus, cum lucis sit ex se ipsa se ipsam multiplicare, aliquod corpus posset se ipsum multiplicare ex se sine appositione materiae aliunde.' All references to Bonaventure are from *Opera omnia*, ed. Bernard a Portu Romatino et al., 10 vols, Quaracchi, 1882–1902. Here *Op. om.* 2, *Sent.* d.13,a.2,q.1,conc.; de Bruyne, 20.

Light is the fundamental form of corporeality as such and constitutes the source and being of perfection in corporeal forms. Therefore, the more that an object shines, the more it approaches a state of perfect simplicity and therefore the more noble and beautiful it is said to be. The instantaneous generative power of light applies as a creative principle; it also transfers remarkably well to the specific environment of love at first sight.

Light evokes the language of love and in thirteenth-century thought this discourse synthesizes corporeality. Bonaventure explicitly states that light is the most beautiful, most delightful and greatest among corporeal bodies.[73] His zealous language suggests that an affective response to beauty has gained ground. E.J.M. Spargo has in fact characterized Bonaventure's aesthetic as 'an aesthetic of love.'[74] It combines a love of beauty that is visually based with a concession to corporeality. We see hints here of the subordination of the intellect to a response of love in matters of beauty. Perhaps the combination of a concession to corporeality and a reordered relationship between love and knowledge encourage Bonaventure to takes pains to distinguish between spiritual and physical beauty. He recognizes that beauty leads to love and that any ambiguity in the language of the beauty of sight could lead to confusion between sensual and spiritual love. Spargo goes so far as to suggest that for Bonaventure concupiscence rather than pride is the root of all evil.[75] She suggests this because love and the aesthetic of visual beauty are central to his thought. The corporeality of light pushes the medieval discussion of the principles of beauty and the love to which beauty gives rise in the same direction.

The Neoplatonic categories of love and knowledge remain complementary; yet it becomes increasingly possible to consider these categories from a more phenomenological point of view, as evinced in the continuing importance of proportion in definitions of beauty. For instance, the beauty of light combines radiance and proportions in the thought of Grosseteste; the primacy that he gives to light incorporates both of these aesthetic emphases. His pleasure in light reaches the logical extent allowed it by the Neoplatonism of Augustine and Dionysius.[76] This fusion of principles reflects the interest in visual phenomena. The medieval passion for sheer colour and glitter, for hue and shimmer, combines with what in Augustine is a more abstract love for mathematical proportion. If Augustine's passion for the beauty of light seems to be more for an ontological category than a sensible reality, in the metaphysical aesthetic theories of the thirteenth century this passion extends more obviously to the enjoyment of proportion and harmony in the visual arts. This is perhaps most obvious in Bonaventure's aesthetic, which implements the principles of *De*

---

[73]   *Op. om.* 6, *Comm. in Librum Sapientiae*, 7.10.
[74]   E.M.J. Spargo, *The Category of the Aesthetic in the Philosophy of St. Bonaventura*, St. Bonaventura, 1953, 15.
[75]   Spargo, 65.
[76]   As de Bruyne writes, 'la couleur et la splendeur aussi bien que la figure et la proportion y sont déduites d'un principe unique: la lumière' (3.124).

musica in terms of light. Bonaventure expresses his commitment to the orders of number, weight, and measure in his *Sentences* commentary.[77] And he relates beauty and harmony bluntly elsewhere: 'Therefore since all things are beautiful and in a way delightful, and beauty and delight cannot be without proportion, and proportion first is in number, it is necessary for all to be numbered.'[78] The priority that he gives to light in the beauty of corporeal things, combined with this definition of beauty, insures an aesthetic of visual proportions. The relationship between subject and object in the sensible realm matters to Bonaventure.[79] That shift towards the sensible realm goes hand in hand with a more avowed passion for beauty, even though the rational definition of beauty remains solid.

Although the invention of linear perspective in art will not take place until the Quattrocento, interest in the problem of the relationship between subject and object stems back to Plato and recurs in the art of the medieval period. The issue is discussed explicitly in the *Liber de intelligentiis*, originally thought to be the work of Witelo but now dated about a generation earlier, closer to the time of Grosseteste. It nonetheless bears both Platonic and Aristotelian influences. This writer describes a pleasure based upon proportions, and the adaptation of the mind and the world to each other.[80] This concept clearly draws the subject and the object together in their phenomenal context, and the emphasis on pleasure here is noteworthy. He goes on to assert the value of light.[81] In a discussion in which he considers a number of the senses, that of sight receives most attention. A generation later, Witelo himself draws attention to the importance of subjective distance in contributing to a pleasing aesthetic experience.

---

[77] 'Sibi non convenit: cum enim summe bonus sit, non potest aliquid facere nisi bonum, et ita non potest facere nisi rem ad se ordinatam. Quoniam igitur ordo praesuppōnit numerum, et numerus praesupponit mensuram, quia non ordinantur ad aliud nisi numerata, et non numerantur nisi limitata; ideo necesse fuit, Deum facere omnia in numero, pondere et mensura' (*Op. om.* 1, *Sent.* d.43,a.1,q.3, conc.; de Bruyne, 3.189).

[78] My translation. 'Cum igitur omnia sint pulchra et quodam modo delectabilia; et pulcritudo et delectatio non sint absque proportione, et proportio primo sit in numeris: necesse est, omnia esse numerosa' (*Op. om. 5, Itinerarium* 2.10; de Bruyne, 3.189).

[79] 'Intrat igitur quantum ad tria rerum genera in animam humanam per apprehensionem totus iste sensibilis mundus. . . . Ad hanc apprehensionem, si sit rei convenientis, sequitur oblectatio. Delectatur autem sensus in obiecto per similitudinem abstractam percepto vel ratione speciositatis, sicut in visu. . . . Omnis autem delectatio est ratione proportionalitatis' (*Op. om. 5, Itin.* 2.4–5; de Bruyne, 192).

[80] Discussed in Eco, 68 and de Bruyne, 3.241. De Bruyne writes, 'Avant toute conscience il existe des proportions entre les choses: certaines choses conviennent à d'autres qui, par nature, y aspirent.' He goes on to discuss the diffusive nature of this desire: 'Avant toute connaissance distincte où s'opposent le sujet actif et l'objet, c'est-à-dire l'image apparente de l'idéal, le premier acte de conscience est un sentiment diffus et vague de l'harmonie de la nature déjà réalisée et d'une tension vers une perfection plus grande.' As he emphasizes, 'Toute vie est diffusive: toute vie se dilate; *toute vie est d'essence lumineuse*' (emphasis added).

[81] 'Lux inter omnia apprehensioni est maxime delectabile.' 'Liber de intelligentiis', in *Witelo: Ein Philosoph und Naturforscher des XIII Jahrhunderts*, ed. Clemens Baeumker, Munster, 1908, prop.12.

He emphasizes the importance of proportions in beauty, and he is particularly concerned with the phenomenon of seeing.[82] Some things, he says, need to be seen from a distance, others observed more closely, and the axis of vision also affects one's perception. This emphasis on the participation of the subject in the visual process in the intellectual climate where the world increasingly matters for its own sake represents a development that foreshadows the aesthetic breakthough of the fifteenth century. The writings of Witelo and others testify both to the heritage of theory and recent developments of natural philosophy, in which commingle tradition, evident in the Neoplatonic appreciation of geometry, and nascent science, demonstrable in the interest in matter.

This fusion of influences complicates our understanding of aesthetics as the psychological understanding of vision expands in the Middle Ages to include a serious discussion of physical aspects of perception. A new confidence in science extends discussions of the psychology of vision; and aesthetics naturally makes extensive reference to vision, specifically on the issue of the apprehension of beauty. Given developments in optics, the role of perspective in the phenomenal act of perceiving becomes increasingly important. Both optics and the inquiry into aesthetics coalesce around questions related to cognition in ways no longer reducible to the doctrine of illumination. In the fifteenth century, aesthetic theory of perspective is expressed through the analogy of the icon of an arrow through the eye. The earliest known optical analysis of linear perspective is Leon Battista Alberti's treatise of 1435, *De pictura*. In supplying instructions for working with perspective, Alberti issues this caveat:

> Never let it be supposed that anyone can be a good painter if he does not clearly understand what he is attempting to do. He draws the bow in vain who has nowhere to point the arrow.[83]

The development of precise formulations of the relationship between the viewing subject and the viewed object occurs fully in this climate of the renaissance, yet it has its roots in aesthetic concerns of the thirteenth century and well-established principles developed in that time. The image of the arrow, which figures prominently in technical writings of the fifteenth century, represents the collocation of a number of medieval concerns. It reveals that the categories of

---

[82] 'Pulchritudo comprehenditur a uisu ex comprehensione simplici formarum uisibilium placentium animae, uel coniunctione plurium uisibilium intentionum habentium ad inuicem proportionem debitam formae uisae' (Baeumker, 4.148).
[83] Leon Battista Alberti, *On Painting*, trans. J.R. Spencer, New Haven, 1966, 59. Michael Kubovy has an instructive discussion of these issues in the introduction to his study *The Psychology of Perspective and Renaissance Art*, Cambridge, 1986, 1–16. He cites as another influential reference Filarete's mid-century comparison of the architect drawing in perspective and the crossbowman taking his aim on a fixed point (14). Leonardo also appeals to archery imagery to describe how linear rays reach the eye. Leonardo da Vinci, *The Notebooks of Leonardo da Vinci*, ed. and trans. E. MacCurdy, London, 1938, 252.

love and knowledge continue to function as a system. The image has potency as a symbol of inquiry into perspective, a rationalistic discipline; we will encounter it again in, at least at first glance, a markedly different context, that of erotic love literature. Concepts related to vision, that of the arrow in particular, have a breadth of application that is disarming. It is not easy for us to reimagine the weight that such allusions carry in their various contexts.

The writings of Aquinas reveal how questions regarding the relationship between love and knowledge remain central and how the categories continue to function as a system in medieval thought. Under the influence of Aristotle, Aquinas approaches the topics of love and knowledge with more systematic inclusion of what happens on the level of the senses. His handling of the subject of light therefore differs from that of those thinkers for whom light is more strictly a metaphysical reality. Nonetheless, he participates in the same discourse of love, beauty, and truth and he uses the imagery of vision to clarify his position. As for the other thinkers we have examined, the system of love and knowledge ultimately concerns the eschatological apprehension of God.

Aquinas follows pseudo-Dionysius in his equation of beauty, goodness, and love. He writes,

> The beautiful is the same as the good, and they differ in application only. For since good is what all seek, the application of good is that which calms the desire; while that which calms the desire, by being seen or known, pertains to the application of beauty.[84]

The concept of desire (*appetitus*) locates this discussion in the context of movement, the activity of the will, which belongs to the realm of love broadly conceived in Aristotelian terms. Aquinas has already concluded that good is the proper cause of love, so that his formula closely resembles that of Dionysius. At this point in his argument Aquinas introduces the senses as important participants in the process of apprehending beauty, and the senses are important for their contributions to cognition: 'Consequently those senses chiefly regard the beautiful, which are the most cognitive, viz., sight and hearing, as ministering to reason; for we speak of beautiful sights and beautiful sounds.'[85] This is the specific contribution of beauty: 'Thus it is evident that beauty adds to a goodness a relation to the cognitive faculty' (2.q27.ar1.r3).[86] The appeal to

---

[84] My translation. 'Pulchrum est idem bono, sola ratione differens. Cum enim bonum sit quod omnia appetunt, de ratione boni est quod in eo quietetur appetitus, sed ad rationem pulchri pertinet quod in eius aspectu seu cognitione quietetur appetitus.' Thomas Aquinas, *Opera omnia 2, Summa theologiae*, ed. Robert Busa et al., Stuttgart, 1980, 2.q27.ar1.r3.

[85] Thomas Aquinas, *The 'Summa theologica' of St. Thomas Aquinas*, trans. Fathers of the English Dominican Province, London, 1914, 2.q27.ar1.r3. 'Unde et illi sensus praecipue respiciunt pulchrum, qui maxime cognoscitivi sunt, scilicet visus et auditus rationi deservientes, dicimus enim pulchra visibilia et pulchros sonos.'

[86] 'Sic patet quod pulchrum addit supra bonum, quendam ordinem ad vim cognoscitivam.'

cognition in the context of a discussion of love and beauty again brings us to the corner where these three meet. And the apprehension of beauty involves, crucially, the senses of maximum cognition, sight and sound. This elevated discourse has the most profound of implications.[87]

In the following article, Aquinas makes the importance of sight in the relationship between love and knowledge increasingly evident. Here he refers to both pseudo-Dionysius and Augustine to answer the question on which of love and knowledge comes first; and the analogy of sight plays an important role as Aquinas formulates his opinion. One of the objections he raises to the idea that knowledge is a cause of love involves an insight from Dionysius, that love can exist where there is no knowledge. But he recognizes that this brings him into contradiction with Augustine, who asserts that no one can love what is not known. Aquinas answers this difficulty by returning to the idea that good is the cause of love and that 'Love demands some apprehension of the good that is loved' (2.q27.ar2.co).[88] The idea of apprehension inspires him to quote Aristotle, and here we see the relevance of physical sight in his handling of the question of knowledge and love:

> For this reason the Philosopher says that bodily sight is the beginning of sensitive love: and in like manner the contemplation of spiritual beauty or goodness is the beginning of spiritual love. (2.q27.a2.co)[89]

Not only does this reference illustrate the importance of sight in love, but coming as it does in the middle of Aquinas' resolution of a conflict between authorities on divine love, it bridges the realms of sensory love and spiritual love, and illustrates the importance of sight in both realms. The relationship between human love and divine love is at once simple and complex, and analogies between the two are at the same time natural and strictly limited.

The information of the senses does give way to transcendent receptivity in contemplation. The conclusion by Aquinas that love precedes knowledge may cause some surprise, since Dominican spirituality rests upon its emphasis on

---

87   Umberto Eco discusses the relationship between the good, the beautiful, and the true with reference to whether or not beauty is a transcendental in Aquinas' 'system.' Umberto Eco, *The Aesthetics of Thomas Aquinas*, trans. Hugh Bredin, Cambridge, Mass., 1988, esp. 37–42. Eco uses the word 'system' in pursuit of the internal logic of Aquinas' thought: 'Every formal system has within it a little logical termite which nibbles away at it and spoils its perfect self-sufficiency' (202). I would argue that in his approach to the relationship between love, knowledge, and sight Aquinas acknowledges the paradoxical nature of this system.

88   'Amor requirit aliquam apprehensionem boni quod amatur.'

89   'Et propter hoc philosophus dicit . . . quod "visio corporalis est principium amoris sensitivi." Et similiter contemplatio spiritualis pulchritudinis vel bonitatis, est principium amoris spiritualis.'

the intellect.[90] At least in one place in the *Summa theologiae* Aquinas does refer
to contemplation as primarily an intellectual activity.[91] His attitude towards the
relationship between love and knowledge becomes more clear through an understanding of what he means by intellect. In a classic study of Christian mysticism, Rowan Williams shows how the concept of the intellect (*intellectus*) is
for Aquinas rich and comprehensive:

> Its central meaning seems to be that it designates the human subject as
> receptive and responsive: receptive to the impressions of 'intelligible
> form,' discernible order and structure, in the realities it encounters, and
> responsive in its *engagement* with objects, working on them and willing
> things about them. *Intellectus*, then, means 'understanding' in a very
> comprehensive sense; and it involves a genuine union of knower and
> known correlative to the union of lover and beloved.[92]

Understanding involves moving and moving involves willing, the realm of desire, of love. Even the beginning of understanding involves the desire to be
completed by the other. It is a system indebted to Aristotle's physics yet, as
Williams points out, places Aquinas very close to Bernard in terms of mystical
outlook. As we would now expect, this tight relationship between love and
knowledge has as its ultimate goal a vision of God. If for Aquinas this process
of apprehending Beauty begins in sense vision, it culminates in a mystical experience of such simplicity that it apparently banishes the intellect. What begins as receptivity and responsiveness becomes enlarged in contemplation
to complete receptivity, transcending sense and reason. He warns that this is a
strange state and that the contemplative relies on grace. It brings both delight
and pain.

Aquinas' thought gives us another indication of the enduring complexity of
the parasitic relationship between love and knowledge in late medieval thought
and the increasing reliance on phenomenal vision to explain metaphysical concepts. As vision becomes more and more interesting as a phenomenon, it contributes to various registers of the discourses of love and knowledge. In
metaphysics it becomes a central term but one which at no time is reducible to
a single meaning. Rather, Neoplatonic texts impress many medieval thinkers
with the ubiquitous importance of what it means to see and participate in the
light. This attitude is transferred to natural philosophy, especially through
Grosseteste. In the latter half of the thirteenth century and in the fourteenth
century vision becomes coterminous with a new kind of knowledge which is
the product of human inquiry into the way things work, including the mind as

90   Simon Tugwell, 'Dominican Spirituality, Dominicans,' in *A Dictionary of Christian
Spirituality*, ed. Gordon S. Wakefield, London, 1983, 119–20.
91   2.2ae.180.i.co.
92   Rowan Williams, *The Wound of Knowledge*, 2nd ed., London, 1990, 125.

it processes information from the sensible world. When we come to Chaucer's poetry, we will see that his appeal to sight has come through the filters both of Neoplatonic categories and interest in the physical phenomenon.

If vision does come to have important links with naturalistic inquiry, the enthusiam for vision in mystical thought continues unabated and positively flourishes in late medieval writings in the vernacular. The same categories apply here regardless of the degree of interest in the details of the philosophical and theological background. English religious and mystical texts of the fourteenth century, such as the practically-oriented writings by and for anchorites and anchoresses, exhibit the ubiquitous and lingering importance of what it means to see and participate in the light in terms easily traceable to Neoplatonic influences. The writings of Richard Rolle, Julian of Norwich, and the author of *The Cloud of Unknowing*, for instance, indicate the widespread appeal of this cluster of ideas. Written in the vernacular and seized upon by readers and writers of both sexes, these texts express powerful ideas of both visual beauty and insight; they provide us with contemporary examples of the appeal of physical and spiritual language of sight and the system this language informs.

Richard Rolle provides beautiful expressions of the vitality of visual concepts in the religious life and especially applies the language of light directly to Jesus. He describes his Lord as his guide into light as well as the object of his desire for a complete vision:

> Heyle Jhesu, leder to lyght! In saule þou ert ful swete.
> Þi luf schynes day and nyght, þat strenghes me in þis strete.
> Lene me langyng to þi sight, and gif me grace til grete;
> For þou, Jhesu, hase þat myght, þat al my bale may bete.
>
> . . . On þe I sette al my desyre, þou ert my luf-langyng.
> Þi luf es byrnand als þe fyre, þat ever on he wil spryng.[93]

The image of the fire conveys the idea of upward yearning, fire being the lightest of the four elements; it also is a source of light and a visual phenomenon. Elsewhere Rolle appeals to this same collocation of concepts and adds an intellectual dimension to his religious fervour:

> Me langes, lede me to þi lyght, and festen in þe al my thoght.
> In þi swetnes fyll my hert, my wa make wane till noght.
>
> . . . Þi wil es my ȝhernyng; of lufe þou kyndel þe fyre,
> Þat I in swet lovyng with aungels take my hyre.[94]

[93] Richard Rolle, 'Heyle Jhesu my creatowre,' in *English Writings of Richard Rolle, Hermit of Hampole*, ed. Hope Emily Allen, Oxford, 1931, 48, 5–8; 10–11.
[94] Richard Rolle, 'Jhesu, God sonn, Lord of mageste,' in *English Writings*, 41, 7–8; 11–12.

In keeping with the metaphysical tradition, he uses light as the nexus for combining intellectual and emotional spiritual responsiveness and indeed for grading the degrees of love.[95] As Julian of Norwich will do, Rolle seizes upon the Passion to elaborate upon physical aspects of vision, as in these lines from 'Jhesu, God sonn, Lord of mageste':

> Whyte was his naked breste, and rede his blody syde;
> Wan was his faire face, his woundes depe and wyde.
>
> (42, 37–8)

Rolle displays his interest in colour and a striking visual contrast, here between the whiteness of Christ's breast and the redness of his bloody side. He incorporates this urgent appeal to the sense of sight into a poem that initially and predominantly focuses upon spiritual forms of sight. Later in the poem he in effect inverts the visual circumstances, enlarging this theme still further, by commenting upon Christ's circumstances in this way: 'Blynded was his faire ene, his flesch blody for bette' (43, 41).

Religious writings for women also refer to the beauty of Jesus as a point of appeal. The guide for anchoresses *Ancrene Riwle* encourages the individual to seek God with the eye of the heart and turn away from worldly things. It nonetheless emphasizes the physical beauty of the son of God. The author describes Christ as a heroic knight who has come to win a damsel's heart, and part of his charm is his attractiveness:

> Hwet wult tu mare he com him seolf on ende. schawde hire his feire neb.
> as þe þe wes of alle men feherest to bihalden.[96]
>
> (What more do you want? At last he came himself; showed her his handsome face, as the most supremely handsome of men.)[97]

The visual attractiveness of Christ finds its way into religious writings in a variety of contexts where it is used to convey notions of truth and love. The treatise on virginity *Hali Meiðhad* employs a variety of arguments to convince the reader of the reasonableness of remaining steadfast in virginity. Among the inducements that the author marshalls is the surpassing attractiveness of Christ,

---

[95]   For Rolle the eye of the heart looking into heaven provides the bridge to the third and highest degree of love, contemplation: 'At þe begynyng, when þou comes þartil, þi gastly egh es taken up intil þe blysse of heven, and þar lyghtned with grace and kyndelde with fyre of Christes lufe, sa þat þou sal verraly fele þe bernyng of lufe in þi hert ever mare and mare, liftand þi thoght to God, and feland lufe, joy, and swetnes.' Richard Rolle, 'Ego Dormio,' in *English Writings*, 69.

[96]   *The English Text of the Ancrene Riwle: Ancrene Wisse, edited from MS Corpus Christi College, Cambridge, 402*, ed. J.R.R. Tolkien, EETS os 249, London, 1962, 198.

[97]   *Guide for Anchoresses*, Part 7, in *Medieval English Prose for Women: Selections from the Katherine Group and* Ancrene Wisse, ed. Bella Millett and Jocelyn Wogan-Browne, Oxford, 1990, 115.

whose beauty the author describes in terms of light. Christ is the pinnacle of beauty and the most desirable of men:

> ʒef þet tu wilnest were þe muche wlite habbe, nim him of hwas wlite beoð awundret of þe sunne ant te mone, upo hwas nebscheft þe engles ne beoð neauer fulle to bihalden; for hwen he ʒeueð feirlec to al þet is feier in heouene ant in eorðe, muchele mare he haueð, wiðuten ei etlunge, ethalden to himseoluen.[98]

> (If you want a husband who is very handsome, take him whose beauty the sun and moon admire, whose face the angels are never weary of gazing at; for when he gives beauty to everything that is beautiful in heaven and on earth, he will have kept inestimably more for himself.)[99]

Treatises aimed at the individual who has chosen a solitary path, as well as those that deal more explicitly with contemplation and revelations, refer to Christ in terms of light and splendour; his beauty serves as a source of visual comfort. Even when the phenomenon of revelations or visions is not central, appealing to visual concepts to teach about Christ remains significant.

Julian of Norwich provides us with an excellent example of the movement from the physical to the spiritual as she reflects upon her goal of pursuing Christ whilst always keeping her sight upon the faith of Holy Church. With this as her measuring rod, she seeks further revelations from God that come to her in various forms of vision:

> For the feyth of holy chyrch, which I had before hand vnderstondyng, and as I hope by the grace of god wylle fully kepe it in vse and in custome, stode contynually in my syghte, wyllyng and meanyng never to receyve ony thyng that myght be contrary ther to. And with this intent and with this meanyng I beheld the shewyng with all my dyligence, for in all thys blessed shewyng I behelde it as in gods menyng.
>
> All this was shewde by thre partes, that is to sey by bodyly syght, and by worde formyde in my vnderstondyng, and by goostely syght.[100]

Julian roots her entire spiritual life in concepts of vision. Even before embarking on a quest to understand her revelations, she articulates her spirituality as one of keeping the faith of the Church before her eyes; she interprets her mystical experience in light of intellectual assent. Building upon this foundation, she affirms that her revelations themselves involve three kinds of vision strictly in keeping with the precedent laid down by Augustine, pseudo-Dionysius, and

---

[98]   *Hali Meiðhad,* ed. Bella Millett, EETS 284, London, 1982, 20.
[99]   *A Letter on Virginity,* in Millett and Wogan-Browne, 35–7.
[100]   Julian of Norwich, *A Book of Showings to the Anchoress Julian of Norwich,* ed. Edmund Colledge and James Walsh, Toronto, 1978, 323.

others. For her, as for them, physical sight serves as the foundation for her mystical insights and she emphasizes the grounding of her experience in physicality; she stresses the act of focusing on a cross before her and emphasizes that she sees the Passion of Christ physically (Ch. 10). That physical touchstone of the Christian religion becomes the touchstone of her spiritual visual experience. As with other religious writers and as we have perhaps now come to expect, the language of vision, insight, and intellectual assent leads naturally to expressions of love:

> Theyse be two workynges that may be seen in this vision. That one is sekyng; the other is beholdyng. . . . For it is his wille þat we know that he shall aper sodenly and blyssydefully to all his lovers. (334–5)

As she brings the account of her revelations to its climax, Julian's language becomes increasingly effusive:

> I had in perty touchyng, syght and feelyng in thre propertees of god, in whych the strenght and þe effecte of alle þe revelacion stondyth. . . . The propertees are theyse: lyfe, loue and lyght. In lyfe is mervelous homely-hed, in loue is gentylle curtesse, and in lyght is endlesse kyndnesse.
>   Theyse iij propertees were seen on oone goodnesse. (722–3)

Julian links love, light, and goodness in a way very reminiscent of pseudo-Dionysius.

The anonymous *Cloud of Unknowing* treats images of light and vision differently for it presents the *via negativa* as the way to closer communion with God. Images of cloud and darkness replace those of brilliance and clarity, but the *Cloud* author nevertheless conceives of the enterprise in striking and engaging visual terms. At times his appeal to visual images is both highly imaginative and rigorous:

> & wene not, for I clepe it a derknes or a cloude, þat it be any cloude congelid of þe humours þat fleen in þe ayre, ne ȝit any derknes soche as is in þin house on niȝtes, when þi candel is oute. For soche a derknes & soche a cloude maist þou ymagin wiþ coriouste of witte, for to bere before þin iȝen in þe liȝtest day of somer; & also aȝenswarde in þe derkist niȝt of wynter þou mayst ymagin a clere schinyng liȝt. Lat be soche falsheed; I mene not þus.[101]

The author draws upon profoundly physical examples of light to drive home the point that the darkness which concerns him is of a different order. His attitude towards spiritual progress and that of writers who refer to an ascent into

---

[101] *The Cloud of Unknowing*, ed. Phyllis Hodgson, EETS os 218, Oxford, 1944, 23.

greater degrees of light and insight give us the two sides of the same Neo-platonic metaphysical coin. The *Cloud* author fully understands the discourse in which he is a participant and recognizes the typical stages of vision which the would-be contemplative expects to negotiate. He warns his reader against them:

> Trauayle not in þi wittes ne in þin ymaginacion on no wise. For I telle þee trewly, it may not be comen to by trauaile in þeim; & þerfore leue þeim & worche not wiþ þeim. (23)

The author does not really put anything in place of the visual paradigm. Indeed, that is precisely his point: he seeks to remove anything that, in his terms, is higher than the individual and therefore comes between the individual yearning for God and God himself. What can threaten to come between the soul and God he conceives of primarily in visual terms; what is most desirable is a state of blind love:

> . . . a blynde steryng of loue vnto God for him-self; . . . & beter þee were for to haue it & for to fele it in þin affeccion goostly, þen it is for to haue þe iȝe of þi soule openid in contemplacion. (34)

As other religious writers attempt to do, the *Cloud* author tries to account for the categories of love and knowledge; his approach, however, differs radically.

In the fourteenth century the tripartite system flourishes both in terms of aesthetics and the pursuit of God. The strands of love and knowledge bind together in the language of vision. The metaphysical basis results in greater emphasis being placed upon spiritual and internal kinds of vision but the physical sense of sight always maintains a place of some importance. And as aesthetic ideas evolve, the coordination of these concepts of love, knowledge, and beauty produces a greater and greater interest in the physicality of vision. Such an interest taps into the Neoplatonic sources, at least in the period that concerns us here; however, fresh ideas on the nature of physical sight will certainly supplement and alter metaphysical notions. The metaphysical tradition to which Chaucer is heir certainly sets a precedent for collocating ideas of love and knowledge and exploring both conflict and complementarity between them, especially in visual terms.

2

A Two-fold Symbol of Knowledge
Sight in Natural Philosophy

> They speken of Alocen, and Vitulon,
> And Aristotle, that writen in hir lyves
> Of queynte mirours and of perspectives,
> As knowen they that han hir bookes herd.[1]

> (Chaucer)

> Look for the parasite who reestablishes a healthy situation.
> . . . Health remains the couple message-noise. Systems
> work because they do not work. Nonfunctioning remains
> essential for functioning. And that can be formalized.
> Given, two stations and a channel. They exchange mes-
> sages. If the relation succeeds, if it is perfect, optimum,
> and immediate; it disappears as a relation. If it is there, if
> it exists, that means that it failed. It is only mediation. Re-
> lation is nonrelation. And that is what the parasite is.[2]

> (Michel Serres)

Vision in natural philosophy extends the parasitic relationship of hostility and symbiosis between love and knowledge. In Chaucer's Squire's Tale, a knight brings four gifts to the court of Genghis Khan, each of which provokes marvel and considerable debate as to its qualities. Of the brass horse, for instance,

> Diverse folk diversely they demed;
> As many heddes, as manye wittes ther been. (202-3)

As each gift in turn comes under scrutiny, speculation on its properties touches

---

[1] Geoffrey Chaucer, *Canterbury Tales,* V.232–5.

[2] Serres, 78–9. 'Cherchez le parasite qui rétablit la santé altérée. . . . La santé demeure le couple message-bruit. Les systèmes marchent parce qu'ils ne marchent pas. Le non-fonctionnement demeure essentiel pour le fonctionnement. Et cela peut être formalisé. Soit deux stations et un canal. Elles échangent, comme on dit, des messages. Si la relation réussit, parfaite, optimale, immédiate, elle s'annule comme relation. Si elle est là, si elle existe, c'est qu'elle a échoué. Elle n'est que médiation. La relation est la non-relation. Et c'est cela, le parasite' (Serres, 107).

on various branches of learning. Chaucer parodies a speculative appeal to authorities and theories at the same time as he gives an indication of the smorgasbord of opinion available in his time. The squire's insistence on recounting the substance of this speculation reflects a narrative style that verges on the interminable: the tale as a whole represents an excess of rhetoric, detail, and learning. At the same time it belongs to an apprentice of chivalry, one whom the Franklin praises only partly ironically for his gentle manner and 'discrecioun' (685). The tale is a romance and the squire blends chivalry, in the courtly context and knightly characters, with love, in the adventure of Canacee and references to heroes of romance such as Lancelot. The Squire's Tale reveals Chaucer's facility for bringing together the popular, in fulfilling the expectations of romance, and the learned, including a parody of learning.

The allusion to Alhazen ('Alocen'), Witelo ('Vitulon'), and Aristotle is part of his focus on knowledge: the names represent intellectual endeavour in a general way, and a sub-discipline of particular interest in natural philosophy. Apart from Witelo, Chaucer could have gotten his list of theorists from *Le Roman de la Rose*. The *Roman*, especially in the continuation by Jean de Meun, offers an encyclopedic collection of facts, in which the sub-discipline of optics figures prominently. That Chaucer includes Witelo suggests at the very least an updated understanding of work in this area and its ongoing ability to attract the attention of non-specialists. Together, the names of Alhazen, Aristotle, and Witelo form a list that suitably represents contemporary optical learning. By Chaucer's time optics has become a powerful symbol of knowledge. Increasingly in the late Middle Ages, it is coterminous with an investigation that explains the deepest mysteries of natural philosophy: this is the first way in which it symbolizes knowledge. The second lies in the rigorous application of this sub-discipline to philosophical and psychological inquiries into how knowledge is acquired.

The French concept of *parasitisme* incorporates an inorganic dimension in that *parasitisme* can mean radio interference as well as an organic hostility/host/hospitality relationship. The overlay of a more scientific discourse onto existing metaphysical interest in this relationship introduces just such an inorganic dimension – rays, geometry, disembodied forms – to the potential meaning of sight. The impress of metaphysics remains and is in fact essential to the development of optical theories in the West in the thirteenth century. This scientific discourse contributes to the ways in which sight, love, and knowledge come together; it increases the resulting dissonance as well. If sight in metaphysics influences scientific thinking, sight as a subject of scientific interest will continue to feed back into theological thinking and influence more secular writings of love and sight as well.

The Rise of a Pivotal Sub-Discipline
The development of optical concepts in the East was dominated by the work of Alhazen, or Ibn al-Haytham (c.965–c.1039). Alhazen achieved this status as a

leading authority through groundbreaking work that successfully combined salient aspects of three leading theories that had competed with one another since Greek antiquity.[3] One theory, which has been labelled extramission, suggested that rays pour out from the organs and travel to the objects. Its greatest proponents were mathematicians such as Euclid and Ptolemy because rays streaming from the eyes allowed for a mathematical understanding of vision. The eye became the apex of a cone made up of the rays as they fanned out to strike the entire object being perceived. The lines that made up this cone allowed for depth perception and kept the object's surface properly organized. (It is a version of this theory that we encounter when we read about the power of the beloved's gaze to transfix the lover.) The problem with extramission, however, was that one could perceive distant objects as soon as the eyes were opened. Unable to provide a satisfactory explanation for this phenomenon, proponents could merely assert the terrific speed of the rays.

The opposite understanding, that whole images or forms stream off objects and penetrate the eyes, is known as the intromission theory, and was developed by Epicurus. It accounted for the immediacy of sight and promoted a physical understanding of vision. But how could the form of a very large object shrink sufficiently to enter the eye? Also, there was no mechanism in this theory to account for perspective. The third theory combined elements of the first two and was attractive to physiologists. In this version the form meets in the air together with a raylike *pneuma* from the eye. Galen developed a version of this theory to explain the function of the optic nerve, which for him served as a conduit for the *pneuma*. The greatest challenge facing visual theory was know-

---

3   David Hahm has traced the development of early Hellenistic theories of vision and he reminds us that we cannot attain a complete history of Greek optics since we lack parts of the optical treatises by such thinkers as Ptolemy and have only glimpses of the intellectual activity in the century after Aristotle. His work, even as it stands, is known only through a Latin translation of an Arabic translation; furthermore, the first part of the work is completely absent. A fragment attributed to Geminus (first century B.C.) reflects the basic options available. In it the writer asserts that optics does not decide whether 'rays are poured out from the organs of sight and effluences travel to the surfaces of objects, or images streaming off from perceptible bodies in rectilinear motion penetrate the eyes, or the intervening air [between the object and the eye] is extended together with, or carried along with, the raylike *pneuma* of the eye.' David Hahm, 'Early Hellenistic Theories of Vision and the Perception of Color,' in *Studies in Perception*, ed. Peter K. Machamer and Robert G. Turnbull, Columbus, 1978, 61. David Lindberg offers a brief introduction to the theories of antiquity, and he sets out a basic correspondence between view and proponents. David Lindberg, 'The Science of Optics,' in his *Studies in the History of Medieval Optics*, London, 1983, I, 338–68. The strength of Lindberg's discussion lies in his demonstration that the three theories represent basic conceptual differences, and this can help us understand the context that was received into thirteenth-century discussions of optics. He puts it this way: 'But to classify ancient theories of vision in terms of the direction of radiation or the role of the medium in vision is to overlook fundamental aspects of ancient optics – and also to make the debate among the various theories seen trivial and those who debated for a thousand years look foolish' (341).

ing what criteria a solid theory of vision ought to satisfy, for which Alhazen came up with the most satisfying answer.

Alhazen almost single-handedly gave the science of optics a more solid footing and showed how it served as the nexus for the three separate disciplines which stood behind the competing optical theories. This capacity of optics to interest mathematicians, those interested in physical forms, and physiologists helped establish it as a symbol of knowledge of nature. Alhazen reconstructed the intromission theory of vision to account for weaknesses in earlier models. In doing so, he applied the principle of the cone from the Euclidean theory, in which the eye is the apex of the cone and the span of the object perceived its base, a principle accepted as crucial to the phenomenon of perspective. The major complaints against the intromission theory had been restated by an earlier Arabic thinker, al-Kindi, whose key argument was a mathematical one. Using the example of a circle laid edgewise before the eye, he interpreted the intromission theory as positing that one should still perceive the full circularity of the object. This should happen because, in al-Kindi's understanding of the intromission theory, the form emitted from the object represents the entire object, not just its surface. The orientation should not matter, since within the eye the laws of perspective no longer apply.[4]

With the challenge of accounting for perspective before him, Alhazen developed another point clearly articulated by al-Kindi, that luminous bodies emit rays in all directions from each point of their surface.[5] For al-Kindi, the behaviour of external light merely served as an analogy for his claim that rays issue forth from every point on the surface of the eye. Alhazen transformed this seemingly simple concept into a conical theory of intromission. To deal with the objection that rays of colour and light from every point on the object would fall indiscriminately on every part of the eye, resulting in total confusion, Alhazen noted that only one ray falling on each point of the eye's surface would be incident perpendicularly. This established a one-to-one correspondence between points on the surface of the object and points on the eye, allowing for clear and organized perception. Furthermore, the object becomes the broad base of a cone and the eye its apex, thus satisfying the basic requirement for perception within a geometrical framework.[6] In subsequent sections of *De*

---

4   Lindberg offers this summary: 'In short, al-Kindi sees no means by which the intromission theory, which for him is the theory of coherent forms, can be made compatible with the laws of perspective.' David Lindberg, *Theories of Optics from al-Kindi to Kepler*, Chicago, 1977, 23.

5   Alhazen, *De aspectibus*, in *Opticae thesaurus Alhazeni Arabis libri septem, nunc primum editi a Federico Risnero*, Basel, 1572, 1.prop.13.

6   'Lineae ergo radiales sunt lineae imaginabiles, et figuratur per eas qualitas situs, super quam patitur uisus ex forma. Et iam declaratum est quod quando uisus oppositus fuerit rei uisae, figurabitur inter rem uisam et centrum uisus puramis, cuius uertex erit centrum uisus, et basis eius superficies rei uisae, et erit inter quodlibet punctum superficiei rei uisae, et inter centrum uisus linea recta, intellecta perpendiculariter super superficies tunicarum uisus' (1.prop.24).

aspectibus, Alhazen concerned himself with, among other matters, the psychology of perception and the physiology of vision, thus tying in all three strands of optical inquiry and securing his place as a significant commentator on the science of optics.

From the formative days of Greek theory, optical theories involved three different conceptual frameworks, the mathematical, the physical, and the physiological. Alhazen gave vision a thorough, naturalistic explanation because of his preoccupation with perspective, a compelling problem articulated by Euclid and the mathematicians, restated in Arabic thought by al-Kindi. The arrival of Arabic theories in the West did not sweep away all opposition; other theories continued to flourish. But the importance of perspective in optical theory now had a fresh, strong basis, and in the writings of Bacon, Pecham, and Witelo this would develop into a tradition of thought, combining geometry and the role of physical forms. It was far from clear before Kepler that this tradition would win the day but the issue of perspective was raised to greater heights in the thirteenth century, and was firmly fixed in the minds of many.

Natural philosophy in the West in the Middle Ages always had paid particular attention to the eyes. The most influential discussion in the West of the phenomenon of sight and the operations of the eyes was that of Plato's in the *Timaeus*. Chalcidius preserved the first half of this work in his translation and accompanying commentary. In the *Timaeus* Plato presents his theory of optics in some depth, with sections on both vision and the properties of mirrors. His ideas on sight constitute what commentators on the history of optics describe as a combined extramission-intromission theory, with outside light as well as light from the visible bodies assisting the fire of light streaming from the eyes and making the eyes active in the visual process.[7] Chalcidius added discussion of other conceptualizations of what sight involved, so that his commentary became an important general source at the same time as it promoted Platonic ideas.[8]

Augustine's references to the processes of vision also carried a great deal of

---

[7]   Lance K. Donaldson-Evans has shown how this theory, which Plato probably developed from Empedocles, accounts for what he calls the 'Aggressive Eyes' topos in medieval literature. 'Love's Fatal Glance: Eye Imagery and Maurice Scève's Délie,' *Neophilologus* 62 (1978), 202–11. Donaldson-Evans explores the importance of sight in Plato's philosophical system. Although these ideas would not have been directly available until late in the medieval period, they are noteworthy. Plato ascribed the greatest value of any of the senses to the eyes in the *Symposium*. Vision plays an important role in the apprehension of beauty, and earthly beauty arouses love as the counterpart to the beauty of divine forms.

[8]   Chalcidius restates the three aspects of the Platonic theory: 'Tribus ergo his concurrentibus uisus existit trinaque est ratio uidendi: lumen caloris intimi per oculos means, quae principalis est causa, lumen extra positum, consanguineum lumini nostro, quod simul operatur et adiuuat, lumen quoque, quod ex corporibus uisibilium specierum fluit, flamma seu color, qui perinde est atque sunt omnia sine quibus propositum opus effici non potest, ut sine ferramentis quae sunt operi faciendo necessaria; quorum si quid deerit, impediri uisum necesse est.' Chalcidius, *Timaeus. A Calcidio translatus commentarioque instructus*, ed. J.H. Waszink, London, 1962, 256.

weight, as we might expect, and when it was useful to do so later medieval thinkers working with considerably advanced theories still quoted him on the subject. His understanding of how sight occurs reflects the Platonic influence. In *De Genesi ad litteram* Augustine has this to say about the process of seeing:

> Now this is certainly a ray of material light that shines forth from our eyes and touches objects so remote with such speed that it cannot be calculated or equalled. It is quite obvious, then, that all those measureless spaces are traversed at one time in a single glance. (4.34.54)[9]

He follows Plato in promoting a theory of the emission of visual rays. His opinion also reveals the concern over the problem of explaining how these rays could travel 'measureless spaces' and see planets, for instance, instantaneously. Following on from this assertion Augustine extrapolates to make a point about the mind. We are now familiar with the fact that interior vision interests him far more than physical sight:

> Now, if vision in the eyes of the body is capable of such speed, what cannot intellectual vision do, even in the case of men, and much more in the case of angels? And what can we say of the speed of the supreme Wisdom of God Himself, which penetrates everywhere by reason of Its purity, and which no stain ever sullies? (4.34.55)[10]

This train of thought depends upon a reference not only to physical sight but to a specific theory of how sight occurs, where the concept of speed garners most attention. Augustine reveals further understanding of the subtleties of sight in his consideration of perception. Medieval debate about vision involves other problems of visual apprehension besides accounting for speed. These include the adaptation of the external to the internal:

> But we ought rather to believe that the nature of the intellectual mind is so formed as to see those things which, according to the disposition of the Creator, are subjoined to intelligible things in the natural order, in a sort of incorporeal light of its own kind, as the eye of the flesh sees the things that lie about it in this corporeal light, of which light it is made to be receptive and to which it is adapted.[11]

[9] 'Et certe iste corporeae lucis est radius, emicans ex oculis nostris, et tam longe posita tanta celeritate contingens, ut aestimari compararique non possit. Nempe hic et illa omnia tam ampla immensaque spatia simul uno ictu transiri manifestum est.'
[10] 'Quod si oculorum carnalium acies celeritate tantum potest, quid mentis acies vel humanae? Quanto magis angelicae? Quid jam de ipsius summae Dei Sapientiae celeritate dicatur, quae attingit ubique propter suam munditiem, et nihil inquinatum in eam incurrit?'
[11] Augustine, *On the Trinity* 12.15.24. 'Sed potius credendum est mentis intellectualis ita conditam esse naturam, ut rebus intelligibilibus naturali ordine, disponente Conditore, sub-

This question of receptivity and adaptation concerns such issues as the problem of how a very large object when seen can fit inside the eye. Augustine takes on important questions in natural philosophy and expresses influential opinions, though his interests ultimately lie in internal and metaphysical processes. His fascination with light and vision inspired grand theorizing along these lines.

In the thirteenth century, Robert Grosseteste (d.1253) enhanced the status of the science of optics by making it no less than the basis for understanding all of natural philosophy in a theory that combined metaphysics with natural philosophy. He describes the theory in detail in *De luce*, which opens with the profound emphasis placed upon the corporeity and effulgence of light. Grosseteste appeals to light to describe the multiplication of forms, to explain the phenomenon of matter:

> Now the extension of matter in three dimensions is a necessary concomitant of corporeity, and this despite the fact that both corporeity and matter are in themselves simple substances lacking all dimension. But a form that is in itself simple and without dimension could not introduce dimension in every direction into matter, which is likewise simple and without dimension, except by multiplying itself and diffusing itself instantaneously in every direction and thus extending matter in its own diffusion.[12]

The understanding of multiplying species derives from the Neoplatonic doctrine of emanation. Plotinus writes in *The Enneads* that

> All things which exist, as long as they remain in being, necessarily produce from their own substances, in dependence on their present power, a surrounding reality directed to what is outside them, a kind of image of the archetypes from which it was produced: fire produces the heat which comes from it; snow does not only keep its cold inside itself. Perfumed things show this particularly clearly. As long as they exist, something is diffused from themselves around them, and what is near them enjoys their existence.[13]

This quotation reveals both the early meaning of the idea and its broad appli-

juncta sic ista videat in quadam luce sui generis incorporea, quemadmodum oculus carnis videt quae in hac corporea luce circumadjacent, cujus lucis capax eique congruens est creatus.'

[12] *On Light*, 10. 'Corporeitas vero est, quam de necessitate consequitur extensio materiae secundum tres dimensiones, cum tamen utraque, corporeitas scilicet et materia, sit substantia in se ipsa simplex, omni carens dimensione. Formam vero in se ipsa simplicem et dimensione carentem in materiam similiter simplicem et dimensione carentem dimensionem in omnem partem inducere fuit impossibile, nisi seipsam multiplicando et in omnem partem subito se diffundendo et in sui diffusione materiam extendendo' ('De luce,' 51).

[13] Plotinus, *The Enneads*, ed. and trans. A.H. Armstrong, London, 1984, 5.1.6.

cation. The precise meaning of the term *species* was to have a profound effect upon the content of intellectual debates in vision and epistemology in late medieval thought. Grosseteste's theory of multiplication is important for optics and indeed for the entire inquiry into natural philosophy. He applies the theory in his treatise *De lineis, angulis et figuris*, which shows the detailed application of the diffusion of light.[14] Since optical concepts lie at the root of creation, to study them is to unwrap the structure and physical dynamics of the material universe.[15]

Augustine's thought is an integral part of Grosseteste's conceptualization and part of what makes it a metaphysical theory.[16] In his *De veritate*, Grosseteste alludes to the Church Father, drawing a parallel between how truth is perceived in supreme light and how corporeal eyes see coloured bodies in the light of the sun. The theological implications provide a significant reason for understanding the value of light and contribute to the status of the discipline of optics, even though later thinkers would concern themselves less with the metaphysical basis. A.C. Crombie acknowledges this, though he goes on to assert Grosseteste's leading role as an empiricist: 'Grosseteste was able to give Augustinian-Platonism a twist which turned the inquiry for God in things into the first systematic experimental investigation of things.'[17] Although Grosseteste may not have had the pivotal role in developing empirical methodology that Crombie ascribes to him, his contribution to optics is indisputable.[18] The narrower question of his contribution to empiricism should not obscure the

---

14 'Utilitas considerationis linearum, angulorum, et figurarum est maxima, quoniam impossibile est sciri naturalem philosophiam sine illis. . . . Valent quidem in actione et passione, et hoc sive sit in materiam sive in sensum; et hoc sive in sensum visus, secundum quod occurrit, sive in alios sensus in quorum actione oportet addere alia super ea, quae faciunt visum.' Robert Grosseteste, 'De lineis, angulis et figuris seu de fractionibus et reflexionibus radiorum,' Baur, 59–60.

15 A.C. Crombie summarizes: 'In the beginning of time God had created out of nothing unformed matter (*materia prima*) and light (*lux*) which, by autodiffusion, had produced the dimensions of space and then all subsequent beings. For this reason Grosseteste believed that the study of optics was the key to the understanding of the physical world; and it was impossible to study optics without geometry, for light behaved according to geometrical laws.' A.C. Crombie, *Robert Grosseteste and the Origins of Experimental Science 1100–1700*, Oxford, 1953, 104.

16 Lawrence Lynch has amply demonstrated the presence of Augustine's epistemology of light in Grosseteste's writings in 'The Doctrine of Divine Ideas and Illumination in Robert Grosseteste, Bishop of Lincoln,' *Medieval Studies* 3 (1941), 161–73.

17 Crombie, 13.

18 Bruce Eastwood has challenged the extent to which Grosseteste can be seen to practise empiricism, emphasizing Grosseteste's reliance on the ontological significance of numbers and mathematics. The use of geometry is not sufficient proof of his empiricism: 'But the geometrical treatment of light could be more than just a method; its metaphysical significance stemmed from the place of mathematics itself in the neoplatonic outlook. When one recalls the high place accorded to mathematics in Plato's ontology and epistemology, the metaphysical suggestiveness of applying geometry to any science is clear.' Bruce Eastwood, 'Medieval Empiricism: The Case of Grosseteste's Optics,' *Speculum* 43 (1968), 306.

fact that he draws several different strands together concerning the topic of light. Besides drawing in Augustinian doctrine and giving the study of light a sound theological foundation, Grosseteste's concept of multiplication promises a high return on the study of optics.

Besides Neoplatonism, *De luce* also shows the influence of Aristotelianism.[19] The only source which Grosseteste notes in the treatise is Aristotle's *De caelo et mundo*, referred to as he lays the foundation for his discussion, and the Philosopher's concepts of the world as a physical system permeate his thinking. Aristotle argues that earth gathers in a sphere around the centre of the universe, a process Grosseteste takes the other way in his concept of multiplication while still retaining the idea of a single, central point. Furthermore, Grosseteste follows the Aristotelian concept of a finite cosmos which light fills evenly, leaving no vacuum in in accordance with Aristotle's dictum that nature abhors a vacuum. In this treatise on light, therefore, Grosseteste synthesizes Neoplatonism with Aristotelian physics, promotes interest in Aristotle and questions of physics with reference to light, and, as James McEvoy has observed, sets the challenge of 'circumscribing Aristotelian scientific understanding within the entirety of revealed truth,' where knowledge and devotion become fused.[20] Evidence from Grosseteste's mature scientific writings and theological works from the period of the late 1220s to the late 1230s suggests that he came to appreciate the importance of light in the physical cosmos as his mind was turning increasingly to theological considerations. In this period Grosseteste could fully conceive that the light of nature was the same as the light of revelation.[21] In his work in training preaching friars he draws upon a vast range of optical and visual metaphors that resonate with this conceptualization of light. Grosseteste also maintained that sense perception, unlike the higher faculties of reason, memory, and imagination, had remained intact after the Fall and could assist in the rehabilitation of those higher faculties. Optical references therefore had added significance for him, practically serving in a literal way in the spiritual objectives of preaching.

The doctrine of multiplication, which is bound up with the first corporeal form light, represents the most important aspect of Grosseteste's contribution. Not only does it spark further interest in light, but it adds to the already broad appeal of optics. In terms of his theory of vision itself, Grosseteste offers

---

[19]   James McEvoy draws attention to the importance of Aristotle in Grosseteste's system of thought in *The Philosophy of Robert Grosseteste*, Oxford, 1982, 149–205.

[20]   McEvoy, 167. McEvoy goes on to suggest that Grosseteste undertook this task in his next major work, the *Commentarius in Libros Analyticorum Posteriorum*. There is disagreement, however, over the dating of these and other works which fall into a time period when Grosseteste's interests were shifting from natural philosophy to theology. See R.W. Southern, *Robert Grosseteste: The Growth of an English Mind in Medieval Europe*, 2nd ed., Oxford, 1992, 125–40 for a brief discussion of the issues.

[21]   Southern makes the case that theology brought Grosseteste's scientific thinking to maturity, 136.

primarily a simple restatement of known views, favouring the Neoplatonic interpretation which combined the theories of intromission and extramission. Interestingly, he does stress the importance of rays issuing from the eye for perspective. In spite of his brilliant achievement in mixing metaphysics and natural philosophy, Grosseteste does not mention Alhazen or incorporate this Arabian's synthesis of earlier theories. It was this natural philosopher who provided the best naturalistic explanation to account for the principal features of vision. From the time of Roger Bacon (c.1214–1292/4),[22] his name became associated with a revolutionary approach to optical problems.

To complete our understanding of the rise of optics in medieval thought, we must consider the influence of Alhazen's writings upon Western theorists, which we find in the writings of the so-called perspectivists. Robert Grosseteste's enthusiasm for optics, a powerful mixture of metaphysics and science, was taken over by Roger Bacon, who combined Grosseteste's ideas with the newly arrived optical theory from Arabia. Like Grosseteste, Bacon believed that optics held the key to understanding all of natural philosophy.[23] Yet although he adapts the same metaphysical framework as Grosseteste, Bacon is more ambitious and advanced than his predecessor; he seeks to achieve a synthesis of all the leading theories, and includes the recently discovered insights of Alhazen. He consistently returns to Alhazen in Book 5 of his *Opus maius*: 'Nevertheless, an irrefutable argument for the opinion of Alhazen can be drawn from his statements in the seventh book;'[24] or 'The anterior glacial humor has many properties. The first and principal of these is that the visual power resides only in it, according to Alhazen and others.'[25] He does not follow Alhazen at all points in the debate over visual rays, however, and maintains the concept of visual rays proceeding from the eye, which Alhazen had dismissed. Though he breaks new ground by including Alhazen's concepts, he tries to reconcile his opinions with those of others; a glance at *Perspectiva* (Bk 5) in the *Opus maius* shows his efforts at inclusiveness. As J.H. Bridges has written, 'A fundamental principle with Bacon was that truth of whatever kind was homogeneous.'[26] This point is as important as the fact that he advances Alhazen's theory: like Grosseteste, perhaps on an even greater scale, he tries to achieve a total system, one that encompasses very recent developments, and optics constitutes a very large part of that effort.

[22]   *CHLMP*, 884.
[23]   Bacon opens his *Opus tertium* boldly: 'Postquam manifestavi mathematice potestatem, aspiravi ad perspective dignitatem. Que quia pulchrior est omnibus scientiis, et utilitates habet respectu omnium sine qua nulla sciri potest.' Roger Bacon, *Un fragment inédit de l'*Opus Tertium *de Roger Bacon*, ed. Pierre Duhem, Quaracchi, 1909, 75.
[24]   Edward Grant, *A Source Book in Medieval Science*, Cambridge, Mass., 1974, 396. 'Potest tamen sumi argumentum insolubile pro opinione Alhazen ex eis quae dicit in septimo.' Roger Bacon, *The* Opus Majus *of Roger Bacon*, ed. J.H. Bridges, London, 1900, 5.1.d9.c3.
[25]   Grant, 400. 'Anterior autem glacialis habet multas proprietates. Nam prima et principalis est, quod virtus visiva est tantum in eo, secundum Alhazen et caeteros' (5.1.d4.c2).
[26]   Bridges, lxxxviii.

Bacon's theory also relies heavily on Grosseteste's doctrine of multiplication and the role played by species. For his part, Bacon describes the nature of the species with clarity:

> But a species is not a body, nor is it moved from one place to another; but that which is produced [by an object] in the first part of the air is not separated from that part, since form cannot be separated from the matter in which it is unless it should be soul; rather, it produces a likeness to itself in the second part of the air, and so on. Therefore there is no change of place, but a generation multiplied through the different parts of the medium; nor is it body which is generated there, but a corporeal form that does not have dimensions of itself but is produced according to the dimensions of the air. (5.1.d9.c4)[27]

His definition comes out of the context of the historical ambiguity of the term;[28] Bacon's concept depends specifically on the distinction introduced by Alhazen that forms radiate from each point on an object's surface.

Bacon follows Alhazen in the important matter of how species come from the individual parts of the object until they reach the eye and establish a one-to-one correspondence that results in the shape of a pyramid. It means in effect that vision is made possible through the replication of the image or form of the thing seen. In scientific thought in the thirteenth century, the term *species* thus comes to have a specific, technical meaning which applies to sight, though not limited to vision. Influenced by Grosseteste's metaphysical idea, Bacon explains that all objects and powers contribute to the multiplication of species:

> Every efficient cause acts through its own power, which it exercises on the adjacent matter, as the light of the sun exercises its power on the air (which power is light diffused through the whole world from the solar light). And this power is called 'likeness,' 'image,' and 'species,' and is

---

[27] Grant, 394. 'Sed species non est corpus, neque mutatur secundum se totam ab uno loco in alium, sed illa quae in prima parte aeris fit non separatur ab illa, cum forma non potest separari a materia in qua est, nisi sit anima, sed facit sibi simile in secundam partem, et sic ultra. Et ideo non est motus localis, sed est generatio multiplicata per diversas partes medii; nec est corpus quod ibi generatur, sed forma corporalis non habens tamen dimensiones per se, sed fit sub dimensionibus aeris.'

[28] Pierre Michaud-Quantin has admirably traced this history. He writes that 'dans les traductions du grec faites a cette époque (the twelfth century) *eidos* est régulièrement rendu par *forma*, mais si le mot vient a travers une version arabe, *species* reparait. . . . Il en va de même dans la *Logique* d'Avicenne, on trouve aussi chez ce dernier l'affirmation, qui sera parfois reprise, que ce sens de forme substantielle est le sens primitif de l'*eidos-species*.' Pierre Michaud-Quantin, 'Les Champs Semantiques de *Species*. Tradition Latine et Traductions du Grec,' in his et al., *Études Sur Le Vocabulaire Philosophique du Moyen Age*, Rome, 1970, 138.

designated by many other names, and it is produced both by substance and by accident, spiritual and corporeal, but more by substance than by accident and spiritual than corporeal. This species produces every action in the world, for it acts on sense, on the intellect, and on all matter of the world for the generation of things.[29]

The species, also called 'forms' and 'images' by Bacon, radiate along straight lines in every direction. They generate additional species in the medium contiguous to them, proceeding from every point on the object's surface. Once these forms impress themselves upon the viewer's eye, they continue to multiply, making their way along the optic nerve until they reach the inner wits of the brain. This same principle applies to the other senses as well.[30] Natural philosophers concerned with optical questions, especially those in the perspectivist tradition, used the term *species* with care. I would also like to draw attention to Bacon's stress that the object generates a corporeal form. On exactly this point, William of Ockham will argue for the logical unnecessity of species in the processes of vision and cognition. His opposition will crystallize a debate that brings the fields of vision and psychology or epistemology even closer together.

Bacon tried to achieve an inclusive synthesis, but insofar as he emphasized Alhazen's theories and espoused them himself, he established the tradition of perspectivist optics which provided the major viable alternative to the Aristotelian theory advanced by Albertus Magnus and which eventually won the day, though this only became clear much later. Pecham and Witelo extend Bacon's work and also show the influence of Alhazen.[31] Both emphasize the argument that sight occurs through lines of radiation perpendicularly incident on the eye. Chaucer may well have known some specifics of the nature of Witelo's achievement. Interestingly, he uses the word 'perspectives' (V.234), which *The Riverside Chaucer* glosses as 'optical lenses,' a possible meaning the word indeed carries. It could as easily have a mathematical meaning, which would

---

[29]   Grant, 393. 'Omne enim efficiens agit per suam virtutem quam facit in materiam subjectam, ut lux solis facit suam virtutem in aere, quae est lumen diffusum per totum mundum a luce solari. Et haec virtus vocatur similitudo, et imago, et species et multis nominibus, et hanc facit tam substantia quam accidens, et tam spiritualis quam corporalis. Et substantia plus quam accidens, et spiritualis plus quam corporalis. Et haec species facit omnem operationem hujus mundi; nam operatur in sensum, in intellectum, et in totam mundi materiam per rerum generationem.' Roger Bacon, *Opus maius* 4.d2.c1.

[30]   As Michaud-Quantin notes elsewhere in his article, however, the term came to have specific connections with the eyes: 'Avec le XIIe siècle, viennent les définitions qui combinent les deux éléments enregistrés par l'oeil' (114).

[31]   Gareth Matthews has, overconfidently, argued for *a* medieval theory of vision. Though he does not adequately account for the influence of Aristotle's theory in the Middle Ages, he nonetheless does see the continuity of a tradition sparked by Alhazen and made up of Bacon, Pecham, and Witelo. Gareth B. Matthews, 'A Medieval Theory of Vision,' in Machamer et al., 186.

be in keeping with the mention of Alhazen and Witelo.[32] Apart from these possibilities, there are a number of points to be gleaned from the existence of this tradition: new information made available from Arabia led to a lasting tradition that became influential almost immediately upon its arrival but not immediately dominant; the name of Alhazen was bound up with these innovations in optics; this tradition focused on the issue of perspective, a mathematical approach that enhanced the study of optics and contributed to developments in scientific methodology.

The relevance of optics as a symbol of innovative thinking in late scholasticism also derives from the appeal to optical principles in other non-optical discourses. Here we see further evidence for the tenacity of Grosseteste's hopes for this science's explanatory powers. One place where optics made an important contribution to the growth of an apparently unrelated scientific idea was in the 'Merton School.' In the fourteenth century, several developments in natural philosophy took place at Merton, as a number of historians have pointed out.[33] Among these was a new theorem on quantification, one of the fundamental components of the scientific method. The Mertonians developed a theorem to cope with changes in qualities observed in optical experiments. It was noticed that intensity of illumination could be made to increase either by the addition of light sources or the increased concentration of a light source on a smaller space. Aristotle's concept of a quality did not allow for this kind of interchange. For him, a quality belonged to a particular subject, and subjects could not exchange qualities. The interchange of adding light sources or increasing the concentration of a light source to intensify illumination therefore taxed Aristotelian ideas of quality.[34] The study of optical phenomena, already on a solid footing theoretically, produced unexpected and interesting results. With perspectivism, optics builds its own basis in mathematics and naturalism; here it contributes to an advancement of the empirical method.

In developments well removed from the *quadrivium*, current optical concepts found their way into sermon illustrations as well. Intricate illustrations gave the medieval preacher, already building on scriptural and patristic metaphors of seeing, new angles from which to approach such material. Optics provided new ways to move from the familiar to the unfamiliar in ways that were nonetheless deemed to be accessible to the audience and pleasing in their abil-

---

[32] The *Riverside's* gloss on 'Vitulon' (V.232) correctly points out that he was an authority on perspective.

[33] Marshall Clagett, *The Science of Mechanics in the Middle Ages*, Wisconsin, 1961; Lynn Thorndike, *A History of Magic and Experimental Science* 3, New York, 1934; J.A.W. Bennett, 'The Men of Merton,' in his *Chaucer at Oxford and at Cambridge*, Oxford, 1974, 58–85.

[34] As Edith Sylla points out regarding the early history of this theorem, 'by references to such physical additions a quantification of qualities based on intensity as an extensive and additive quantity could develop.' 'Medieval Quantification of Qualities: The "Merton School," ' *Archive for the History of Exact Sciences* 8 (1971), 9–39.

ity to spark interest and appeal to the intellect. The Franciscans developed a style of preaching to the laity famous for earthy and provocative analogies and illustrations deliberately designed to pierce sophisticated indifference, and in the late thirteenth century the Franciscan Peter of Limoges compiled an exemplum book entitled *De oculo morali*.[35] Over 100 manuscripts of this exemplum book exist in European libraries, attesting its widespread popularity. Drawing notably on Alhazen in a number of different sections, Peter makes analogies throughout on every aspect of vision from the anatomy of the eye to causes of error in physical perception to the power of visual rays, which he still maintains. Based in Paris, Peter would almost certainly have known Bacon and Pecham, both fellow Franciscans, when they were at the University of Paris in the 1260s. The *De oculo morali* could date from that time period, with a *terminus ad quem* early in the fourteenth century. In well-developed and imaginative ways, therefore, very recent optical theories were being transmitted to educated laity.

The language of optics also enters into the theology of John Wyclif. He uses current ideas from this field to explain a variety of concepts, some of them Augustinian in nature and therefore already aligned with visual metaphors, but others as well not so aligned. One such concept is his interpretation of the Eucharist. As Wyclif moved away from the doctrine of transubstantiation, he took pains to explain the presence of God in the elements in the most positive language possible. He insisted on the presence of God by using the analogy of an image in the mirror.[36] Wyclif makes a precise comparison of the way species of light multiply without a multiplication of body and an analogous multiplication of the species of the body of God.[37] The ideas and language of optics find their way into a broad range of contexts, and this phenomenon strongly suggests a widespread learned interest in the range of ideas associated with sight. In all of these cases the mechanics of sight serves as the basis for discus-

---

[35] [Peter of Limoges], *Johannis Pithsani archiepiscopi Canthuariensis liber de oculo morali foeliciter incipit*, Augsburg, 1475. The work was initially attributed to John Pecham. David Clark discusses the Franciscan style of preaching and Peter of Limoges' contribution in 'Optics for Preachers: the *De oculo morali* by Peter of Limoges,' *The Michigan Academician* 9 (1977), 329–43.

[36] In late medieval sermons, the mystical nature of the host is often expressed in terms of its ability to shine brightly. In one anti-semitic sermon it blinds unbelieving Jews who have cut up a clerk who has just partaken of the Lord's Supper. *Middle English Sermons from MS Royal 18.B.23*, ed. Woodburn O. Ross, EETS os 209, London, 1940, sermon 11, 65. See also sermon 22.

[37] 'Si enim secundum perspectivos corpus multiplicatur intencionaliter vere presens, ubicunque species eius agitur, et habet ibi efficaciam operandi; quod magisterium Deo facere corpus suum esse ad omnem punctum hostie sacramentaliter et effectus spirituales efficaciter operari!' John Wyclif, *Tractatus de benedicta incarnacione*, ed. Edward Harris, London, 1886, 191. Heather Phillips discusses Wyclif's recurrent use of contemporary optical ideas and also argues for their widespread appeal in 'John Wyclif and the Optics of the Eucharist,' in *From Ockham to Wyclif, Studies in Church History* Subsidia 5, ed. Anne Hudson and Michael Wilks, Oxford, 1987, 245–58.

sion or analogy, and this tendency points to the usefulness of optics and reinforces this innovative sub-discipline as a symbol of learning.

Sight and Epistemology

In a series of epistemological questions in the late medieval period, vision influences cognitive theory as well, symbolizing rational endeavour in a second distinct and pervasive way.[38] Armed with an understanding of Augustinian illumination and related ideas, we are in little danger of underestimating the psychological component of vision. In late medieval thought, however, there is a close relationship between the psychology of vision and developments in physical optical theory. The way Robert Grosseteste and Roger Bacon combine metaphysics and natural philosophy in their work alerts us to the implications of making any sort of allusion to vision since their works aim at integration, not least of Neoplatonic and Aristotelian thinking. While it can be very fruitful indeed to apply, for instance, Augustine's theology of light to Chaucerian poetics, to bypass the rise of naturalistic theories of vision and light in the West and the profound implications of Grosseteste's and Bacon's assertions must render such a connection partial and in need of further elucidation. Reference to vision also reflects both highly specialized advances in natural philosophy and increasing philosophical interest in the ways knowledge is obtained.

The early encyclopedic tradition[39] indicates the power of naturalistic visual concepts to convey respect for reason. Adelard of Bath's *Naturales questiones* contains a dialogue between Adelard and his nephew on the topic of optics that includes a description of the various schools of thought while reaffirming the Platonic viewpoint, very similar to Chalcidius' commentary. At one stage, the nephew asks one of the questions most problematic for the extramission theory that Augustine had himself felt compelled to tackle, namely how the visual breath can travel from the eyes to the distant stars and return almost instantaneously. Adelard's answer attests the theory's resilience, but more than that it suggests the reverence accorded visual matters. That respect is at once bounded and enhanced by the relationship between empirical inquiry and reason, and the master's answer also reflects this tension. He begins by comparing speed with size, emphasizing that just as the vulgar mind has difficulty in conceiving the very large, it also has difficulty imagining the very swift. He then continues:

> They think that the size of the sky exactly coincides with the earth, and
> that the bulk of the moon and sun and other things, which true reason

---

[38] Hans Jonas discusses philosophical reasons for the grandeur of sight in 'The Nobility of Sight: A Study in the Phenomenology of the Senses,' *Philosophy and Phenomenological Research* 14 (1954), 507–19. He points to three qualities: simultaneity of presentation; dynamic neutralization, or the choice whether or not to engage with the scene seen; and distance.

[39] So called in Grant, 378.

would show them to exceed in size the earth, are not one whit greater than they seem to their bleary eyes. Those, however, who in matters of this sort are more apt to use reason, the incorporeal eye of the mind as their guide, just as they see clearly the magnitude of the external continent, or boundary, and the almost infinite extent of its diameter, so also see clearly the revolution of the heavens and the unutterably swift movement of the visible breath – and this in both cases, thanks to the use of reason. Just as the mind of the external sphere excels all created beings in the execution of virtues, so also this visible breath is more subtly perfected by the wonderful energy of creative virtue than all things compounded of elements[40]

Adelard conjoins reason with a profound interest in the natural world, and with phenomena related to visual processes in particular. This passage powerfully illustrates the interest in vision on two planes: as a metaphor, where 'the incorporeal eye of the mind' serves as an infallible guide; as a physical reality, with the visible breath being 'more subtly perfected ... than all things compounded of elements.' On this fairly popular level of scientific discussion, vision plays a double role and has obvious importance as a naturalistic phenomenon in questions of perception and understanding.

The *Speculum maius* by Vincent of Beauvais also pays considerable attention to the importance of sight. The writer asserts that the most important among substances is light, and refers to Augustine as his authority.[41] One of Vincent's main objective is to collect learning for preachers, and in his handling of light and vision he reveals his primary interest in light metaphysics. Illumination is primarily divine, transmitted through angelic hierarchies; light expands and propagates itself like God's goodness and beauty. Vincent does venture into brief discussions of physical topics such as the anatomy of the eye, the emission of visual rays, and perceptual interference. His encyclopedia includes, at least in a tentative fashion, some facts from the realm of natural philosophy along with the discourse of light metaphysics.

The *De proprietatibus rerum* of Bartholomaeus Anglicus, compiled

---

[40] Grant, 379. 'Metitur enim, immo ut verius dicam, mentitur omnia secundum hoc, quod iuxta terram sibi fallaces promittunt sensus aestimatque caeli ambitum terrae undique versum insidere tantaeque nec maioris quantitatis, quam lippientibus oculis eius videtur. Formas lunae et solis caeterorumque non potest iudicare, cum ipsa vera ratione terrae ambitum excedant. Illos vero, qui magis in huiusmodi rebus incorporeo animi oculo ratione duce utuntur, sicut amplitudo extimae continentiae eiusque diametri fere infinita spatiositas non latet, sic et ipsius uranicae conversionis visibilisque spiritus velocissimus motus latere non potest. Quod utriusque rationis merito accidere puto. Sicut enim illa extimae sphaerae anima omnibus conditorum animabus virtutum executione praestantior est, sic et hic visibilis spiritus omnibus elementariter compositis mirabili creatricis virtutis opera subtilius elimatus est.' Adelard of Bath, *Die Quaestiones Naturales Des Adelardus Von Bath*, ed. Martin Müller, Münster, 1934, 32.

[41] Vincent of Beauvais, *Speculum quadruplex sive Speculum maius*, Graz, Austria, 1964 (Douai, 1624), 2.35.

c.1230–c.1240, slightly earlier than the *Speculum maius*, presents a discussion of matters related to optics on a level that one historian of science, perhaps unfairly, has called 'extremely general and elementary.'[42] At any rate, or perhaps for that very reason, it provides useful information. Bartholomaeus first refers to the eyes in the context of his discussion of the soul, where he calls attention to the position of the eyes in the body. The importance of this physical, hierarchical localization goes back at least as far as Isidore of Seville, to whom he refers. He then elaborates on the matter:

> Pronaque cum spectent animalia cetera terram
> Os homini sublime dedit celumque videre
> Iussit et erectos ad sidera tollere vultus.

> Þe menynge is þis: oþir bestis lokeþ donward to þe erþe, and God ȝaf to man an hiȝe mouþ and hete hym loke vp and se heuen, and he ȝaf to men visagis arerid toward þe sterres. Also a man schal seche heuen and nouȝt putte his þouȝt in þerþe and be obedient to þe wombe as a best.[43]

Often, the relationship between heaven and vision entails a purely spiritual understanding of sight, but here the connection emphasizes the fundamental level of physical orientation. The passage clearly indicates the significance accorded to the eyes: their position in the body sets humans apart from animals, allowing us to 'look vp and se heuen;' and they also have a function in encouraging spiritual reflections. The encyclopedist's reference to vision comes in the context of his discussion of the soul and has epistemological as well as metaphysical implications. This fact illustrates the respect with which medieval commentators normally treated sight, pointing to the ways vision, thought, and spiritual insight were considered to be connected. When Bartholomaeus later sets about describing the 'outer witte' of vision and its relationship to the other outer wits, he stresses the preeminence of sight:

> Þe siȝt is more sotile and more lifliche þan þe oþir wittis. *Visus* 'þe sight' haþ þe name of *uiuacitas*, þat is 'liflichness'. Also he is more worthi þan oþir wittis. Also in dede, as it were a vertu of fire, he is more myȝti þan oþir wittis. (111–12)

For all the developments in optics that take place in Bartholomaeus' time and shortly after, the common knowledge that he has collected already points out the value of the study of vision, especially its usefulness in connection with other studies such as those of the mind and soul.

---

[42] Grant, 383.

[43] *On the Properties of Things. John Trevisa's translation of Bartholomaeus Anglicus*, De proprietatibus rerum vol. 1, ed. M.C. Seymour et al., Oxford, 1975, 90–1.

Bartholomaeus offers some general insights into how the physical location of the eyes increases the importance of vision in connection with what the eyes communicate to and about the soul or mind. The eyes hold the position in the body that is closest to the soul and this fact further shows the importance of sight, since the soul separates humans from irrational beasts. We have already seen how their position in the body gives humans a spiritual and rational advantage: the position of the eyes relative to the soul augments this. Indirectly, the relationship between eyes and soul encourages study of the eyes as the best way to gain access into the most enigmatic part of a person. The eyes hold out much promise for the discovery of that which is especially meaningful. As Bartholomaeus says, the eyes do give away some of the soul's secrets, telling whether or not it is disturbed or glad. Since 'in þe yȝen is iknowe and iseye al þe dome of mynde,' they hold forth the greatest promise for psychology.

In the Middle Ages, the discussion of vision and light leads into consideration of the psychology of perception, specifically into the realm of the *anima sensibili*. Bartholomaeus introduces the subject and its sub-categories in this way:

> *De anima sensibili* 'of þe soule þat ȝeueþ felinge' somwhat schal be schortliche iseide, touchinge þe diuersite of þe myȝtis and vertues þerof. For þe vertue of felinge haþ place in þe most subtile chambres of þe brayn and ȝeuep wilful meuynge and felinge in alle þe lymes, and þat by synewis and smale veynes þat springit out of þe braine and spredip into alle þe parties of beste. Þe soule sensible þat ȝeuep felinge haþ double myȝt and vertu of apprehendinge and of meuinge. Þe vertu of apprehend-inge, þat is maner knowinge, is departid atwinne. Þat o partie haþ þe comyn and þe inner witte. Þat oþir hatte particulare and þe vtter wit. (98)

The inner wits consist of the three compartments of the brain. The foremost is the cell of the imaginative faculty: 'Þerin þingis þat þe vtter witte apprehendiþ without beþ i-ordeyned and iput togedres withinne' (98). The middle cell contains the estimative faculty, while the third holds the faculty of memory. What medieval commentators called the outer wits we know as the five senses. The common wit mediates between these two realms. Albertus Magnus ascribes to it two functions: ' "It judges of the operation of a sense so that when we see, we know we are seeing"; it puts together the data given by the five senses, or Outward Wits, so that we can say an orange is sweet or one orange is sweeter than another.'[44] C.S. Lewis makes a useful point of clarification when he tells us that the common wit turns 'mere sensations into coherent consciousness of myself as subject in a world of objects.'[45]

---

[44] *De anima*, pt1,i,m2,subs.7, quoted in C.S. Lewis, *The Discarded Image*, Cambridge, 1964, 164.
[45] Lewis, 164–5. In his book *Chaucer and the Imagery of Narrative: The First Five*

Vision is the most worthy of the five outer wits, and the place of the senses in the process of cognition is the first of four stages. Boethius explains the hierarchical process of achieving knowledge in the *Consolation of Philosophy*, where Lady Philosophy clarifies how free will can exist with God's foreknowledge. She uses the example of perceiving a man:

> the wit comprehendith withoute-forth the figure of the body of the man that is establisschid in the matere subgett; but the ymaginacioun comprehendith oonly the figure withoute the matere; resoun surmountith ymaginacioun and comprehendith by an universel lokynge the comune spece that is in the singuler peces. But the eighe of intelligence is heyere, for it surmountith the envyrounynge of the universite, and loketh over that bi pure subtilte of thought thilke same symple forme of man that is perdurably in the devyne thought. . . . The heyeste strengthe to comprehenden thinges enbraseth and contienith the lowere strengthe; but the lowere strengthe ne ariseth nat in no manere to the heyere strengthe. (5.pr4)

This explanation establishes the relationship between sensory perception and the complete process of cognition. It shows the relevance of the data of the outer wits, yet the preeminence of inner processes of the mind.[46] This passage also provides a high calling for the study of cognition, which applies to God and man alike; although God alone possesses intelligence, the 'heyeste strengthe to comprehenden thinges,' that ability simply extends the hierarchy of which the human mental processes are a part.

Roger Bacon's *Opus maius* reveals an interpretation of theories that reflects

---

Canterbury Tales, London, 1984, V.A. Kolve explains that both the first and third cells play a role in recall and he draws attention to the ability of the imagination to see images by virtue of the mind's eye. This is his point of departure for his study: 'The images that will be our subject are located "in the head" rather than in paint or wood or stone, and they are created by the mind's inner eye' (20). The illustration that he uses to emphasize this point, interestingly enough, accurately reproduces the process of seeing an external phenomenon although its function apparently is to illustrate how the imagination works. The *oculus imaginationis*, with a variety of images to choose from, sees the ship in a storm by virtue of rays that have their apex in the eye and fan out to form a cone that extends from the top of the highest mast to the waterline of the hull. Much more than simply connecting the eye with the chosen image, the drawing faithfully reproduces something of the full act of seeing, including the idea of perspective embodied in the cone. Furthermore, Kolve goes on to quote Chaucer's reference to 'thilke eyen of [the mynde]' from the Man of Law's Tale and in an endnote provides more of the verse where Chaucer describes how Hermengyld healed an old blind Christian: 'That oon of hem was blynd and myghte nat see,/ But it were with thilke eyen of his mynde/ With whiche men seen, after that they ben blynde' (II.551–3). Kolve's reference is perfectly relevant to his own discussion, but the context emphasizes vision rather than images. The *oculus imaginationis* is invoked in a discussion of physical sight; the image of the eye and its functions here matter at least as much as what the inner eye might see.

46   It is a similar hierarchy that Grosseteste endorses though he ascribes to sense perception a greater role in rehabilitating the higher faculties.

the importance of both mathematical and psychological aspects of visual theory. While the perspectivists may have concentrated on geometrical problems, the psychology of vision figured prominently in the Aristotelian commentaries.[47] We have briefly looked at an example of this interest in the *De proprietatibus rerum*, where Bartholomaeus asserts that 'in þe yȝen is iknowe and iseye al þe dome of mynde.' Bacon's *Opus maius* provides an excellent example of how the processes of optics were seen in an integrated way. Very near the beginning of *Perspectiva* he devotes a number of chapters to the psychology of visual perception. Here his favourite authorities are Aristotle and Avicenna, though he does also refer to Alhazen's *De aspectibus* as well.[48] While Alhazen set about solving the problems facing the intromission theory in *De aspectibus*, he presented a full-orbed discussion of optical theory, including implications for psychology, at the same time. Nonetheless, the perspectivist tradition tended to emphasize mathematical aspects of optics, while the Aristotelians encouraged more discussion of psychological aspects.

When Bacon states that a species or image acts on sense and on the intellect, he is applying the multiplication of species to the realm of psychological processes. Once inside the brain, the species journeys through the five internal wits, beginning with the common sense. This is where information from all the outer wits is collected, hence its name. After that, the species makes its way into the imagination, which occupies the back part of the first cell. In the middle chamber, the 'estimative' and 'discriminative' senses cause judgement to occur, while in the last chamber sense-memory is stored.[49] Although species journey

---

[47]   Lindberg makes this admission himself, and provides examples, including John Buridan's *Questiones* on Aristotle's *De anima* and *De sensu*, Albertus Magnus' *De homine*, and Nicole Oresme's *Questiones super quatuor libros meteorum*.

[48]   Harry Wolfson has shown at length the study of internal senses in both Latin and Arabic texts. Harry A. Wolfson, 'The Internal Senses in Latin, Arabic, and Hebrew Philosophical Texts,' *Harvard Theological Review* 28 (1935), 69–113. On the complexity and variability of medieval descriptions of the internal senses, see Mary J. Carruthers, *The Book of Memory: A Study of Memory in Medieval Culture*, Cambridge, 1990, esp. 47–60. She outlines in particular the 'essentially somatic nature of the memory's images' (50) and draws upon the tension between spiritual and material elements, especially with reference to sight (54ff.). Janet Coleman also stresses the emphasis upon the body in the development of theories of perception and intellection. She has a particularly clear discussion of the roles of form and matter in Aquinas' understanding of perception and intellection. Janet Coleman, *Ancient and Medieval Memories: Studies in the Reconstruction of the Past,* Cambridge, 1992, esp. 422–64. See also Ernest N. Kaulbach, *Imaginative Prophecy in the B-Text of* Piers Plowman, Cambridge, 1993, 39–76, where Kaulbach discusses the applications of Avicenna's *vis imaginativa*.

[49]   This exhausts the faculties of the sensitive part of the soul, but the soul also has an intellectual realm, where rational and discursive operations occur. This bipartite structure originated with Aristotle and survived in Avicenna's interpretation of the Philosopher's work on the soul. Some thinkers considered sensible species unworthy of the intellectual part of the soul, and so posited intelligible species as their counterpart that impressed themselves on this part of the soul. On this distinction, Roger Bacon shows ambivalence (see

to the common sense from all five wits, and from there to the cells of the mind, the term became prominent in connection with optical theories. The term played a crucial role in Grosseteste's and Bacon's conception of natural philosophy as a unified field of endeavor; it also contributed significantly to investigations in psychology, so that optics and cognition became tightly interwoven.

Ockham (b. ca 1285; d. 1347/9)[50] developed his theory of cognition in counterpoint to the perspectivist tradition. With him, optics as a symbol of mental processes and of knowing becomes fully developed and widely influential. Commentators before him, such as Henry of Ghent, Peter Olivi, Scotus, and Durand of St Pourçain, had called into question the necessity for mediating forms or species. Ockham returned to this issue and asserted the direct knowledge of an object's existence as the first stage of cognition. This stage is known as intuitive cognition. He concludes that nothing can come between the knower and the known object:

> For intuitive cognition one need not posit anything besides the intellect and the thing known, with no intermediary species. It is useless to achieve by more what can be achieved by less. But by the intellect and thing seen, without any species, intuitive cognition can occur.[51]

This assertion expressly eliminates species, which Ockham argues would impede direct intuitive cognition. Given that by intuitive cognition we know that an object exists, if species exist we would have direct knowledge of them. This, however, is not the case in the accepted perspectivist explanation: the species represent the object seen, providing knowledge of the object, not of themselves. Against this concept Ockham argues that not only are the representatives, or species, unnecessary but that they do not lead to cognition of the object.[52] Ockham totally eradicates species from his system. The clarification made by Bacon and others that the forms emitted by objects do not qualify as

---

Opus maius 5.1,d4,c4). It is important to keep in mind, however, if only for those cases when modern explicators emphasize the difference.
[50] *CHLMP*, 891.
[51] My translation. 'Ad cognitionem intuitivam habendam non oportet aliquid ponere praeter intellectum et rem cognitam, et nullam speciem penitus. Hoc probatur, quia frustra fit per plura quod potest fieri per pauciora. Sed per intellectum et rem visam, sine omni specie, potest fieri cognitio intuitiva, igitur etc.' All references to Ockham are to the critical edition, Guillelmi de Ockham, *Opera philosophica et theologica ad fidem codicum manuscriptorum edita*, St. Bonaventure, ed. Gedeon Gál et al., 1967–85. Here, O th 5, 2Rep.q13, 268. Elsewhere, *Opera theologica* 1–4, *Scriptum in librum primum sententiarum: ordinatio*, ed. Gedeon Gál et al., 1967–79; *Opera theologica* 5–7, *Questiones in librum secundum, tertium, et quartum sententiarum*, ed. Gedeon Gál et al., 1981–4; *Opera theologica* 9, *Quodlibeta septem*, ed. Joseph C. Wey, 1980.
[52] 'Item, repraesentatum debet esse prius cognitum; aliter repraesentans nunquam duceret in cognitionem repraesentati tanquam in simile' (O th 5, 2Rep.q13, 274).

bodies but rather as 'corporeal forms' encouraged consideration of other degrees of being, so that extramental species could be said to have either corporeal or intentional being. Ockham, however, does not allow for any fine distinctions.[53]

Ockham replaces species with an impressed quality (*qualitas impressa*) as the only requirement for vision. Nothing having independent existence passes into the eye, from which an intelligible species can be extracted for the intellectual part of the soul. Impressed qualities alone induce the faculty to act.[54] This inducement returns us to the volitional aspect of Ockham's understanding of cognition. He draws upon Aristotle and clarifies the Philosopher's use of species in a way that coordinates with his own emphasis on will:

> I say that the Philosopher uses 'species' in place of act or habit. This is clear, because the Commentator never names the species, but where the Philosopher says 'species,' [Averroes] always calls this 'form;' and he uses 'form' for 'intention' or 'habit.' And when he says that the intellect is the place of 'species,' it is true, because [the intellect] is the subject for intentions and habits.[55]

Intuitive cognition occurs in the direct contact between the intuiter and the intuited object. Ockham applies his famous razor to do away with intermediary representatives since no assimilation of intellect to object occurs. The same technique applies to the second stage of cognition which takes place entirely in the mind, known as abstractive cognition. No assimilation occurs there either, only the duplicate operations of the intuitive cognition and the intellect giving rise to abstractive cognition and the production of habits.[56] In fact, Ockham treats the two types of cognition together, and describes abstractive cognition in relation to intuitive cognition.[57]

---

53 'Item, illa species non habet esse intentionale et spirituale, quia hoc dicere includit contradictionem, quia omne ens extra animam est vera res et verum esse reale habet suo modo, licet non ita perfectum sicut unum castrum vel domus. Et per consequens est vere substantia vel accidens. Et si sit accidens, vere informat subiectum. Igitur dicere quod est res extra animam, et cum hoc quod tantum habet esse spirituale et intentionale est dicere opposita' (O th 6, 3Rep.q2, 60).
54   O th 6, 3Rep.q3, 98–129.
55   Translation by Katherine Tachau, whose discussion of Ockham on sight has been instructive. *Vision and Certitude in the Age of Ockham: Optics, Epistemology and the Foundation of Semantics 1250–1345*, Leiden, 1988, 126. 'Ad omnes auctoritates Philosophi dico quod accipit speciem pro actu vel habitu. Hoc patet, quia Commentator nunquam nominat speciem, sed semper ubi Philosophus dicit "speciem," ipse nominat "formam," et accipit formam pro intentione vel habitu. Et quando dicit quod "anima est locus specierum," verum est, quia subiectum intentionum et habituum' (O th 5, 2Rep.q13, 291–2).
56   See 2Rep.q12–13 but cf. q14, 251–337.
57   'Una est quod quaedam est cognitio intuitiva, et quaedam abstractiva. Intuitiva est illa mediante qua cognoscitur res esse quando est, et non esse quando non est. Quia quando

Vision occupies a comprehensive place in Ockham's epistemology. He spends a great deal of time clarifying how vision occurs and eradicating species from the process. In choosing this as the focal point for his discussion of vision, and by returning to the topic of species again and again, Ockham shows his concern with the topics raised by perspectivism. Although *species* has a long history of usage in western medieval thought, that Ockham engages with the term in the context of optical questions shows his indebtedness to thirteenth-century developments in this field. The influence is pervasive; it does not stop with consideration of intuitive cognition. Just as Bacon had, in the fifth book of the *Opus maius*, considered some of the effects of species in the mind, so too does Ockham extrapolate his epistemology on the basis of their absence. While it is true that for Ockham and the moderate nominalists knowing has other connections with willing and naming, knowing is also fundamentally a matter of seeing. There is no urgent need, especially for our purposes, to press the question to ascertain which of these plays the more important role in Ockham's epistemology. However, insofar as knowing can be said to be a nominalist question of general interest in the fourteenth century, it is inextricably bound up with concepts of sight.[58]

The very close relationship between Ockham's epistemology and vision underscores the importance of natural philosophy in the fourteenth century and the science of optics in particular. This field plays an important role in the intellectual climate, connecting a number of concepts bound up with late scholastic concerns. Ockham's radical redefinition of fundamental optical principles does not mean that his theory necessarily gained widespread approval; we now know better than to assume that Ockham's ideas define the age. Katherine Tachau has pursued this question and found that perspectivist adherence to the importance of species continued to flourish well after Ockham's ideas began to be disseminated. Having investigated the writings of Oxford-trained theologians usually designated as followers of Ockham, she reports that Ockham 'did not succeed in displacing visible species from accounts of cognition even in *Sentences* commentaries. On the contrary, most scholars defended such media-

---

perfecte apprehendo aliqua extrema intuitive, statim possum formare complexum quod ipsa extrema uniuntur vel non uniuntur; et assentire vel dissentire. . . .

Sciendum tamen quod licet stante cognitione intuitiva tam sensus quam intellectus respectu aliquorum incomplexorum possit intellectus complexum ex illis incomplexis intuitive cognitis formare modo praedicto et tali complexo assentire, tamen nec formatio complexi nec actus assentiendi complexo est cognitio intuitiva. . . . Et tunc, si ista duo, abstractivum et intuitivum, dividant omnem cognitionem tam complexam quam incomplexam, tunc istae cognitiones dicerentur cognitiones abstractivae; et omnis cognitio complexa [diceretur] abstractiva, sive sit in praesentia rei stante cognitione intuitiva extremorum sive in absentia rei, et non stante cognitione intuitiva' (O th 5, 2Rep.q13, 256–7).

[58]   Katherine Tachau has recently posited a link between optics, epistemology, and semantics. If she is right, that connection opens up a new direction for Chaucerians to follow in exploring the historical context of Chaucer's interest in linguistic issues. Examining such a link goes beyond the scope of this study.

tors precisely because they thought the perspectivist account of vision, and the psychological processes originating in vision, more adequately accounted for the observed phenomena than did the alternative that Ockham posed.' As she logically goes on to conclude, 'This indicated that medieval optics was much more important to late medieval intellectual life than we had generally supposed.'[59] This conclusion contributes to our understanding of the power of visual concepts in the intellectual milieu. Regardless of the position they took, individual commentators addressed the questions raised by Ockham directly. Many commentators positioned themselves relative to Ockham's clear denial of species, a position not in all points original to him but for which he became the major figure. The enduring nature of the issue speaks perhaps as loudly as does the fact that perspectivism endured: both perspectivism and Ockham's attack on species gave optics a currency that we have undervalued, and the predominance of optical and cognitive questions after Ockham dramatically illustrates their combined centrality.

Currents in Late Medieval Thought

It may be tempting to evaluate interest in sight in the fourteenth century strictly on the basis of changes in the philosophical scene that contributed to advances in science. However, sight continues to be relevant as a vivid theological and spiritual concept as well as a physical phenomenon with profound implications for understanding the material world. It is true that the fourteenth century came increasingly to be dominated by nominalism,[60] which coincided with the emergence of the *via moderna*.[61] Traditionally, nominalism has served as the umbrella term for late medieval thought, with which have been associated the

---

[59]   Tachau, xv. This conclusion, while substantiated by her investigation into a number of supposed Ockhamists, also rests upon one or two opposing assumptions. In the first place, Tachau appropriately reacts against the purported fact the Ockham was the predominant influence upon fourteenth-century thought and she combines this purported fact with another fallacy, that scepticism characterized nominalism. However, she does not take stock of the fact that not only have both of these ideas been abandoned, but also that Ockham is not associated with radical nominalism. Several historians have shown that his views tend to be moderate and make a positive contribution. Secondly, she strikes out against 'a new skeptical or empirical epistemology derived from Ockham' (xiv). Scepticism and empiricism do not go hand in hand in Ockhamism; rather Ockham's doctrine of the unimpeded *potentia Dei ordinata* enhances empiricism.

[60]   One of nominalism's basic features is the proposition that real links between objects, man, and God do not exist, but that universals are only concepts, which we refer to by names or terms.

[61]   In recent years scholars have tried to define both of these terms, nominalism and *via moderna,* more precisely. Though some have abandoned nominalism as a label, most historians still value it highly but are more careful to distinguish which branch of nominalism they have in mind. The revaluation that has taken place regarding nominalism has resulted in a description that includes three branches. William Courtenay, 'Nominalism and Late Medieval Religion,' in *The Pursuit of Holiness in Late Medieval and Renaissance Religion,*

notions of decline and fragmentation, and especially that of a deep rift between matters of faith and matters that required a scientific attitude of scepticism.[62] For the past half-century or so, however, this view has undergone considerable revision as historians underscore the connections between late medieval thought and later movements, between the influences of theological method and that involved in a careful scrutiny of nature. Along this line, Heiko Oberman speaks of the harvest of medieval theology,[63] while in a reassessment of

ed. Charles Trinkaus with Heiko Oberman, Leiden, 1974, 34–5. Courtenay would like scholars to abandon the term altogether. The most radical of these branches of nominalism aligns closely with the traditional view of late scholasticism, and includes such figures as Robert Holcot, Adam Wodham, Nicholas of Autrecourt, and John of Mirecourt. A conservative branch is made up of Augustinian thinkers, including Thomas Bradwardine and Gregory of Rimini. Moderate nominalism includes Ockham, Pierre d'Ailly, and Gabriel Biel. Recent work on the thought of some of the radical nominalists, however, has suggested that a further revaluation of its adherents needs to take place. Scepticism and fideism have become more and more marginalized as forces in late medieval thought, the products of twentieth-century philosophers and historians more than those of late scholastic thinkers.

The label *via moderna* has the value of suggesting new elements and continuity between late scholasticism and changes that culminate in the Renaissance and Reformation. Discussion of the concept is not new to Chaucer criticism. Laurence Eldredge developed its relevance for reading Chaucer in 'Chaucer's *Hous of Fame* and the *Via Moderna*,' *Neuphilologische Mitteilungen* 71 (1970), 105–19, though our understanding of the intellectual issues of the time has undergone revision since then. The growth of science in the fourteenth century makes this term attractive to me. However, the phrase has difficulties of its own. As a label, it first appears in the fifteenth-century university and scholastic documents and does not refer back to specific fourteenth-century schools of thought. One scholar has traced its roots to the theology of the realist Wyclif but the term *moderni* has other related uses that pre-date Wyclif. In the early fourteenth century, *modernus* referred to an exact contemporary. As such, it had a neutral tone, though Courtenay believes that it acquired a slightly negative tone since one usually only mentioned a contemporary opinion to attack it. Examining documents from this period onward, Courtenay has recently noted that *moderni* did not immediately become *antiqui* for the next generation. Adam Wodeham, writing in the 1330s, calls Duns Scotus (lecturing in 1300) 'antiquus,' while Richard Campsdale and William of Ockham, active a decade later, he calls 'moderni.' This division does not shift with passing decades. Scotus remains an *antiquus* and Ockham a *modernus*: 'Thus,' concludes Courtenay, 'gradually in the fourteenth century *modernus* ceased to mean an approximate contemporary and came to mean someone "of our age" ' (5). As such, it could refer equally to a contemporary with whom one agreed as a product of the same age, as much as it could refer to an opponent. See William Courtenay, '*Antiqui* and *Moderni* in Late Medieval Thought,' *Journal of the History of Ideas* 48, (1987), 3–10. On the fourteenth-century intellectual context see also his magisterial *Schools and Scholars in Fourteenth-Century England*, Princeton, 1987.

62   The old view of nominalism had a number of characteristics that were accepted as axiomatic: atomism; immoderate stress on the absolute power of God; scepticism; and fideism. J. Huizinga offers a central thesis of decline in *The Waning of the Middle Ages*, trans. F. Hopman, Harmondsworth, 1924. This notion is also present in R.W. Southern's cut-off date for humanism at 1320. See his *Medieval Humanism and Other Studies*, Oxford, 1970.

63   Oberman also uses the language of childbirth: cf. Heiko Oberman, 'The Shape of Late Medieval Thought: The Birthpangs of the Modern Era,' in Trinkaus, 3–25.

one of the major figures of fourteenth-century thought, Gordon Leff has admitted that he underestimated the positive contribution made by William of Ockham.[64] Although a number of studies have shown the complexity of nominalist thought ideas of fragmentation have persisted in some quarters, not least in literary criticism, where it has been difficult to nurture ideas that combine natural philosophy and religion. With reference to Chaucer and other late medieval writers, it is important to consider sight in a context of complexity and continuity between metaphysical and scientific realms of interest.[65]

As an example of the ongoing integration of theology and scientific inquiry in the late medieval period, one of the most convincing achievements of moderate nominalism was its contribution to the study of science, and in this regard the theological distinction between the *potentia Dei absoluta* and the *potentia Dei ordinata* made a valuable contribution. The traditional view of nominalism encouraged an inconclusive view of the relationship between God's absolute power and his ordained power. The *potentia ordinata*, in this view, referred to the way God had willed to act normally in the natural order, while the *potentia absoluta* allowed for his extraordinary and miraculous intervention. The arbitrariness of God's potential involvement in the natural world militated against the study of nature as a closed system.[66] In the traditional evaluation of nominalism's relationship to science, this distinction in the thought of Ockham and

---

64   Gordon Leff, *William of Ockham*, New York, 1975, xiii.

65   The earlier tendency to see the period in terms of disintegration has pertinence for medieval literary studies, where the nuances of changing historical interpretation sometimes travel slowly. Sheila Delany focuses on scepticism and fideism in her study of Chaucer's *House of Fame* and produces a reading that stresses the limitations of Chaucer's trust in tradition, dream lore, and science. Her analysis invites further discussion, as a number of literary critics have noticed in passing, though few have taken advantage of her groundbreaking work in Chaucer's intellectual context. Her dismal outlook, especially as it relates to scientific developments, requires rethinking. Another pertinent example from the field of literary criticism is to be found in Kathryn Lynch's *The High Medieval Dream Vision*, in which she applies Leff's three stages of the destruction of a paradigm to help locate the genre which interests her. Given her adherence to Leff's construct, Lynch interprets Chaucer's time as being further along the road to decline and abandonment. See Sheila Delany, *Chaucer's* House of Fame: *The Poetics of Skeptical Fideism*, Chicago, 1972; Kathryn L. Lynch, *The High Medieval Dream Vision*, Stanford, 1988, 9.

66   The condemnations of 1277 asserted the absolute power of God, which meant that God could do anything at any time. This insistence ran counter to a cause-and-effect understanding of nature, and the date was therefore convenient for some historians as a marker of decline. Edward Grant has argued that natural philosophers used the assertion as a tool to consider plausible and implausible alternatives to current explanations of natural phenomena. By couching their arguments in hypothetical circumstances, allowed by the absolute power of God, they could consider many controversial propositions. Having arrived at one heretical conclusion, Albert of Saxony excused himself by reminding his reader that he had proposed a hypothetical situation: 'The natural philosopher is not much concerned with this argument because when he assumes the eternity of the world, he denies the resurrection of the dead' (quoted in Edward Grant, 'Science and Theology in the Middle Ages,' in *God and Nature*, ed. David C. Lindberg et al., Berkeley, 1986, 68).

others caused confusion. It was seen to encourage science because only par-
ticulars of this world had being and therefore inquiring into the natural world
could only be undertaken for its own sake. However, an atomistic view of the
universe – one of the assumed basic features of nominalism – would not encourage the study of causality.[67] Natural philosophers from the eleventh century onward, however, distinguish between the two powers of God quite
differently.[68] God's absolute power refers to the total possibilities initially open
to God, some of which he realized in creation, some of which are now only
hypothetically possible. The *potentia Dei ordinata*, on the other hand, refers to
his complete plan for creation.[69] Ockham and others still believe in miracles
but these are not examples of God's absolute power. Rather, they prove that the
causal principles of day to day life, such as fire always burning, are contingent
and not absolute in themselves. The reliability of the natural order resulting
from this system, an understanding which does not differ greatly from Aquinas', encouraged rather than discouraged empiricism, and did so through adherence to principles from both natural philosophy and theology.

The science of sight attracted a great deal of attention from different
philosophers and was seen by some to hold the secrets for explaining all of
natural philosophy for the same reasons that sight and light already had pride
of place in metaphysics. In the late medieval period, a variety of thinkers
worked to incorporate its terms into their frameworks. Optical concepts
achieved a currency they would not have again until the seventeenth century[70]
and posed challenges on a number of fronts the way that computer technology

---

67   Indeed, the symbolist outlook had already encouraged a kind of atomism that limited
the search for connections in this realm. For a description of the 'symbolist mentality,' see
Marie-Dominique Chenu, *Nature, Man, and Society in the Twelfth Century*, ed. and trans.
Jerome Taylor and Lester Little, Chicago, 1968, 99–145.
68   Edward Grant, 'The Condemnation of 1277, God's Absolute Power, and Physical
Thought in the Late Middle Ages,' *Viator* 10 (1979), 211–44, esp. 215.
69   'Circa primum dico quod quaedam potest Deus facere de potentia ordinata et aliqua de
potentia absoluta. Haec distinctio non est sic intelligenda quod in Deo sint realiter duae
potentiae quarum una sit ordinata et alia absoluta, quia unica potentia est in Deo ad extra,
quae omni modo est ipse Deus. Nec sic est intelligenda quod aliqua potest Deus ordinate
facere, et aliqua potest absolute et non ordinate, quia Deus nihil potest facere inordinate'
(Ockham, O th 9, Quod.6.q1.a1, 585–6).
70   Seventeenth-century men of letters also responded to optical concepts and referred to
them to express a similar confidence in the findings of science. In his 'Essay of Dramatic
Poesy,' Dryden has Crites say, ' "Is it not evident, in these last hundred years . . . that almost
a new nature has been revealed to us – that more errors of the school have been detected,
more useful experiments in philosophy have been made, more noble secrets in optics,
medicine, astronomy, discovered, than in all those credulous and doting ages from Aristotle
to us? So true it is that nothing spreads more fast than science, when rightly and generally
cultivated." ' John Dryden, 'Essay of Dramatic Poesy,' in *John Dryden*, ed. Keith Walker,
Oxford, 1987, 80. Consider also these lines from Milton:

> The broad circumference
> Hung on his shoulders like the moon, whose orb
> Through optic glass the Tuscan artist views

has gripped the imagination in recent years. The nuances of fourteenth-century thought rightly induce a cautious attitude towards making overgeneralizations about the age based on the thought of certain individuals. Nonetheless, the trends have implications for how we consider vision, as William Courtenay suggests:

> If the fragmentation of the medieval synthesis can no longer be used as the hallmark of nominalism around which to build a theory of the development of late gothic art, the increased importance given to empiricism in the nominalist system should have some implications for the development of the visual and plastic arts, if not architecture. Ockhamist epistemology is not simply empirical; it is based on visual experience, and it takes the eye as the primary sense organ around which to build a theory of knowledge. . . . Knowing in Ockhamism is primarily 'seeing.' Such an epistemology certainly parallels the emphasis in late medieval and early Renaissance art on rendering the visual world with increasing accuracy.[71]

Given the roots of optics in metaphysical doctrines of illumination and beauty, interest in visual experience also has implications for theology.[72] Reference to sight in late medieval theology continues to convey the tension between love and knowledge. In natural philosophy sight emphatically symbolizes knowledge in two different ways: the attractiveness of innovative applications of sight in theology, especially popular preaching, helps disseminate sight as such a symbol and return it to contexts where love is also an operative term. The widespread interest in sight and visual experience has implications for poetry as well, in terms of sensitivity to naturalistic processes of vision, perceptual issues, and in the ways sight conveys a tension, in no way limited to theology alone, between love and knowledge.

At evening, from the top of Fesole,
Or in Valdarno, to descry new lands,
Rivers, or mountains, in her spotty globe.

John Milton, *Paradise Lost*, in *John Milton,* ed. Stephen Orgel and Jonathan Goldberg, Oxford, 1991, 1.286–91.

71   Courtenay, in Trinkaus, 57.

72   Charles Davis chides Courtenay for venturing to make broad applications when Courtenay has devoted so much energy to decrying that habit, but in fact he agrees about nominalism's contact with science: 'But this is the last and most irresistible temptation even of the historian who believes himself to be skeptical and hard-boiled, indeed something of an Ockhamist. How can he resist drawing parallels between the chief object of his interest and the other important cultural aspects of the period? So Courtenay links Ockham with the new art, the new humanism, and (most convincingly) the new empirical science.' Charles T. Davis, 'Ockham and the Zeitgeist,' in Trinkaus, 64.

Naturalistic Knowledge and the Containment of Love
The power of vision as a two-fold symbol of knowledge contributes to efforts to understand what happens in love. Here too Arabic thought exerts tremendous influence. The universal understanding of how love at first sight occurs is itself based partially on principles from optical theory. Furthermore, through medical treatises natural philosophy makes a concerted effort to organize the spontaneous energy of love into the reasoned medical category called lovesickness: love becomes subject to serious treatment as a disease. Additionally, certain metaphors for the relationship between lover and beloved depend on an understanding of the processes of the mind, to which visual concepts make a vital contribution.

For a naturalistic concept of the eye acting as an agent in love, a line of continuity runs between the Greeks and the Arabs, both of whom present the dual role of the eye in love as perceiver and agent. The motif's importance in Greek literature begins, not surprisingly, with the writings of Plato. In the *Phaedrus*, he sets forth the importance of the eyes among physical senses and their concomitant importance in love:

> But beauty, as I said before, shone in brilliance among those visions; and since we came to earth we have found it shining most clearly through the clearest of our senses, for sight is the sharpest of the physical senses, though wisdom is not seen by it, for wisdom would arouse terrible love, if such a clear image of it were granted as would come through sight, and the same is true of the other lovely realities; but beauty alone has the privilege, and therefore it is the most clearly seen and loveliest.[73]

The motif of love at first sight appears to be ubiquitous in the love poetry of several different cultures. In the concept of the apprehension of beautiful forms, however closely linked to love at first sight, we have a theme to which writers from Plato to Aquinas return again and again. The concept of eyes playing a role in love as agents has roots in Greek thought; however, it is less clearly developed here than in later Arabic writings. Plato speaks of a stream flowing between the eyes of the lover and the beloved, but this is a stream of beauty. The description suggests primarily that both receive the beauty of the other in their eyes. Nonetheless, the passage emphasizes a purity that overwhelms, with the suggestion of a severe sharpness of experience. The reference to physical sight induces Plato to consider wisdom, and to imagine in the conjunction of sight and wisdom a 'terrible love.' If love, knowledge, and sight were to come together a kind of pain would accompany the event. Plato tacitly submits that love and wisdom do not come together, at least not in their purest forms.

The importance of beauty is well articulated in Arabic literature. Ibn Hazm's

---

[73] Plato, *Phaedrus*, ed. and trans. Harold North Fowler, London, 1953, 1.485.

The Dove's Neck-Ring contains this declaration: 'As regards the cause of love which ever occurs in most cases, it is an outwardly beautiful form: because the soul is beautiful and passionately desires anything beautiful, and inclines to perfect images.'[74] In the tenth-century poem 'The Porter and the Three Ladies of Baghdad,' the woman blames her lover's eyes for her love, evidence of the concept of the eyes as agents as well as perceivers:

> 'Go ask his glorious eyes,' I said,
> . . .
>
> On my mind's mirror sun-like sheen he cast
> Whose keen reflection fire in vitals bred.[75]

Arabic literature refers to the power of the eyes in ways that, with the possible exception of Greek literature, none of the other traditions do. One critic has concluded that Arabic literature provides the sole source for the motif of the eyes as active agents as it appears in twelfth-century Western poetry.[76] Given the heritage of Arabic poetry, in which eye imagery was evidently well developed by the twelfth century, there is a strong suggestion of continuity and borrowing between the Arabic and Western cultures. The development itself signals a growing appeal to precise visual concepts in the context of love in Western love literature.

The notion that the eyes are active agents renders the role of vision in love more literal and naturalistic. Interest in vision's role in love represents a development in keeping with the accepted importance of the eyes among the senses and with theories of how we perceive. The idea of the gaze of the beloved striking the eye of another recalls a very popular theory of vision, in which the eyes play an active role in perception by sending out rays. It would be easy for us to interpret passages involving vision merely metaphorically, but the accepted understanding of how sight occurs should make us pause. Love involves principles of natural sight: mechanisms of transmission from the soul to the ether outside the eye; speed; and the force of the rays that travel from the eyes to the object beheld. The concept of rays *demystifies*, at least partially, the medieval interpretation of the nature, processes, and power of love. The relationship between the eyes and the heart is also in keeping with the expectations created by commentators who trace the journey of visual rays into the domain of the soul. Obviously the poet is not completely fettered by natural philosophy but he pursues familiar pathways in the ways he connects exterior and interior experience. Plato had brought the science and romance of vision together to a

---

74 Quoted in Ruth H. Cline, 'Heart and Eyes,' *Romance Philology* 25 (1972), 280.
75 *Arabian Nights*, ed. and trans. Richard F. Burton, Beirut, 1966, 1.99.
76 Ruth Cline, 289. Cline notes a curious absence in Latin literature of the connection between heart and eyes. There is, however, a thin body of Latin literature on optics, including Seneca's *Questiones naturales* and Pliny the Elder's *Naturalis historia*. Also, in *De rerum natura*, Lucretius makes a number of references to perspective and visual perception.

certain extent, but in *The Dove's Neck-Ring* and *Arabian Nights* this connection is considerably strengthened, although philosophical discussions do not impinge upon the love poetry in obvious ways. Peter Dronke writes of the poetry of *amour courtois* that in terms of the feeling expressed it is a universal experience; he draws on a breadth of poetry from different ages and cultures to illustrate that point.[77] The feeling of pain in love would seem to be part of this universal experience. References to the eyes fit into a general context where the eyes are commonly ascribed an important role in the beginning of love. However, their lineage reveals a precise use of language accounted for by the idea in Arabic sources that the eyes strike as agents and the currency of optical theories in Arabic thought. Natural philosophy contributes to the language of love.

Arabic thought exerts itself upon Western love literature and bridges the worlds of natural philosophy and love in another way. One specific set of treatises from Arabia that gains much popularity in the West pertains to the problem of lovesickness, to which the Arabs ascribed a material basis and for which they sought material cures. The translation work of Constantine (d. c.1087), to whom Chaucer refers in the General Prologue and the Merchant's Tale, plays a pivotal role in the transmission of these ideas.[78] Mary Wack provides a good indication of the place of medical texts on lovesickness in this milieu, although she overestimates the newness of interest in love at the time and is drawn to the idea of 'the discovery of love': 'In this supersaturated mix of texts, ideas, and behavior, the conception of love in the *Viaticum* and other medical texts, couched in a more precise technical vocabulary, crystallized new ways of interpreting and controlling erotic behavior.'[79] Some of this precise technical vocabulary concerns the role of vision in love.

The conflict between reason and love takes the form of a disease requiring psychosomatic treatment. Very near the outset of its chapter on lovesickness, the *Viaticum* explains that

---

[77]   Peter Dronke, *Medieval Latin and the Rise of the European Love Lyric* 1, Oxford, 1965, 46. Concerning the claim that Arabic poetry makes a specific contribution, he offers considerable latitude for shared knowledge and the oral transmission of songs, but rejects the premise that the 'notions and motifs and images occur so suddenly and mysteriously in Western Europe that they must have been borrowed, that basically the character of European secular songs is determined from outside, by another culture, at one particular point in time' (1.50). Dronke is speaking of the phenomenon of *amour courtois* as a whole, but this generalization needs to be balanced by the evidence that some notions and motifs appear to have a fairly specific lineage. He indeed goes on to explore aspects of the Western intellectual contribution.

[78]   'The Arabic medical texts that Constantine translated stimulated a new emphasis on the materiality of the human organism.' Mary Frances Wack, *Lovesickness in the Middle Ages: The* Viaticum *and its Commentaries*, Pennsylvania, 1990, 31. See also my review in *Medium Aevum* 60 (1991), 295–7.

[79]   Wack, 30.

> Sometimes the cause of eros is . . . the contemplation of beauty. For if the soul observes a form similar to itself it goes mad, as it were, over it in order to achieve the fulfilment of its pleasure.[80]

This observation has clear connections with the literary motif of loving beautiful forms and it further endorses the importance of vision in the processes of love in Arabic culture, not simply as a pleasant motif but as a probable cause of physical illness. The disease of *ereos* takes its toll on the eyes:

> Since this illness has more serious consequences for the soul, that is excessive thoughts, their eyes always become hollow [and] move quickly because of the soul's thoughts [and] worries to find and possess what they desire. Their eyelids are heavy [and] their color yellowish; this is from the motion of heat which follows upon sleeplessness. (1.20)[81]

Naturally enough, the *Viaticum* also provides a prescription for the eyes as part of the remedy for lovesickness:

> What better helps erotic lovers so that they do not sink into excessive thoughts: temperate and fragrant wine is to be given; listening to music; conversing with dearest friends; recitation of poetry; looking at bright, sweet-smelling and fruitful gardens having clear running water; walking or amusing themselves with goodlooking women or men. (1.20)[82]

Later commentaries on the *Viaticum*, such as the two versions of Peter of Spain's (d.1277) *Questiones*, would add that showing both ugly and beautiful women to the patient could be efficacious.[83]

The cause noted in the *Viaticum* has a psychological analogue. In the earliest commentary on the *Viaticum*, probably written in the last quarter of the twelfth century, Gerard of Berry explains that

---

[80] Constantine the African, *Viaticum* 1.20, in Wack, 189. 'Aliquando . . . eros causa pulchra est formositas considerata. Quam si in sibi consimili forma conspiciat, quasi insanit anima in ea ad uoluptatem explendam adipiscendam' (Wack, 188).
[81] Wack, 189. 'Cum hec infirmitas forciora anime subsequentia habeat, id est cogitationes nimias, fiunt eorum oculi semper concaui, cito mobiles propter anime cogitationes, sollicitudines ad inuenienda et habenda ea que desiderant. Palpebre eorum graues, citrini ipsorum colores. Hoc ex caloris fit motu qui ex uigiliis consequitur' (Wack, 188).
[82] Wack, 191. 'Quod melius eriosos adiuuat ne in cogitationes profundentur nimias: uinum est temperatum et odoriferum dandum et audire genera musicorum; colloqui dilectissimis amicis; uersus recitacio; luciferos uidere ortos, odoriferos et fructiferos, currentem habentes aquam et claram; spatiari seu deducere cum femina seu maribus pulcre persone' (Wack, 190).
[83] Wack, 251.

The estimative [faculty], then, which is the nobler judge among the perceptions on the part of the sensible soul, orders the imagination to fix its
gaze on such a person.[84]

The discussion of the causality of lovesickness becomes more focused on the
eyes as time progresses. Bona Fortuna (fl. c.1300) qualifies Constantine when
he writes,

The author gives two causes, namely the beauty of a woman and the
necessity to expel superfluity. But I say that there is, however, one principal cause, namely an extrinsic apprehension that is thought fitting and
congenial, such as the form of any woman that is so strongly apprehended
and so firmly embraced by the thought that it pleases the patient above
everything.[85]

For Bona Fortuna, the apprehension of beauty plays a more important role than
beauty itself. Wack explains the importance of this emphasis at some length,
and draws attention to his idea of species as that which is fitting and desirable
at the moment of perception: '*species* plays the crucial role of moving the fan-
tasy or practical intellect and consequently the reason to desiring and pursuing
the desired object.'[86] The term *species* reminds us of the terminology of
Grosseteste and Bacon in their elaboration of optical principles. Wack provides
us with an indication of the fruitfulness of visual concepts related to lovesickness in the thirteenth century: 'With the revival of interest in optics in the second half of the thirteenth century, physicians discussed the role visual images
played in the disease's causality. Arnold of Villanova, Dino del Garbo, and
Gerard de Solo all commented on the *species* or *apprehensum* that the imagination or *phantasia* must store in order for the mind to reflect upon it. Bona
Fortuna makes the *species vel passio* – a likeness of an object that mediates
between the material world and the mind – the principal cause of lovesickness.'[87]

From cause to cure, the *Viaticum* pays attention to the eyes in its discussion
of lovesickness. Though visual concepts do not reach the West as a package
from the East, Arabic concepts contribute to the supersaturated conditions in

---

[84] Gerard of Berry, *Notule super Viaticum*, in Wack, 199. 'Estimatiua ergo, que est nobilior
iudex inter apprehensiones ex parte anime sensibilis, imperat imaginationi ut defixum habeat intuitum in tali persona' (Wack, 198).

[85] Bona Fortuna, *Tractatus super Viaticum*, in Wack, 257. 'Auctor ponit duas causas, scilicet pulchritudinem mulieris et necessitatem expellendi superfluitatem. Sed ego dico quod
est tamen una causa principalis, scilicet extrinsicum apprehensum quod putatur conveniens
et amicum, sicut forma alicuius mulieris que est ita fortiter apprehensa et ita firmiter a
cogitatione amplexata quod placet ipsi patienti super omnia' (Wack, 256).

[86] Wack, 134.

[87] Wack, 132.

the West. The saturated state of twelfth-century Western culture involved love as well as other concepts that had links with the conceptualization of love, including vision and optics: several different scientific theories strove for prominence, especially in the East where they had recently been substantially reconciled by Alhazen; Augustine had elevated the discourse of light and developed a metaphysics of illumination; mystics saw in light/dark imagery a useful analogue to experiencing the inexpressible love of God; love literature actively engaged in visual language; the Arabs gave to the West technical and scientific discourse that encouraged interest in materiality and a view of love as a possible disease which required analysis partially in terms of vision. The efforts of the medical tradition imported from Arabia to explain, to rationalize, to subdue what happens in love rely upon sight as a key to meet these goals even as they consolidate the interdependency of love, knowledge, and sight.

A popular medieval model of intellection further entwines the discourses of love and knowledge. The human potential to obtain knowledge of forms entails the interaction of two forces: the divine principle irradiating knowledge, sometimes called the *intellectus activus*; and the human mind, with a potential knowledge, called the *intellectus possibilis*. Depending on the way these forces interact, the *intellectus possibilis* will become activated to a greater or lesser extent and share accordingly in the active knowledge of things as they really are. The concept derives ultimately from Aristotle, who in *De anima* describes the process with reference to light as a constant power and its activating effect upon colour:

> This is a sort of positive state like light; for in a sense light makes potential colours into actual colours.[88]

In many of the descriptions of the operations of the active and potential intellects, light serves as the metaphorical starting point. Aristotle describes the active intellect in *De anima* and relies upon light imagery: the active intellect is a positive state like light, which makes colours that exist potentially into actual colours. The relationship between the higher power of the *intellectus activus* and the lower power of the *intellectus possibilis* in Aristotelian thought also serves as a paradigm in the language of love.[89] There is a close connection between descriptions of love and the apprehension of knowledge. Just as the active intellect is above the passive one, and the sun shines down on thick air or other surfaces to produce colours, so too the beloved in the noble love of the court is above the lover and ennobles the lover. The analogy binds together the two concepts of love and knowledge, since the resolution to a problem of love-

---

[88]   Aristotle, *De anima*, trans. J.A. Smith, in *The Works of Aristotle* 3, ed. W.D. Ross, Oxford, 1931, 3.5 (430a). Dronke quotes from this section (72), but from the twelfth-century translation of James of Venice.

[89]   Dronke has a useful discussion of this analogy (see esp. 71–2).

language is found in a theory of how intellectual forces combine. Light plays an influential role in this collocation of ideas: it operates within the intellectual paradigm and permeates related ideas from metaphysics and *fin' amor* as well.

This situation gives us an important clue to how love and knowledge can be separate yet dependent upon one another, ultimately forming a system. The idea of the separation of the two intellects is crucial: mind is always separable, the active always above the potential or passive.[90] In this analogy for noble love the quality of separation remains between love and reason. The beloved, who has become the active force, is the source of beauty and inspirer of love; the lover, the potential or passive force, is associated with reason, which is overcome. But just as the active and potential intellects engage in spite of this separation, so too do love and reason engage whenever one tries to describe love, even poetically.[91] These connections reinforce the relationship between love and knowledge. They come together in descriptions of metaphysical or physical love. Sensible phenomena make important contributions in the discourse of light, beauty, and love. The analogy of the two intellects, for instance, has strong appeal in the universities, and shapes the thinking of poets such as Dante. A number of these strands of philosophical thought reach Chaucer. To a considerable extent, medieval poetry addresses the topics of love, knowledge, and beauty as an integrated construct and develops precise formulations on their interconnections. The analogies used to describe love develop along the lines of current paradigms. Where these discussions occur, concepts of light consistently appear as well. In fact, the appeal to light contributes a measure of exactness as a philosophical assumption and as a crucial phenomenon in the natural world. If we read Chaucer in the context of this intellectual climate we can ask more nuanced questions about the ways in which natural philosophy and other clear interests of his, such as philosophy and metaphysics, interpenetrate.[92] The two-fold association with knowledge outlined here is revealed in

---

90 The interaction of intellects is not unique in each individual case. Different individuals can comprehend the same universal truth, just as some grapes respond the same way to the sun. To accommodate this reality, the concept of unity-in-diversity evolved. The active intellect combines all knowledge in itself but preserves it in its manifold nature, while the potential intellect can be one as it unifies with the active intellect yet many as it operates in many individuals.

91 Extrapolations of this conclusion take us well into the realm of medieval cosmology. The best guide to the relationship between love and knowledge on this scale is Anders Nygren, *Agape and Eros*, trans. Philip S. Watson, London, 1953, 49–52. This problem besets all medieval discussions of creation after Plato's *Timaeus*. Alain's *De planctu Naturae*, for example, introduces characters that mediate between God and his creation. It is easy to see the place of light in such Platonic discussions of the problem of this separation.

92 Thomas Hoccleve goes so far as to call him the 'universal fader in science' and 'hier in philosophie to Aristotle.' Caroline F.E. Spurgeon, *Five Hundred Years of Chaucer Criticism and Allusion 1357–1900* 1, Cambridge, 1925, 21–2. Natural philosophy has a very prominent place in Chaucer's discursive interests. If Walter Clyde Curry merely scratched the surface with his study of Chaucer's scientific learning, the investigations by J.D. North, J.A.W. Bennett and others have increasingly shown the poet's profound interest in this

Chaucer's poetry as fascination with knowledge, from the ways in which people speculate, as in the Squire's Tale, to issues of perception.[93] More broadly, knowledge takes its place in tension with love.

world. See Walter Clyde Curry, *Chaucer and the Mediaeval Sciences*, New York, 1926; J.D. North, *Chaucer's Universe*, Oxford, 1988. Chaucer gives us a hint of his philosophical connections when he mentions the names of men who had associations with Merton, 'philosophical' Strode and Bishop Bradwardine. These references do not substantiate Chaucer's awareness of any particular ideas being promulgated by that school. Indeed, Chaucer's exact connections with Merton, and the universities generally, remain elusive. As Bennett reminds us, we cannot know if Chaucer ever visited Merton or even knew of its resources through his Oxford acquaintances. Norman Davis, in his review of Bennett's *Chaucer at Oxford and at Cambridge* in *The Review of English Studies* ns (1976), 336–7, seizes upon the equal value of Bennett's further insight that if we want to understand the nature of Chaucer's learning we need to find out what his acquaintances and other contemporaries read. One of the benefits of Bennett's study of resources at Merton is that it attests the similarity between fourteenth-century culture at Oxford and fifteenth-century humanism, a reminder for us not to fall back upon traditional interpretations of the nominalistic environment.

93 Peter Brown has shown Chaucer's sensitivity to space and perception in his fine thesis 'Chaucer's Visual World: A Study of His Poetry and the Medieval Optical Tradition,' York University, York, England, 1981.

3

The Hostility of Love and Knowledge
Sight in Medieval Love Poetry

'Oh what a labyrinth!'[1]
(Anonymous)

Love at first sight produces the hostility of love and knowledge. This is the fundamental convention of medieval love poetry; it is also the basis for more complex considerations in literature of the relationship between love and knowledge. Investigation of a relationship of symbiosis ensues from the established importance of hostility based on sight. The hostility/host/hospitality system of *parasitisme* in metaphysics and natural philosophy provides several medieval poets, including Chaucer, with a model of complexity beyond that which the convention of love at first sight would otherwise suggest. For poets such as Dante, Jean de Meun, the *Pearl*-poet, and Chaucer, the convention of love at first sight often leads into a presentation of love that incorporates a range of applications of sight and becomes a discourse of metaphysical and naturalistic knowledge as well. Such a development in some ways denies the simplicity of love at first sight.

The relationship between religious language, naturalistic concepts, and the literature of *fin' amor*, or what has commonly been called 'courtly love,' is difficult to define, perhaps even to discern.[2] Efforts to tease out cause and effect between the two and resulting speculations on the meaning of (especially) secular love literature have led to a critical morass.[3] Most critics have come to

---

1   Dronke, 388. 'O qualis laborintus!' 'O quam formosa,' Dronke, 387, 5a.8.
2   Part of the problem concerns definitions of 'courtly love.' Henry Kelly indicates some of the options in 'Gaston Paris's Courteous and Horsely Love,' in *The Spirit of the Court*, ed. G.S. Burgess and R.A. Taylor, Cambridge, 1985, 217–23. Tracing the sources of any aspect of *fin' amor* is fraught with difficulty. One scholar has divided the theories on the origin of 'courtly love' into no fewer than seven categories. Roger Boase, *The Origin and Meaning of Courtly Love: a critical study of European scholarship,* Manchester, 1977.
3   The problems have been exacerbated by especially aggressive impositions of clear meaning. The unremittingly ironic readings of Exegetics have assumed a clear and singular intention of love literature in keeping with the ideal of *caritas*. Some critics have called for a moritorium on seeking out the sources of 'courtly love' and its degree of fictionality. See,

emphasize analyzing expressions of love in context, while guarding against forced ironic interpretations.[4] The relationship between love, knowledge, and sight benefits from such an emphasis yet also points to a clearer conceptual relationship between religious and naturalistic principles and literature of *fin' amor*.[5] This relationship creates awareness of the realm of the intellect even as it patently fails to point to a univocal meaning.[6] On its own, the concept of sight transfers readily from the realm of human love language to that of divine love. The developed *parasitisme* of love, knowledge, and sight in medieval theology and natural philosophy, however, contributes to the unanticipated complexity of love literature, with its longstanding convention of love at first sight.[7] The metaphysical and naturalistic discourses both signal and help the poet draw attention to a complexity in giving expression to erotic love beyond that which the convention of love at first sight warrants.[8] The question most often asked,

for example, Nathaniel B. Smith and J.T. Snow, ed., *The Expansion and Transformation of Courtly Literature*, Athens, Ga., 1980, 7. Many more have expressed frustration with Exegetics. See F.X. Newman, ed., *The Meaning of Courtly Love*, Albany, 1968; Tony Hunt, 'Irony and the Rise of Courtly Romance,' *German Life and Letters* n.s. 35 (1981), 98–104; Lee Patterson, 'Historical Criticism and the Development of Chaucer Studies,' in his *Negotiating the Past: The Historical Understanding of Medieval Literature*, Madison, 1987, 3–39.

[4]   Joan Ferrante and G.D. Economou point in this direction when they note that 'the presence of courtly love in medieval literature warrants close study of the effects of that presence in the various genres and poets involved,' although this still leaves the problem of defining what exactly is present. Joan M. Ferrante and G.D. Economou, ed., *In Pursuit of Perfection*, Port Washington, 1975, 2.

[5]   The term 'knowledge' encompasses the *possibility* of meaning.

[6]   Exegetics correctly perceives the relevance of the category of meaning, though even this category is not so widespread in love poetry as the project of Exegetics assumes. It incorrectly overlooks and tacitly denies that the mere possibility of meaning is problematic for several medieval love poets.

[7]   Peter Dronke divides the opening two chapters of his study on the European love lyric into an analysis of 'emotional content' and 'intellectual content.' He notes a similarity between the twelfth and thirteenth centuries and earlier ages and various cultures in the feelings expressed in love literature. However, he draws attention to differences in expression, in intellectual content, which he finds 'startling' (58). The organizational division that suggested itself to him is symptomatic of an increasingly complex relationship between love and knowledge in this literature. Douglas Kelly's work on medieval imagination provides insight into the nature of that complexity. He argues that 'abstracted from religious, scientific, and moral concerns, Imagination could be applied to secular subjects, including courtly love.' Douglas Kelly, *Medieval Imagination: Rhetoric and the Poetry of Courtly Love*, Madison, 1978, 26. He goes on to assert that 'appropriate visual representations gave access to ideas and sentiments which ultimately defied rational scrutiny and analysis' (28). Kelly appeals to the imagination to account for the fascinating and somewhat inscrutable connections between love and knowledge, in which visual representation plays an important role. It is interesting to note that he goes on to emphasize alchemy, an aspect of natural philosophy (see esp. 232–4).

[8]   Critical exasperation over the pursuit of origins, and the implications of posited answers with reference to intention and meaning, not to mention critical frustration with Exegetics, has contributed to a lack of interest in the mere possibility of meaning as potentially a searching issue for medieval authors.

especially but not exclusively by Exegetics, has been 'What does this expression of love mean?' It clearly has not led to a satisfying answer, but the question and the critical row surrounding it suggest the more reflexive question, 'Why does this expression of love suggest meaning when the convention of love at first sight supposedly annuls meaning?' When we ask that question we are asking the same question which, among others, Chaucer posed.

At the base of this potentially complex system, visual concepts make at least three contributions to the conventional discourse of erotic love which I wish to present in this chapter and trace in Chaucer's poetry. In the first place, vision provides some of the most prevalent imagery which medieval poets use to describe the beloved. Descriptions of medieval beauty address matters of proportion and shape; where the beloved is concerned they deal in terms of colour and luminescence above all. Secondly, visual concepts introduce the notions of force, conflict, and devastation that accompany the experience of falling in love. Thirdly, these disruptions and polarizations find their most basic expression in the binary opposition of love and reason. Visual concepts give substance to the claim that love is a labyrinth. The poetic claim at the head of this chapter expresses both supreme frustration and exultation, acknowledgement that love denies philosophical consideration and that such a denial adds to the pleasure of love even as it signals that it is love that is at issue.

The Pleasing Vision

The conjunction of vision, beauty, and love proliferates in courtly poetry as it does in metaphysics. In the poetry of the troubadours and some others it is ubiquitous, and as it grows the convention becomes more complex and richly suggestive. Its roots trace back to very early sources. The Bible furnishes Western love literature with one of the most erotic descriptions of love in the much-read Song of Songs. In the hands of commentators, Solomon's book leads us to the complicated question of the continuity between divine and human love, since exegetes universally interpreted it as a spiritual allegory. The Song of Songs, however, also provides powerful images of love that contributed to the formation of secular courtly lyrics. The biblical poem offers a number of visual images and, as part of its eroticism, focuses on physical beauty. The lover rhapsodizes to his beloved:

> How beautiful art thou, my love, how beautiful art thou! Thy eyes are doves' eyes, besides what is hid within. (4:1)[9]

With equally evocative language he goes on to describe his beloved's hair, teeth, lips, temples, neck, and breasts, obviously entranced by her physical

---

[9] 'Quam pulchra es amica mea quam pulchra es oculi tui columbarum absque eo quod intrinsecus latet.'

appearance. Elsewhere, the writer uses the lavish image of a garden, an image that becomes dominant in medieval love discourse; here he appeals to a number of senses with the varied attractions that a garden offers. The description verges on a taxonomy of love. The pleasure that the lover has in gazing upon his beloved becomes a delightful mental game as he attempts to draw attention to every aspect of her beauty with adequate comparisons. Hiddenness is an important component of this activity. The eyes provide a link to the heart; they also spur him on to keep seeking that which he knows eludes his understanding. This quality, of course, also serves well the allegorizing impulse of the exegetes. This well-known and well-loved biblical source lingers over details of physical beauty and endorses an awareness and celebration of such beauty, if only as a handmaiden for understanding spiritual beauty. The Song of Songs serves as an example of early, influential literature in which visual beauty is important, where already the eyes attract special attention for the pleasure associated with them. And this source contributes significantly to the courtly poetry of the Middle Ages.

The situation is similar in secular literature. Ovid, for example, provides a number of examples of the role of beauty in the initiation of love. In the *Ars amatoria* he notes the importance for the would-be lover of settling in his mind what kind of woman he would like to fall in love with, and then assures him that many such specimens will come before his eyes. In the erotic poetry Ovid makes a more poignant connection between beauty and light. He relates an episode during his siesta that begins with his contemplating the afternoon light coming through the window:

> Illa verecundis lux est praebenda puellis,
>   qua timidus latebras speret habere pudore.
>
> (It was such a light as shrinking maids should have whose
> timid modesty hopes to hide away.)[10]

The physical light prompts these musings. Corinna then comes into the room and he provides a detailed account of her naked body. Although the beautiful sight fascinates him, he does not revere the role of vision the way medieval poets do. He does not linger over the pleasure of his vision: 'Why recount each charm?' (1.5.23). But he does delight in the light, which he identifies with a kind of light that his ideal shrinking maids exude and try in vain to hide. The beloved gives off a special light which the maid herself does not have the power to contain.[11] She tries to hide it, and here again the quality of hiddenness, the unknown, is part of a description of visual beauty.

---

10   Ovid, *The Amores*, ed. and trans. Grant Showerman, London and Cambridge, Mass., 1947, 1.5.7–8.
11   Theresa Krier has an excellent discussion of Ovid on the 'invasive eye' and the 'sufferance of exposure,' arguing that for Ovid hiddenness is difficult to obtain. Theresa M. Krier,

In the medieval period many poems express the lover's delight over his beloved's physical beauty. In these it is the appeal to visual detail that I wish to emphasize, especially the recurrence of a description of the beloved's eyes, clearly an important part of the total impression. *Le Roman de la Rose* treats the subject of erotic love both in the original part by Guillaume de Lorris and the massive addition by Jean de Meun. The *Roman* poets indulge a love of colour and light and play with visual concepts through the mechanism of a dream-vision. In fact, the framing device of the dream provides the initial stress on the importance of sight in the poem, a theme that both poets will develop in a variety of ways. In Guillaume's poem visual concepts have a fundamental role in the love drama, with beauty and eye contact making important contributions. Shortly after he has begun to dream, the lover comes to a garden which he describes in lavish visual detail. The initial message that he receives about the nature of love, namely the qualities that render one ineligible to participate in the activity in the garden of love, reaches the dreamer in the form of images on the wall. Amans takes note of not only the nature of the characters depicted but also the fact that they stand out in blue and gold. The visual emphasis helps lay the groundwork for later, more specific appeals to vision; the description at this early stage simply indicates the medieval love of iconography and visual beauty in terms of colour, light, and feminine shape.

The first person that the dreamer encounters is Idleness; he perceives her in a way that sets the precedent for the lover's appreciation of all the beautiful women he will encounter in the garden:

> Cheveus ot blons cum uns bacins,
> La char plus tendre qu'uns pocins,
> Front reluisant, sorcis votis.
> Li entriaus ne fu pas petis,
> Ains iere assés grans par mesure;
> Le nes ot bien fet a droiture,
> Et les yex vairs cum uns faucons
> Por fere envie a ces bricons.
> . . .
> Sa gorge estoit autresi blanche
> Cum est la noif desus la branche. (527–34; 45–6)

> (Yellow her hair as burnished brazen bowl –
> Tender her flesh as that of new-hatched chick –
> Radiant her forehead – gently arched
> Her brows – as gray as falcon's her two eyes,
> And spaced so well that flirts might envy her.
> . . .

Gazing on Secret Sights: Spenser, Classical Imitation, and the Decorums of Vision, Ithaca and London, 1990, 41–65.

Her throat was white as snow
Fresh fallen upon a branch.)

Idleness' features are those of the typical medieval beauty of literature. Much of Guillaume's description involves details of light and colour, including that of her hair, her forehead, her eyes, and her neck. The passage has an avowedly visual emphasis, yet it also engages the sense of touch to create the sensation of intimacy. The whiteness of the figure's throat, 'cum est la noif desus la branche,' conveys the idea of a gentle touch, an effect achieved almost exclusively through a visual image. The impression of beauty and fineness created by the poet is all-embracing. The characters populating the garden are not only beautiful in their bodies but in their clothes and accessories. Idleness, for instance, wears a golden chaplet, a rich green silk coat, and white gloves. Guillaume's introduction of the reader to the garden scene continues in this visually indulgent vein, mixing visual stimuli with similar appeals to hearing and the other senses. It is a broad foundation upon which both poets will build yet no less remarkable for this. Other poems, such as *Pearl*, follow this example and use a strong visual basis to advance more specific themes.

The general appeal to vision appears in a wide variety of medieval poetry. In the poem 'Bytuene Mersh ant Aueril' the poet offers a succinct visual summary of his impression of the subject, Alison:

On heu hire her is fayr ynoh,
    hire browe broune, hire eȝe blake;
wiþ lossum chere he on me loh,
    wiþ middel smal ant wel ymake.[12]

He sees Alison in terms of hue and colour, a series of shades descending from blonde to black as he casts his eye downward from her hair to her brow to her eyes. It is an unusual account of the beloved's eyes, which as we shall see are often associated with light sources, but perhaps not out of keeping with the emphasis on mystery and enchantment. In some poems, the description of a woman's internal as well as her physical beauty also finds visual expression. The refrain of another poem from about the same time, 'Blow, northerne wynd,' echoes the beloved's call to the north wind in the Song of Songs that it blow on her garden and spread its fragrance abroad. This poem offers an indulgent appeal to the sense of sight as well as to that of smell:

Ichot a burde in boure bryht
Þat sully semly is on syht,

---

[12]   *The Harley Lyrics: The Middle English Lyrics of MS. Harley 2253*, ed. G.L. Brook, Manchester, 1968, 33, 13–16.

menskful maiden of myht,
    feir ant fre to fonde.
    . . .
Wiþ lokkes lefliche ant longe,
wiþ frount ant face feir to fonde,
wiþ murþes monie mote heo monge,
    þat brid so breme in boure,
wiþ lossum eye grete ant gode,
wiþ browen blysfol vnder hode.
He þat reste him on þe rode
    þat leflich lyfe honoure!
        Blou, &c.

Hire lure lumes liht
ase a launterne anyht,
hire bleo blykyeþ so bryht,
    so feyr heo is ant fyn.
    . . .
Heo is coral of godnesse,
heo is rubie of ryhtfulnesse,
heo is cristal of clannesse,
    ant baner of bealte;
heo is lilie of largesse,
heo is paruenke of prouesse,
heo is solsecle of suetnesse,
    ant ledy of lealte. (5–8;14–26;47–54)[13]

The poet describes many of his beloved's features in terms of colour and then
provides an overall impression of her face that brings out its radiance 'as a
launterne anyht.' The next line reinforces how her face shines brightly. This
illuminating quality of the beloved's face and especially her eyes suggests the
pleasure and the comfort she brings to her devotee; the connections between
light and mental faculties suggest an emphasis on the mind here rather than the
heart. The description culminates in an elucidation of spiritual qualities, characteristics developed in an illumined soul. Interestingly, the poet here retains
the same appeal to the sense of sight, furthering the rich visual display and he
also draws upon the garden here for visual analogies. He conveys the sense that
the beloved's inner qualities are desired as much as her physical graces, and he
does so through images of colour and light that have both deep sensual and
spiritual appeal.

The fourteenth-century poem *Pearl* illustrates the handling of these common visual concepts on a very sophisticated level where the writer merges

[13] Brook, 48–50.

secular and religious connotations to great effect. The premise of *Pearl*, the loss of a lustrous pearl by the narrator, establishes the poem's agenda as the elaboration of this image from the outset:

> Perle, plesaunte to prynces paye
> To clanly clos in golde so clere,
> Oute of oryent, I hardyly saye,
> Ne proued I neuer her precios pere.
> So rounde, so reken in vche araye,
> So smal, so smoþe her sydeȝ were,
> Quere-so-euer I jugged gemmeȝ gaye,
> I sette hyr sengeley in synglere.
> Allas! I leste hyr in on erbere;
> Þurȝ gresse to grounde hit fro me yot.
> I dewyne, fordolked of luf-daungere
> Of þat pryuy perle wythouten spot.[14]

This opening illustrates the owner's attachment to his jewel as one in which visual beauty plays an important role. Although the poet eventually develops an extended spiritual allegory, the choice of metaphors allows the reader to associate the description of the pearl with a person along the lines of first physical, then internal beauty. Here too visual description draws in other senses. This pearl is round, radiant, small, and smooth: each adjective applies visually yet smoothness suggests further the intimacy of touch. Vision in this opening also connotes discriminating judgement, a pleasing comparison that results in his setting 'hyr sengeley in synglere.' The corresponding pain of loss is also expressed visually, the pearl having fallen through the grass to the ground. The hiddenness here does lead to the joy of discovery, but the process is excruciating. Both physical and spiritual interpretations clearly establish the poet's relationship to the pearl as one of love: 'I dewyne, fordolked of luf-daungere/ Of þat pryuy perle wythouten spot.' The poet encourages a reading of these lines as indicative of noble, erotic love.

Like the *Roman*, *Pearl* lays its foundation by appealing to the sense of sight. Given the enigmatic yet obviously loving relationship between pearl and speaker, the whole poem contributes images of beauty in keeping with a love lyric.[15] The garden in which the pearl has been lost is among the most important of these, and anticipates as a scene of visual richness both the landscape of his dream and ultimately the celestial city:

---

14   *Pearl*, ed. E.V. Gordon, Oxford, 1953, 1–12.
15   Sarah Stanbury discusses the importance of vision in *Pearl* as a key component to the 'joyful yearning' of the poem. Sarah Stanbury, *Seeing the* Gawain-*Poet: Description and the Act of Perception*, Philadelphia, 1991, 17.

> Þat spot of spyse3 mot nede3 sprede,
> Þer such ryche3 to rot is runne;
> Blome3 blayke and blwe and rede
> Þer schyne3 ful schyr agayn þe sunne.
> Flor and fryte may not be fede
> Þer hit doun drof in molde3 dunne. (25–30)

The garden resembles that of the Song of Songs, where it is an image of the beautiful woman herself. In this way it recalls the spiritual eroticism of the biblical text. It also resembles the garden of the *Roman de la Rose* and elicits the sensuous fervour and devotion of *fin' amor*.

The garden setting belongs firmly to this earth. This is perhaps the best reason why it inspires thoughts of earthly love. In this scene the sun brings radiance and colour: natural light creates a beautiful scene, but one that is circumscribed by being only natural. It provides the springboard for the rest of the poem, a shadowy analogue for the brilliant marvels of the landscape and spiritual experience infused with an altogether higher order of light. As the *Roman* unfolds, the emphasis on vision has particular applications in terms of earthly love that render the painting of the garden scene merely introductory; as *Pearl* unfolds, the painting of the opening scene leads to a particular spiritual vision. Physical vision becomes contrasted with spiritual vision and the dreamer's experience of illumination and understanding. Jean's purpose in using vision as his reference point is to instill a greater appreciation of the benefits of human love; the *Pearl*-poet's is to instill a greater appreciation of divine love.

The transition comes, of course, when the narrator falls asleep. The first stages of his new quest are still ambiguous and display the continuity of a profound visual emphasis. The quality of light, however, gradually reveals a transcendent land and city-scape; ultimately the source of this light in the Lamb is also revealed. The way the poet describes the wood is nothing short of dazzling. It is a scene full of light and colour:

> Dubbed wern alle þo downe3 syde3
> Wyth crystal klyffe3 so cler of kynde.
> Holtewode3 bry3t aboute hem byde3
> Of bolle3 as blwe as ble of Ynde;
> As bornyst syluer þe lef on slyde3,
> Þat þike con trylle on vch a tynde.
> Quen glem of glode3 agayn3 hem glyde3,
> Wyth schymeryng schene ful schrylle þay schynde. (73–80)

The crystal cliffs, unbelievable light, and 'bolle3 as blwe as ble of Ynde' initiate us into an experience of transport and enlightenment. That last line, 'Wyth schymeryng schene ful schrylle thay schyndes,' encapsulates the continuing sensual appeal of vision and its ability to draw in other senses. Here it combines well with sound to create a moving effect. The narrative, controlled almost entirely by such descriptions, moves on to the appearance of the child herself, which has an effect on the dreamer very much like that of a beloved on the lover:

> Þenne vere₃ ho vp her fayre frount,
> Hyr vysayge whyt as playn yuore:
> Þat stonge myn hert ful stray atount,
> And euer þe lenger, þe more and more. (177–80)

This develops into another lengthy description of physical beauty but this initial description neatly captures the tension he feels. His gaze becomes focused on her face and the extraordinary confusion of his spirit finds the beginning of its rest in her ivory-white visage. For the moment it pierces his heart and arrests his sense of time. Vision of her face becomes his eternal now. The context has changed and the poem has shed some of its initial associations with the garden of the *Roman* in favour of a still more luminous landscape. The dreamer's vision has become increasingly complex but it finds its impetus in some basic ideas of the place of vision in the experience of human love. As we shall see, other medieval poetry also shares this feature of increasing complexity expressed in terms of vision. The foundation in poems as divergent as the *Roman* and *Pearl* depends upon concepts that reflect the ubiquitious interest in visual phenomena.

The Painful Vision
Beyond the pleasure of beholding beauty, the encounter between the lover and beloved is often characterized in terms of power, conflict, and pain. The beauty of the lady is often irresistible, especially in the power of her gaze. The lover usually has no choice and simply finds himself taken over. Natural philosophy contributes to this conflict images of power and assault associated with the arrow or dart.[16] Visual imagery engages primordial oppositions as old as the archetypal fight between light and darkness; it effectively communicates the idea of hostility even where opponents are unidentified. Vision itself fits the metaphor of parasitism well for it contains in itself the seeds of hostility.

Respect for the power of the eyes appears in the influential Song of Songs:

> Thou hast wounded my heart, my sister, my spouse: thou hast wounded my heart with one of thy eyes (4:9)[17]

and later,

---

16   Medieval theorists also discussed the pain that looking at extremely bright objects, such as the sun, could cause.

17   'Vulnerasti cor meum soror mea sponsa vulnerasti cor meum in uno oculorum tuorum.'

Turn away thy eyes from me, for they have made me flee away (6:4)[18]

The repetition of the phrase *vulnerasti cor meum* underlines the damage done by the eyes, expressed with surprise, as well as the penetrating nature of the damage: the eyes hurt the heart. The eyes are not simply a source of pleasure but of pain, a juxtaposition that becomes increasingly complex in medieval literature. As early as the twelfth century the importance of vision in Western love poetry can be more pronounced and intricate than the foregoing examples indicate. A natural emphasis on beauty becomes combined with a more specific consideration of the role of the eyes. This represents a greater poetic sophistication in dealing with beauty, an elaboration of what had been an aspect of love from time immemorial.

The twelfth-century poet Bernard de Ventadorn provides perhaps the earliest example of power ascribed to the eyes in Western love literature:[19]

> Anc non agui de me poder
> Ni no fui meus de l'or'en sai
> Que.m laisset en sos olhs vezer,
> En un miralh que mout me plai.
> Miralhs, pus me mirei en te,
> M'an mort li sospir de prëon,
> C'aissi.m perdei com perdet se
> Lo bels Narcisus en la fon.

> (Never have I had power over myself, nor have I to this day been mine, since the hour when she let me look into her eyes, into a mirror which pleases me greatly. Mirror, since I gazed at myself in you, sighs from deep down have killed me; and so I lost myself, just as the beautiful Narcissus lost himself in the fountain.)[20]

The image of the mirror allows Bernard to combine the concept of the perceiving eye with that of the eye of the beloved as agent. Fundamentally, by looking into the lady's eyes the lover finds himself overpowered; the mirror which is her eyes has killed him. Bound up with this experience is a marked awareness of time, the day and the hour when this transforming encounter occurred, an emphasis suggestive of the instantaneous nature of visual processes.[21] The

---

18 'Averte oculos tuos a me quia ipsi me avolare fecerunt.'
19 Ruth Cline suggests that he is the first in Western literature to refer to the power of the eyes (289).
20 Bernard O'Donoghue, *The Courtly Love Tradition*, Oxford, 1982, 116, 17–24, and translation, 117.
21 This probably reflects natural philosophy's pervasive fascination and need to explain the speed involved in vision.

importance of vision makes this initially an experience of beautiful appearances. The appearances involved include both the beloved and the lover, a self-reflexiveness that cannot easily be passed over given the analogies of the mirror and the god Narcissus. The lover presumably sees himself as his beloved sees him; one could also say that her eyes communicate the intentions of love. The craftsmanship involved in producing good mirrors suggests in this context that the woman plays a role in providing a clear reflection. The passage interweaves ideas of optical knowledge and understanding that grow simultaneously out of the emphasis on sight. The concept of the mirror in medieval thought carries with it associations with insight and close study. Narcissus' experience involves a lesson in self-knowledge as he suddenly realizes but too late who it is that he gazes upon in the pool. That medieval love poetry should seize upon the icon of Narcissus usefully indicates the importance and the complexity of vision in love discourse. While it does not explain the mechanics of what is going on, it does suggest the layers of involvement between the participants.

Chrétien de Troyes discusses the importance of vision at length in the romance *Cligés*. There, the eyes serve a double function as perceivers of beauty and as active agents. As agents, they strike through the eyes and enter the heart of the person whose gaze they meet. Soredamors complains about her eyes that they have committed treason against her heart:

> Ses ialz de traïson encuse
> Et dit: «Oel, vos m'avez traïe;
> Par vos m'a mes cuers anhaïe,
> Qui me soloit estre de foi.»[22]

> (She accuses her eyes of treason, saying: 'My eyes, you have betrayed me! Through you my heart, which used to be so faithful, has come to hate me.')[23]

This finger-pointing offers an interesting variation on the Song of Songs. There the lover blames his beloved and the power of her eyes, with the role of his own eyes unmentioned. Here Soredamors blames her own eyes as receptors. In both cases the effect is similar, an altered state of heart. Later, Alexander utters a similar lament. This is the language of profound political upheaval, of an irrevocable breach of faith. Eventually both will absolve the eyes but the immediacy of the event makes the eyes the first to blame, given the way they work and their associations with temptation. Lovers appeal to the eyes to express the upheaval of their hearts. Of the relationship between beauty and vision, Chrétien writes,

---

[22] Chrétien de Troyes, *Cligés*, ed. Alexandre Micha, Les Classiques Français du Moyen Âge, Paris, 1957, 468–71.
[23] Chrétien de Troyes, *Cligés*, in *Arthurian Romances*, trans. D.D.R. Owen, London, 1987.

Li penon sont les treces sores
Que je vi l'autre jor an mer,
C'est li darz qui me fet amer. (782–4)

(The feathers are the fair tresses I saw at sea the other day.
That is the arrow that inspires my love.)

For Chrétien the arrow of love is the arrow of beauty, which pierces the lover's
heart via the eyes. The analogy of the arrow here seems literally to involve the
whole of the beloved's head, with the feathers at the tail of the shaft being her
fair tresses that complete his impression of her visage.[24] Chrétien shows an
interest in entire forms, not only the rays of the eyes, though he adapts arrow
imagery. The gaze of the beloved exerts an even more powerful influence,
again associated with light:

Mes an tot ce n'a riens a dire,
Qui la clarté des ialz remire;
Car a toz ces qui les esgardent
Sanblent deus chandoiles qui ardent. (803–6)

(But all this is as nothing if one looks at the brilliance of the
eyes; for to all those who see them they seem like two burning
candles.)

A burning candle can cause pain or damage and the poet conveys the idea that
candlelight has a life of its own. The image of candles, it will be recalled,
appears in the theories of how sight occurs, where it is associated with the
power of visual rays. The complex possibilities inspired by Bernard's allusion
to Narcissus appear here as well: the lanterns of the eyes provide the light for
learning, perhaps the knowledge of self and sexual initiation.

Amans' entrancement in the *Roman de la Rose* with the crystal stones in the
pool of Narcissus closely resembles the experience of the lover in Bernard de
Ventadorn's poem. There the poet describes the beloved's eyes as a fountain
and mirrors, and his rapture like Narcissus' losing himself in the fountain. Here
too the crystals act as mirrors:

Aussi cum li mireoirs montre
Les choses qui li sont encontre
Et y voit l'en sans couverture
Et lor color et lor faiture,
Tretout aussi vous di por voir

---

24   M.B. Ogle discusses the movement from eyes to hair as the snare of love in 'The Classical Origin and Tradition of Literary Conceits,' *American Journal of Philology* 34 (1913),
129–30. See also 130–46 for other aspects of the importance of the eyes in love.

Que li cristal, sans decevoir,
Tout l'estre du vergier accusent
A ceus qui dedens l'iaue musent. (1555–62)

(Just as a mirror will reflect each thing
That near is placed, and one therein can see
Both form and color without variance,
So do these crystals undistorted show
The garden's each detail to anyone
Who looks into the waters of the spring.)

This similarity between the two poems suggests that the fountain and crystals represent the woman's eyes. They reflect 'tout l'estre du vergier': the woman's eyes communicate all the subtleties of love and leave the lover the pleasing task of discovering and cataloguing each of these details. The passage makes capital out of the confidence placed in optics, that mirrors can reflect form and colour without variance. Guillaume focuses on a product that illustrates human craftsmanship as well as a natural phenomenon rather than solely the natural phenomenon of light. As with Bernard, here there is at least the suggestion of the woman's ability to craft a good mirror though the metaphor undoubtedly depends on existing theories of how vision occurs. Additionally, the effect of these mirrors upon Amans also resembles the effect of eye contact on a lover in other poetry:

Cis mirëors m'a deceu:
Se j'eüsse avant cogneü
Quex sa force ert et sa vertus,
Ne m'i fusse ja embatus,
Car mentenant ou las chaï
Qui maint homme a pris et trahi. (1609–14)

(The mirrors me deceived. Had I but known
Their power and their force, I had not then
So close approached. I fell within the snare
That sorely has betrayed and caught full many a man.)

As C.S. Lewis remonstrates, 'The equivalences are very easy, and even approach dangerously near to that physiological allegory which burdens Spenser's *House of Alma*.'[25] The dreamer twists the idea of straightforward

---

[25] C.S. Lewis, *The Allegory of Love*, Oxford, 1936, 128. Elsewhere, he writes dismissively, 'I have known readers long familiar with the fragmentary Middle English version of the Romance who had never noticed that the fountain of Narcissus represented the heroine's eyes' (117). To this, however, should be added the self-love implicit in looking in the pool of Narcissus.

knowledge. He has just praised the mirrors for their ability to reflect without distortion; now he blames them for deceiving him. He has become trapped, as he admits, in a deceptive relationship between love and knowledge.

The visual encounter in the *Roman de la Rose* causes the sensual struggle that the lover then undergoes. The god of love eventually makes the lover his man by piercing his heart with an arrow that enters through the eyes:

> Et quant la corde fu en coche
> Il entesa jusqu'à l'oreille
> L'arc qui estoit fort a merveille,
> Et trait a moi par tel devise
> Que parmi l'oel m'a ou cors mise
> La saiete par grant roidor. (1690–5)

> (He quickly chose an arrow; nocking it,
> He pulled the cord back to his ear. The bow
> Was marvelously strong, and good his aim,
> And when he shot at me the arrow pierced
> My very heart, though entering by my eye.)

This arrow represents the beauty of the woman. Guillaume extrapolates to include the archer and the action of drawing the bow. In doing so, he accentuates the aggression, danger, and pain involved in love at first sight. The lover tries to overcome its effects but soon concedes defeat:

> Mes la saiete barbelee
> Qui Biautés estoit appellee
> Fu si dedens mon cors fichie
> Qu'ele n'en puet estre errachie. (1715–18)

> (But still the golden barb named Beauty stayed
> Fixed in my heart, never to be removed.)

Beauty, the arrow, receives all the attention at this point; the archer no longer matters. Guillaume follows convention by emphasizing the two-fold importance of vision: the effect of the woman's beauty and the power of her eyes to transfix the lover.

Dante similarly celebrates the conjunction of sight and love and the turmoil sight produces. In the *Vita Nuova* he recounts his experiences of devastation upon seeing his beloved Beatrice, and handles the convention in masterly fashion, developing it in both canzoni and commentaries. He writes, for instance:

> Bieltate appare in saggia donna pui,
>   che piace a li occhi sì, che dentro al core
>   nasce un disio de la cosa piacente.[26]

---

[26]   Dante Alighieri, *Vita Nuova*, ed. Marcello Ciccuto, Milan, 1984, 20.5.

> (Then beauty in a virtuous woman's face
>   Pleases the eyes, striking the heart so deep
>   A yearning for the pleasing thing may arise.)[27]

Beatrice has both a disarming gaze and great physical beauty, and for both these reasons vision plays an impressive role in the beginning stages of love. Beauty enters the heart via the eyes and it strikes the heart, an aggressive activity that forces a reaction.

The writer of 'A wayle whyt ase whalles bon' also focuses on the effect of the woman's eyes. He offers a description of her complete physical beauty, then locates the source of the pain she has caused him in her eyes:

> Gret hire wel, þat swete þing
> wiþ eȝen gray.
>
> Hyre heȝe haueþ wounded me ywisse,
> hire bende browen, þat bringeþ blisse. (23–6)[28]

Like the other poems we have examined, this one draws attention to the beauty of the woman's eyes. Here the description of her arched brow as well extends the arrow imagery through a pun on the bent brow as the bent brow. The eye and the brow also function as opposites, the one causing a wound and the other bringing bliss, expressing the conventional paradox of the sweet pain of love. A roundel from the later part of the fourteenth century, which may be the work of Chaucer, opens with a similar complaint against a woman's eyes:

> Your yen two wol sle me sodenly;
> I may the beautee of hem not sustene,
> So woundeth hit thourghout my herte kene. (1–3)[29]

Another example, from one of Chaucer's short poems, that clearly shows his thorough familiarity with the conventions of love poetry can be found in his complaint to his purse, where he asserts that

> To yow, my purse, and to noon other wight
> Complayne I, for ye be my lady dere. (1–2)

He then proceeds to complain in the language of love, and here he appeals specifically to the beauty of the object of his affections and his utter dependence:

---

[27]   Dante Alighieri, *La Vita Nuova*, trans. Barbara Reynolds, Harmondsworth, 1969.
[28]   Brook, 41.
[29]   *The Riverside Chaucer*, 659.

Now voucheth sauf this day or hyt be nyght
That I of yow the blisful soun may here
Or see your colour lyk the sonne bryght
That of yelownesse hadde never pere.
Ye be my lyf, ye be myn hertes stere.
Quene of comfort and of good companye,
Beth hevy ageyn, or elles moot I dye. (8–14)

Chaucer draws an extensive analogy and plays especially with the colour of money, which is 'lyk the sonne bryght,' and just like the blonde hair of the ideal beautiful woman. He conjoins this motif with that of death, isolating visual beauty and pain as the two focal points of the courtly experience of love. It is a playful poem, and certainly an example of the poet's cleverness. It is also an example of Chaucer's willingness to press the specific set of conventions into service for a particular purpose, here a translucent appeal to King Henry IV for patronage.

Religious lyrics directed especially to Mary constitute another popular strain of poetry in the Middle Ages that inverts the theme of the look and pain. An example of this type of love poetry is 'Levedy, ic thonke thee,' a short thirteenth-century piece that concludes with the following stanza:

Moder, loke one me,
Wid thine swete eyen,
Reste and blisse gef thu me,
My levedy, then ic deyen.[30]

The writer addresses Mary tenderly and lovingly, and looks for sustaining comfort from her gaze. The line 'Wid thine swete eyen' extends the idea of watchfulness and contributes a sense of adoration on the part of the petitioner in keeping with the language of noble love. Here too vision plays an important part in the expression of devotion. He inverts the relationship between the gaze and its effect as expressed in secular literature: the look will result in rest, salvation, and bliss in death rather than result in death-for-love. Death waits to take him and forms part of the experience of love and adoration. In terms of vision there is latitude for mutual influence between secular and sacred sources, a point that contributes to the functioning of *parasitisme* in ways that go beyond mere hostility. The language of metaphysics provides a very adequate source for spiritual love language incorporating the notions of beauty and vision.

[30] R.T. Davies, ed., *Middle English Lyrics*, London, 1963, 64, 13–16.

Love and Knowledge Opposed

The notion of conflict associated with vision becomes internalized and appears in its most fundamental form as a breach between love and knowledge. This opposition has an ancient pedigree, going back at least as far as the conflict between vulgar eros and philosophical eros in Platonic thought.[31] The eyes are linked specifically with this binary opposition. In *Cligés*, Chrétien conjoins the heart and the eyes and the imagery of light suggests many readings. But while the eyes effectively transmit the emotions of the heart, in certain circumstances they have very limited abilities:

> Li ialz n'a soin de rien antandre,
> Ne rien ne puet feire a nul fuer,
> Mes c'est li mereors au cuer,
> Et par ce mereor trespasse,
> Si qu'il ne le blesce ne ne quasse,
> Le san don li cuers est espris.
> Donc est li cuers el vantre mis,
> Ausi com la chandoile esprise
> Est dedanz la lenterne mise. (702–10)

> (The eye is not concerned with comprehending anything and is totally incapable of doing so; but it is the mirror for the heart, and through this mirror there passes, without damaging or breaking it, the fire that sets the heart ablaze. For is not the heart placed in the breast just like a lighted candle placed inside the lantern?)

The eyes simply accept the incoming information, in this case the two burning candles of the beloved's eyes, reflecting the material to the heart where the fire from the candles sets the lover's heart ablaze. In this passage Chrétien directly attacks the associations of the eye with insight and understanding: 'Li ialz n'a soin de rien antandre/ Ne rien ne puet feire a nul fuer.' By addressing this issue, he admits the layers of meaning that might otherwise be read into this situation; he effectively polarizes the possible associations of the eyes into the classical opposition of love and reason. The lover has no facility to keep the burning candles out of the heart or to prevent the conflagration there.

The opposition of love and knowledge finds expression in various strains of medieval poetry, including the following examples from Latin love lyrics. The first, from the thirteenth-century poem 'O quam formosa,' illustrates the confusion caused by the wound of love:

---

[31] For a useful discussion of this dualism see Anders Nygren, *Agape and Eros,* 49–52.

O quam formosa,
quam decens quam diligo!
rubet ut rosa
in qua visum figo.
. . .
In me thelum iaties,
mortis et spem vite quaties,
hiemps non, nix neque glacies
me infrigidaret.

Figo in te oculorum acies,
te diligo: foris paret!

Intuitum oculorum saties –
cor deficit cum te caret.

O deus, quid agam?
iam plagam
amoris, iam foris
monstro, tolero intus;
fero mentem vagam,
presagam
maioris doloris
O qualis laborintus![32]

(O how beautiful, how comely is she I love – she is like a red
rose, on whom I fix my gaze!
. . .
You will pierce me with a dart, make tremble my hope of life
and death. No winter, snow or ice would cool me (then).
I direct all the strength of my gaze on you, I love you – as can
well be seen.
May you utterly fill my field of vision: when you are not in it
my heart fails.
O God, what shall I do? That wound of love – I show it without, endure it within. My mind is distraught, foreboding
greater grief.
Oh what a labyrinth!)[33]

The motif of the gaze of love utterly fills our vision here. The poet returns
compulsively to that experience and describes his state in terms of superlatives

---

[32] Dronke, 387, 1a; 3b–5a.
[33] Dronke, 388.

and extremes of opposition; he craves the sight of his beloved with an obsessiveness that itself indicates that his mind is not his own. And that is the only conclusion that he can draw about his condition. Love is a labyrinth, taxing his mind beyond its limits, leaving him wondering helplessly what he can do. On labyrinths, Boethius' prisoner also complains to Lady Philosophy when he cannot follow her reasoning that she has

> 'so woven me with thi resouns the hous of Didalus, so entrelaced that it is unable to ben unlaced.' (3.pr12)

The meter following this section in *The Consolation of Philosophy* relates the story of Orpheus, which tidily expresses the complete opposition of love and rationality. The metaphor of the labyrinth applies quite specifically to this convention.

The suitability of Orpheus for this kind of depiction has roots in the commentary tradition on this mythical figure. Orpheus, like Narcissus, stands as an icon of the potency of vision. In the concluding meter of book 3 of *The Consolation of Philosophy*, Lady Philosophy reflects upon Orpheus as an example of the battle between love and reason. For Boethius, in the true Platonic tradition, the quest for understanding is a quest for sight:

> Blisful is that man that may seen the clere welle of good! (3.m12)

This beatitude is followed by the negative example of Orpheus, who used his sight to achieve the opposite ends in accordance with 'the most ardaunt love of his wif [that] brende the entrayles of his breest.' Boethius interprets the conflict of love and reason as here hinging upon which vision Orpheus values. After he has negotiated freedom for his wife and himself, the god of the underworld gives Orpheus the command not to look at his wife behind him as they leave. This injunction produces the question,

> But what is he that may yeven a lawe to loverys? (3.m12)

Love denies rational controls and Orpheus illustrates this fact by looking back. This famous incident encapsulates the conflict of love and reason in terms of vision.

Another Latin poem, written down in 1358, develops the contrast between love and intellectual pursuits and the power of love over philosophy in the experience of Orpheus. Although the eyes are chief among the physical senses and closest to the faculty of reason, they serve the cause of love:

> Predantur oculos, captivant animum
> vocalis Orphei
> siderei
> vultus et simplices risus Euridices.

Qui solis animos luneque menstruos
rimari solitus
circuitus,
celo fugam siderum
per numerum
notatam,

Iam nunc ad alteram traductus operam,
mutato studio,
de basio,
de amplexu loquitur
et sequitur
amatam

In flammam abiit totus philosophus,
amantis spiritum
solicitum
tacente cithara stupebant Ismara.[34]

(Eurydice's starry looks and innocent laughter ravish the eyes
of singing Orpheus, captivate his mind.
Orpheus, whose habit was to research into the spirits of the
sun, the monthly orbit of the moon, the numerically established courses of the stars in heaven, now led to a pursuit of
another kind, his studies modified, speaks of kissing, of em-
bracing, and follows his beloved.
The philosopher has quite gone up in flames – Ismarus stood
amazed at his love-lorn spirit, while his lute lay still.)[35]

The poem sustains oppositions throughout. It opens with two aggressive, mili-
taristic verbs which in turn contrast with the starry looks and simple laugh of
Eurydice. That appeal to the stars introduces the central *volte face*, Orpheus'
transformation from studying the stars to undertaking other pursuits. With his
studies changed, the philosopher now engages in activity that reflects his sub-
mission, succinctly expressed in the deponent verbs *loquitur* and *sequitur*. The
wry observation 'In flammam abiit totus philosophus' captures the truism in
medieval love poetry that love and reason oppose each other with consuming,
painful effects. Orpheus has had his eyes ravished and his mind captivated.

The classic medieval exposition of this binary opposition occurs in the *Roman de la Rose*. After the god of love has made Amans his servant, the lover
faces a number of challenges as he tries to pluck the rose. These include the
persuasions of Reason, who scans the countryside with eyes like two stars. She
incarnates intellectual sight and has the power

[34] 'Predantur oculos, captivant animum,' Dronke, 403, 1–20.
[35] Dronke, 404.

> De garder homme de folie,
> Par quoi il soit tex qu'il la croie. (2994–5)

> (To rescue men from rash and foolish acts
> Provided that her counsel they'll believe.)

Reason's argument is straightforward. She attacks love as unrewarding folly:

> «C'est li maus qui amors a non,
> Ou il n'a se folie non.
> Folie, si m'aïst Diex, voire!
> Hons qui aime ne puet bien faire
> N'a nesun bien du monde entendre;
> S'il est clers, il pert son aprendre;
> Et se il fet autre mestier,
> Il n'en puet gueres esploitier.» (3041–8)

> ('Nothing but foolishness is this disease
> Called love; 'twere better it were folly named.
> A ne'er-do-well is every man in love;
> No profitable task he undertakes.
> He leaves his learning if he be a clerk;
> Nor can he thrive in any other craft.')

By picking on clerks Guillaume heightens the sense of conflict between love and reason. Reason objects that love forces one to abandon learning and all other crafts. The basis of her argument is true and reasonable, which is of course the point, but she does not influence the lover, whose response is equally uncompromising:

> «Vous me dites que je refraigne
> Mon cuer, qu'Amors plus ne le praigne.
> Cuidiés vous dont qu'Amors consente
> Que je refraingne et que je dente
> Le cuer qui est tretous siens quites?
> Ce ne puet estre que vous dites.» (3077–82)

> ('You tell me that I should oppose my heart,
> Which Love now dominates. But do you think
> Love would consent that I the heart should rule
> Which I have ceded to him utterly?
> You counsel what can never come to pass.')

The repetition of the thought of opposition (*refraigne*) emphasizes the nature of the contest. Amans' response begs the question when he apparently assumes he would need the god of love's consent to reject him: he is indeed under his sway and well beyond Reason's reach.

The unfinished quality of Guillaume's poem further embodies the complete opposition of love and knowledge. Although the poem has a clear beginning as a dream-poem and lacks a similarly clear ending to the dream, David Hult makes a convincing case for the suitability of 'allegory and incompletion,' of the inability to tell one's own ending.[36] This feature of the poem serves as an analogy for the central conflict of the poem between love and reason. The essential lesson that Amans learns is that love denies containment in systematic statements. Like the dream, it simply unfolds and folds back into itself with inherent circularity. The lack of an ending indicates the eternality of the hostility between these terms.

Reason makes a reappearance in Jean de Meun's continuation of the quest, and engages the lover in a much more convoluted dialogue. The lover, however, still faces an either/or choice because love and reason do not cohabit. And the lover's answer remains unchanged:

> «Et quant aillors penser me faites
> Par vos paroles ci retraites
> Que je sui ja touz las d'oïr,
> Ja m'en verrés de ci foïr
> Se ne vous en taisiés a tant,
> Puis que mon cuer aillors s'atent.» (7223–8)

> ('Now oft by your reiterated words
> You irk me so that my thoughts fly away
> And tempt me to achieve escape by flight
> Unless you'll quiet keep; for still my heart
> Is in attendance on another one.')

This is Reason's final attempt, and with this speech the lover sends Reason packing:

> Quant Raison m'ot, puis si s'en torne,
> Et me lessa pensant et morne. (7229–30)

> (When Reason heard this speech, she turned aside
> And left me pensive – lonely – most disconsolate.)

Far from resulting in a resolution, Reason's departure fixes the hostility. As an afterword to this conflict, the god of love later chastizes the lover for listening to Reason. Amans quickly assures his master of his redoubled commitment:

---

36 Hult asks searchingly, 'Is the . . . possibility of ending a dream as unproblematical as it seems? Must the dreamer always state programmatically that he has awakened? In a more general sense, what does it mean to pass from dream to wakefulness? When a dream prophesies the dreamer's future experience, can one tell one's own dream *and* complete it?' (emphasis his). David F. Hult, *Self-fulfilling Prophecies: Readership and Authority in the First Roman de la Rose*, Cambridge, 1986, 109.

«[Si pri qu'il me soit pardonné,
Car je, por ma vie amender,
Si cum vous plest a commander,]
Or vuel, sanz plus Raison ensivre,
En vostre loi morir et vivre.» (10364–8)

('For that I beg your pardon. 'Tis my will
So to amend my life as to conform
To what it may e'er please you to command –
Never again to follow Reason's words,
But always in your service live and die.')

Aspects of Jean's presentation add another dimension to the relationship between love and knowledge, and make a contribution to the system as hospitality
as well as hostility. Like Guillaume, though, he perfectly understands and ca-
pably articulates the opposition. The allegory of the *Roman de la Rose* dramatically represents the gulf separating love and reason. The two are diametrically
and eternally opposed, and this is a fundamental fact of passionate love as
understood in medieval literature.

The most entrancing example of Dante's understanding of the role of vision
in love occurs in the episode where he relates how he saw Beatrice at the house
of friends. He divides the *Vita Nuova* into poetry and technical discussions,
suggestive of a separation between the ineffability of experience in love and a
disquisition on such an experience; interestingly, the distinction between can-
zone and prosaic analysis in this case blurs. He introduces the sonnet by describing the event:

Levai li occhi, e mirando le donne, vidi tra loro la gentilissima Beatrice.
Allora fuoro sì distrutti li miei spiriti per la forza che Amore prese veg-
gendosi in tanta propinquitade a la gentilissima donna, che non ne rimasero in vita più che li spiriti del viso, e ancora questi rimasero fuori de
li loro istrumenti, però che Amore volea stare nel loro nobilissimo luogo
per vedere la mirabile donna. (14.4–5)

(I raised my eyes and as they rested on the women gathered there I saw
among them the most gracious Beatrice. Then my spirits were routed by
the power which love acquired on finding himself so close to this most
gracious being that none survived except the spirits of vision; and even
they were driven from their organs because love himself desired to oc-
cupy their noble place in order to behold her who inspired such wonder.)

Dante emphasizes the effect on his spirits, cleverly moving from the general
and perhaps metaphorical to the specific and physical, increasingly describing
love's devastating effects in terms of what can be intellectually apprehended.
He does not analyze the sonnet that follows since its meaning is clear from the

introduction he has given to it, but he does comment on his reference to the visual effect:

> Vero è che tra le parole dove si manifesta la cagione di questo sonetto, si scivono dubbiose parole, cioè quando dico che Amore uccide tutti li miei spiriti, e li visivi rimangono in vita, salvo che fuori de li strumenti loro. E questo dubbio è impossibile a solvere a chi non fosse in simile grado fedele d'Amore; e a coloro che vi sono è manifesto ciò che solverebbe le dubitose parole. (14.14)

> (I admit that among the words in which I set forth the occasion of the sonnet there are some whose meaning is obscure, for instance, when I say that love slays all my spirits, except the spirits of vision, which survive but are driven from their organs. It is impossible to explain this to anyone who is not to the same extent a faithful follower of love; and to those who are it is obvious what the meaning is.)

Dante clearly affirms the importance of vision in love and treats it in familiar ways, but in his description of what happens to his spirits he realizes that he has moved beyond convention. It is an example, as Barbara Reynolds observes, of his moving beyond the barriers of convention to write directly from experience.[37] Here, Dante focuses on the affinities between vision and love to the point that he disdains technical analysis, a concession to the truism that love denies the processes of ratiocination.

The love in question in all of these examples is also known as *fin' amor*. The adjective *fin'* in this phrase has a range of meanings that apply aptly to this separation. Delving into the meaning of the root *fin'*, J.D. Burnley points out that the word includes the notions of purity and intensity. Though the word can be used in a moral context, Burnley argues that the essence of the meaning of the phrase has little to do with its sexual or divine orientation, or with the marital or extramarital context of the love; rather it concerns the quality and the intensity of the love itself.[38] The adjective commonly describes metals free of impurities and is also used of colour. Interestingly, the *MED* records that the cognate Middle English adjective *fine* can also be used to describe a weapon as 'thin-edged; sharp,' a meaning in keeping with the piercing and rather concentrated effect of love at first sight. Both of these concepts, purity and intensity, accurately describe what happens to the soul in love. The way in which passion totally dominates reason signals a kind of purity. In the *Roman*, Amans wavers for awhile but eventually turns his back on Reason, and the god of love stresses the importance of the purity of his resolve. The literature on love-sickness indicates the intensity of passion, both in controlling the brain and in

---

37 Reynolds, 17.
38 J.D. Burnley, '*Fine Amor*: Its Meaning and Context,' *Review of English Studies* n.s. 3 (1980), 129–48.

causing it to produce excessive thoughts. The term *fin'*, therefore, accurately describes the conflict between passion and reason, a conflict that is a recurring, basic part of medieval conceptions of erotic love.

The interference between love and reason centers on the eyes. It is a conflict reminiscent of the tension between physical and spiritual ways of seeing in Christian theology. If the eye of the heart could see God or be illumined to see spiritual truth, the physical eye could be tempted by worldly enticements. The Sermon on the Mount provides an example of the uncompromising language used in Christianity to reveal the conflict between the spirit and the flesh:

> And, if thy right eye scandalize thee, pluck it out and cast it from thee.
> For it is expedient for thee that one of thy members should perish rather
> than that thy whole body be cast into hell. (Matt. 5:29)[39]

In medieval preaching, the eye was commonly picked on as the cause of much sin, especially sexual offences. This may have been partly due to the popularity of the lyrics that promoted the role of the eye in love, though the tension already exists in the Judeo-Christian scriptures. A fourteenth-century preacher's handbook, the *Fasciculus morum*, represents sight as the first occasion for lechery with this pronouncement: 'Sight and speech, touching and kisses, finally the deed.'[40] The eyes can immediately lead to spiritual trouble, as they apparently do for Augustine, who finds the temptation set before the eyes especially strong. He confesses that even after rediscovering the love of God in his memory, he continues to find beautiful shapes and bright and attractive colours enticing.[41] One insight from our investigation into the place of sight in metaphysics has been to recognize the everpresent ambivalence in Christianity regarding physical sight. It can lead to useful knowledge, but blessed are those who have not seen and yet believed; it provides the language with which one can express the emotional transport of a vision of God, but one ought to have no knowledge of such transport in a human love. The eye can always get one into a great deal of trouble since it serves as a window onto the sensual world. In medieval Christianity this power of sight to lead inexorably to 'the deed' and the conflict between sensual and spiritual love means that the eyes habitually produce conflict. The power of the eye of another could also cause internal conflict and the overthrow of reason, but this concept finds little resonance in Latin and Christian literature.[42] With the possible exception of the erotic language of the Song of Songs, the Bible contributes relatively little to

---

[39] 'Quod si oculus tuus dexter scandalizat te erue eum et proice abs te expedit enim tibi ut pereat unum membrorum tuorum quam totum corpus tuum mittatur in gehennam.'

[40] *Fasciculus morum: A Fourteenth-Century Preacher's Handbook*, ed. and trans. Siegfried Wenzel, University Park, Penn. and London, 1989, 649. 'Visus et alloquium, contactus et oscula, factum' (648).

[41] Augustine, *Conf.* 10.34.

[42] Cline usefully points out that in these traditions the emphasis falls on one's own eye:

subsequent interest in the active role played by the eyes, especially where that relates to their ability to strike into the eyes and heart of another. But it does contribute to the association of the eyes with the binary opposition of love and knowledge.

We have already seen that although they are the chief among the five senses and closest to reason, the eyes capitulate to beauty just as reason capitulates to love. This parasitic hostility is energized by other sources of tension. In theology, vision represents a spiritual capacity to see God but is a source of conflict when one uses the outer eye to focus on the sensory world. In natural philosophy, the ray of the eye is another source of power. Interest in the role of the eyes in love has persisted in modern discourse but now the phenomenon, if thought about at all, is cast simply in terms of a conflict between passion and reason. The theological and optical notions of power and conflict have lost their currency. The importance of vision in medieval love literature is due to a combination of these influences. None on their own adequately explains the complicated use of vision or its capacity to represent love so richly in love lyrics; but together they attest a profound and in some ways literal understanding of the power of vision.

Visual Hostilities in Chaucer's Poetry

The Book of the Duchess develops these simple motifs into a study of love as visual pleasure and love as pain. It opens with a disturbing sense of physicality that is specifically based on light:

> I have gret wonder, be this lyght,
> How that I lyve, for day ne nyght
> I may nat slepe wel nygh noght. (1–3)

The off-handed contrast of 'lyght' and 'nyght' immediately establishes a kind of tension between two different realms: the one all too real, filled as it is with 'so many an ydel thoght' (4) and 'sorwful ymagynacioun' (14), all verifiable 'be this lyght;' the other, a place of subliminal release and potential insight, inaccessible. When he finally does fall asleep, the narrator predictably dreams of what he has just read. Through the dreamer's exaggerated problem Chaucer establishes the naturalism of every day experience as a reference point:

> And wel ye woot, agaynes kynde
> Hyt were to lyven in thys wyse,
> For nature wolde nat suffyse
> To noon erthly creature

'In the cultural tradition of Latin writers, particularly the Christian philosophers, the eye to be feared, the eye that could bring harm upon one, was one's own eye' (Cline, 294).

Nat longe tyme to endure
Withoute slep and be in sorwe. (16–21)

He contrasts the narrator's condition with the normal experience of 'kynde' and any 'erthly creature' in the domain of 'nature.' By setting the scene in terms of light Chaucer anticipates the pleasure of the knight's experience of falling in love, exacerbates the present problem since light is the last thing the insomniac wants or needs, and establishes the structure upon which he will hang the concepts appropriate to the solemn occasion.

In this dream-poem Chaucer treats other-worldly agencies with a touch of comic lightness. His account of the trip that Juno's messenger makes to Morpheus is for me one of the funnier descriptions in his poetry. The messenger is on serious business as Juno wants to respond to Alcyone's lament and provide her with a vision of her drowned husband; but he runs into the ludicrous problem of having to wake up the god of sleep, in the end managing only to get him to open one eye. The vision that Alcyone receives is appropriately serious but Chaucer makes it difficult to take the actual idea of a vision seriously because of his depiction of the machinery behind the event. This is not subversive enough to undermine his objectives for the poem as a whole; on the contrary, this early piece of humour disarms his audience and allows him to lead his listeners gently into the grave subject matter of the occasion for the poem. Perhaps it even contains the element of a message to John of Gaunt to be wary of quick solutions to the grieving process. Chaucer will treat this potentially weighty and meaningful matter of dreams with even more irreverence in the Nun's Priest's Tale. When Chauntecleer tries to find comfort in telling Pertelote about his dream of the fox, the hen dismisses dreams as an imbalance of the humours and summarily tells him, 'For Goddes love, as taak som laxatyf' (VII.2943). Chaucer does not declare himself in these situations: Alcyone receives her vision and Chauntecleer's comes true. But he does tend to demystify the idea, to approach dreams and visions from the point of view of ordinary experience.

In his earliest poetry Chaucer develops the theme of love common to dream-poems after the *Roman de la Rose*. The dreamer in *The Book of the Duchess* claims to belong to the great tradition of dreamers with his 'so ynly swete a sweven' (276) and in keeping with this tradition Chaucer appeals to the sense of sight. His description of May is indebted both to the *Roman* and to Machaut's *Dit dou Roy de Behaingne*.[43] Chaucer refers to the *Roman* explicitly:

---

[43] Barry Windeatt has collected the influential passages in *Chaucer's Dream Poetry: Sources and Analogues*, Cambridge, 1982. He introduces the material by stressing the artistic process of distillation undertaken by Chaucer (ix). Far from being a slave to the material, Chaucer shows brilliance in knowing what to develop, what shows promise where often it is left undeveloped in the source (x).

And alle the walles with colours fyne
Were peynted, bothe text and glose,
Of al the Romaunce of the Rose. (332–4)

In this context, sight plays the important role we have seen it plays in love literature generally. Convention supplies the stained-glass scenes of Troy, the 'bryghte bemes' (337), and later the 'floury grene' (398) and the forest scene. The dreaming frame and the idea of vision particular to it increase our sensitivity to the appeal to sight that now unfolds as the dreamer describes his experience primarily in terms of sight and sound. This emphasis points to a consolation not of anguished reasoning but of remembrance, of treasured moments perceived in all their 'colours fyne,' of aspects of a love as it grew and blossomed.

When the dreamer follows the whelp and discovers the 'man in blak,' Chaucer establishes one of the central themes of this occasional poem, the contrast in colours between him and the 'lady bryght' whom he describes. For all his blackness, the knight can be described by his colours:

and that made al
Hys hewe chaunge and wexe grene
And pale, for ther noo blood ys sene
In no maner lym of hys. (496–9)

As in the poem 'Blow, northerne wind,' there is a correspondence between colour and the individual's emotional condition. The description of the knight becomes especially meaningful as the focus shifts to the Lady White, who symbolizes Blanche:

'And goode faire White she het;
That was my lady name ryght.
She was bothe fair and bryght;
She hadde not hir name wrong.' (948–51)

Such a dependence upon colours is not unusual in dream-poetry, yet the pun on the name Blanche adds a gracefully simple touch to the way Chaucer handles his subject here. He reinforces the imagery of light, which he uses to describe his love when he eventually discloses himself to the wandering dreamer:

'For I dar swere, withoute doute,
That as the someres sonne bryght
Ys fairer, clerer, and hath more lyght
Than any other planete in heven,
The moone or the sterres seven,
For al the world so hadde she
Surmounted hem alle of beaute.' (820–6)

The surpassing brightness of the sun finds its analogue in the description of the lady's golden hair and the brightness of her visage. He likens her to a bright torch from which every man takes light:

> 'she was lyk to torche bryght
> That every man may take of lyght.' (963–4)

Potentially, of course, the torch could pass into the lover's heart and set it ablaze and so it does. But it also can serve as the light of solace and reflection.

The capturing of the knight by this woman is almost identical to what happens to Amans. The lover becomes transfixed by the beloved's beauty, especially by the power of her eyes:

> 'She had so stedfast countenaunce,
> So noble port and meyntenaunce,
> And Love, that had wel herd my boone,
> Had espyed me thus soone,
> That she ful sone in my thoght,
> As helpe me God, so was ykaught
> So sodenly that I ne tok
> No maner counseyl but at hir lok
> And at myn herte; for-why hir eyen
> So gladly, I trow, myn herte seyen
> That purely tho myn owne thoght
> Seyde hit were beter serve hir for noght
> Than with another to be wel.' (833–45)

This passage reminds the audience of the ideals for an experience of *fyn lovynge*. Chaucer idealizes the experience of John of Gaunt and Blanche and reminds John of the transport of his love, its power to nullify all questions: he highlights love as a phenomenon in which vision plays this familiar role.

Chaucer elaborates the conjunction of love and reason to underscore the positive influence the Lady White had upon the knight's mind and, by implication, the positive effect she can still have as the bereaved lover remembers her and acknowledges their splendid love. The knight freely admits that he put himself in love's service from an early age, and proceeds to provide a careful analysis of the development of his understanding:

> 'Syr,' quod he, 'sith first I kouthe
> Have any maner wyt fro youthe,
> Or kyndely understondyng
> To comprehende in any thyng
> What love was, in myn owne wyt,
> Dredeles, I have ever yit

Be tributarye and yive rente
To Love.' (759–66)

'Understondyng' refers here specifically to his interest in love and does not indicate the opposition of those terms but the language used here prepares the ground for the meeting which will shortly occur. Chaucer develops this collocation further, advancing an epistemological concept:

'Paraunter I was therto most able,
As a whit wal or a table,
For hit ys redy to cacche and take
Al that men wil theryn make.' (779–82)

This passage has contributed to much speculation on Chaucer's philosophizing attitude in this poem.[44] Whatever it suggests about Chaucer's understanding of how the mind works, in the context of a love poem and on an occasion of consolation allusions that could degenerate into pedantry primarily draw attention to the separation between the twin foci, love and knowledge. The knight's self-analysis orients the reader's mind to such matters, but renders the story of his falling in love more impressive and reorienting. If the temptation to lament Fortune's prowess at chess seems too great for the knight, reflection on the Lady White and the way she possessed his mind from the moment he saw her indicate the way consolation may also occur. We have here an early indication of Chaucer's awareness of the ways in which love and knowledge function together.

Chaucer works within the confines of the conventions of love-literature and happily accepts the normal emphasis on the eyes, and the association of the beautiful lady with light inspires an almost transcendent feeling of comfort. The love-vision cannot give John of Gaunt his wife back in any meaningful way, and Chaucer realizes this. When Alcyone asks for some token of her husband's fate, the answer to her prayer crushes her and she dies. At the end of the poem nothing spectacular has happened, but life, at least for the public-figure king, carries on hopefully. Chaucer's insistent repetition of the word 'sweven' at the end, three times in the last five lines, calls attention to the tentativeness of what he has just tried to achieve. Not a signal of his own lack of confidence, it reemphasizes the ephemeral nature of reflection, of the glimpses into the past seen in grieving, and of the nature of life itself as expressed in the poem's leitmotif, 'To lytel while oure blysse lasteth.'

The hostility of love and reason appears as a function of sight in at least two of Chaucer's mature works, the Knight's Tale and *Troilus and Criseyde*. The Knight's Tale recreates a world of erotic sights and elucidates the opposition

---

[44]   See, for instance, Russell Peck, 'Chaucer and the Nominalist Questions,' *Speculum* 53 (1978), 745–60.

between passion and reason to investigate Boethian ideals of cosmic order. Passion develops from sight; Chaucer is faithful to his source, Boccaccio's *Il Teseida*, and consistent with the way he presents love's beginnings elsewhere. He expresses Palamon and Arcite's experience in language and imagery that recall the *Roman de la Rose*. As we know, the *Roman* depends heavily on the use of colours and images and sets the standard in medieval literature for establishing the role of the eyes in love. Both the *Teseida* and the Knight's Tale take their cue from it. When Chaucer introduces the reader to Emily in the castle garden, he plays freely with the French model:

> This passeth yeer by yeer and day by day,
> Till it fil ones, in a morwe of May,
> That Emelye, that fairer was to sene
> Than is the lylie upon his stalke grene,
> And fressher than the May with floures newe –
> For with the rose colour stroof hire hewe,
> I noot which was the fyner of hem two – (I.1033–9)

He calls attention to her 'yelow heer' and to the red and white flowers she gathers for a garland. The incident is set in May and Emily clearly is the rose. When the two prisoners see Emily, they are totally transfixed by her beauty and immediately become her servants in love. Palamon lets out a sharp cry and exclaims,

> 'But I was hurt right now thurghout myn ye
> Into myn herte, that wol my bane be.
> The fairnesse of that lady that I see
> Yond in the gardyn romen to and fro
> Is cause of al my criyng and my wo.' (1096–1100)

Arcite suffers the exact same fate:

> 'The fresshe beautee sleeth me sodeynly
> Of hire that rometh in the yonder place;
> And but I have hir mercy and hir grace,
> That I may seen hire atte leeste weye,
> I nam but deed; ther nis namoore to seye.' (1118–22)

Their confessions have several typical features: they suffer painfully from the beloved's beauty, instantaneously become dependent upon her grace, and become emotionally and intellectually captive.

As a result, both knights suffer the deleterious effects of love. Arcite becomes an icon of the lovesick man, his appearance symptomatic of *ereos*:

His slep, his mete, his drynke, is hym biraft,
That lene he wex and drye as is a shaft;
His eyen holwe and grisly to biholde,
His hewe falow and pale as asshen colde. (1361–4)

He visibly represents the parasitic effects of love in his system. The disease overtakes his mind:

And in his geere for al the world he ferde
Nat oonly lik the loveris maladye
Of Hereos, but rather lyk manye,
Engendred of humour malencolik
Biforen, in his celle fantastik. (1372–6)

This is the only place where Chaucer refers to the disease of lovesickness directly. He takes care to describe the process of falling in love completely here to establish its anti-rational nature. He takes us right inside the brain, along a pathway followed by optical theorists and philosophers as well, to show us the devastating effects of love's rays.

Both knights rebel against the constraints of the law imposed by Theseus. They illustrate the opposition of passion and reason as understood by Boethius in his recounting of the myth of Orpheus. Palamon prays to Venus for help to escape and thereby break the bonds of Theseus' civil order:

'Out of this prisoun help that we may scapen.
And if so be my destynee be shapen
By eterne word to dyen in prisoun,
Of oure lynage have som compassioun.' (1107–10)

Arcite also rebels, denying any legal or familial ties to Palamon that may conflict with his desire to gain Emily's love. Verbal echoes of the poem of Orpheus in Boethius mark his reasoning:

'Wostow nat wel the olde clerkes sawe,
That "who shal yeve a lovere any lawe?" ' (1163–4)

This is almost exactly the same as Orpheus' question and he broke the law by turning to see Eurydice. Chaucer appeals to sight in a variety of ways, all well-known in medieval love discourse, to establish the same conflict of this poem: the dialectic between Theseus as arbiter of rationality and the two knights as the thralls of passion.

With the long poem *Troilus and Criseyde*, Chaucer follows in the footsteps of Boccaccio in elaborating upon this favorite epic material, the fall of Troy. Like Boccaccio, he focuses upon a specific set of events within the larger epic context, a love affair between two citizens of that doomed city that defies rational understanding. *Il Filostrato* provides Chaucer with much of the material for his own poem; it is easily his single most important source, though Chaucer has apparently taken pains to familiarize himself thoroughly with the historical material and sets himself up as something of an authority on the subject. The tactic is useful, for by it Chaucer appears to gain what every historian wants, an authoritative voice on the past.[45] By this device the poet effectively reinforces his status as an authority on the more specific subject of love. He declares his objective in the poem at the outset to be that of reporting the double sorrow of Troilus in loving and he describes his larger role in life in similar terms – 'For I, that God of loves servantz serve'[46] – taking on more authority through that parallel with the papal office. The firmness with which Chaucer maintains this purpose gives the poem its main strength and is the chief benefit that he derives from his source. Though Chaucer dramatically embellishes the story as he receives it from Boccaccio, and transforms the poem into something uniquely his own, he has *Il Filostrato* to reinforce the fundamental theme and provide him with the liberty to explore in the directions of philosophy, social ambiguity, and the absence of closure. Chaucer relies heavily upon familiar love discourse to pursue these various pathways; the importance of vision particularly helps the poem both to cohere and to open up at the end. The parasitic relationship of love and knowledge in *Troilus* makes the poem relevant from a number of different angles: allusions to light and vision hold the possibility of polyvalent readings. While Boccaccio leaves these options unfulfilled, Chaucer exploits them to create an intricate pattern in his poem that reflects the changing balance of interests in late medieval thought.

He begins, however, in the same way as Boccaccio, establishing the power of sight to transfix the lover. Like many others before him, Boccaccio makes full use of the importance of vision in love. He writes to his own (probably fictional) love in the proem,

Dico adunque, se Iddio tosto coll'aspetto del vostro bel viso gli occhi miei riponga nella perduta pace, che poscia che io seppi che voi di qui partita eravate e in parte andatane dove niuna onesta cagione a vedervi mi doveva mai potere menare, che essi, per li quali la luce soavissima dei vostri Amore mi menò nella mente.[47]

(I say therefore, an it please God soon to replace mine eyes in their lost peace by the sight of your beautiful countenance, that when I knew that

45   Morton Bloomfield discusses how Chaucer uses this device of the historian to achieve the realism of an authenticating voice. 'Chaucer's realism,' in *The Cambridge Chaucer Companion*, ed. Pietro Boitani and Jill Mann, Cambridge, 1986, 179–93.
46   Geoffrey Chaucer, *Troilus and Criseyde: A New Edition of 'The Book of Troilus,'* ed. B.A. Windeatt, London, 1984.
47   Windeatt, 78.

you had departed hence and gone to a place whither no proper reason for seeing you could ever lead me, these eyes of mine, through which the very gentle light of your lover entered my mind. . . .)[48]

This is the language that he applies to the love affair between Troiolo and Criseida. His description of the love affair is dominated by chiaroscuro, a painting dominated by the various shades and effects of love's light. When Boccaccio invokes his lover's guidance as a muse, he appeals to the light of her eyes specifically for the inspiration to write:

> o vaga luce de' begli occhi in cui
> Amore ha posto tutto il mio diletto. (1.4)

> (O lovely light of those fair eyes in which love hath set my
> whole delight.)

Focusing his attention on the lovers in the poem, Boccaccio introduces Criseida as the woman who outshines all others:

> . . . cotanto era questa
> piú ch'altra donna, bella; ed essa sola
> piú ch'altra facea lieta la gran festa. (1.19)

> (So much fairer was she than other ladies, and she alone more
> than others made bright the great festival.)

It is the natural activity of the would-be suitors to gaze upon the object of their love, a habit Troiolo lightly mocks. Even though he apparently does not seek love himself, he nonetheless spends most of his time gazing at the women. In this, Boccaccio seems to suggest that the habits of men naturally encourage the possibility of love, and therefore that love is as immediate a possibility as the act of sight itself; it is just as common, necessary, and potentially dazzling. This ground-level association informs the entire poem. The effect upon him of seeing Criseida is typical of what happens in medieval accounts of romance: Troiolo enjoys her from a distance, enchanted by her 'occhi lucenti' and 'l'angelico viso' (1.28). We have seen the poetic explanation of what has happened to Troiolo in countless places. Boccaccio's is no different:

> Né s'avvedea colui, ch'era sí saggio
> poco davanti in riprendere altrui,
> che Amor dimorasse dentro al raggio
> di quei vaghi occhi con li dardi sui. (1.29)

48   Giovanni Boccaccio, *Il Filostrato*, ed. and trans. Nathaniel Edward Green and Arthur Beckwith Myrick, Philadelphia, 1929, 118.

(Nor did he who was so wise shortly before in finding fault
with others, perceive that love with his darts dwelt within the
rays of those lovely eyes.)

Unsurprising though this language may be, it is nonetheless integral to how
Boccaccio conceives of *Il Filostrato* as a whole. Already he has layered the
love affair of Troiolo and Criseida over his own, and made the parallels explicit
in terms of light and vision.

Dante maintains the vision of Beatrice as a central theme throughout the
Commedia; in a more limited way Boccaccio does the same here. The role of
vision is most pronounced in the early stages of romance, resulting in love at
first sight and the immediate imprisonment of the heart; later references to the
lady's beauty and the lover's state of being continually smitten with her beauty
sustain this theme. *Il Filostrato* employs this convention in a number of places,
including a very brief but telling window scene. The episode takes place in the
space of merely one stanza and lacks any kind of descriptive flourish, but the
scene reestablishes the importance of vision in the structure of the poem. It
represents the culmination of the first round of Pandaro's interloping and a
return to the kind of circumstances that sparked the love affair in the first place.
When the night on which Troiolo and Criseida will become lovers arrives,
Boccaccio presents the event in terms of light and darkness. In the temple or at
the window, the visual encounter creates a self-contained world in a welter of
unimportant details: people milling about at the temple or carrying on their
daily routines on the street. On this night, the whole scene is one of various
shades. The night provides the contrast for their love, not merely a cover for
their affair but a marker of the terms here that matter most: 'Era la notte oscura
e tenebrosa' (3.24). When the two lovers are alone, Troiolo declares,

> 'sempre davanti m'è stata la stella
> del tuo bel viso splendido e lucente.' (3.29)

> ('Ever have I had before me the star of thy fair visage in all
> its radiant splendor.')

and as they dissolve in love he kisses her on the eyes:

> 'voi mi tenete e sempre mi terrete,
> occhi miei bei, nell'amorosa rete.' (3.36)

> ('You hold me and ever will hold me in love's net, bright eyes
> of mine.')

Boccaccio sustains the basic and essential motif of love at first sight throughout
the poem, a measure of his clear focus. In the denouement of their affair, at one
point Troiolo thinks that Criseida has died and he almost takes his own life so
that he can follow her. Finally, at the moment of their parting the lovers

exchange one last glance; their love affair ends effectively as it had begun. Afterwards, they have only their tears, 'un'amara fontana' (6.2). Boccaccio consistently gives priority to the theme of vision, though this does not represent much of a development in the way medieval poets treated love. *Il Filostrato* effectively focuses attention on an affair of the heart in the midst of the Trojan War and it expresses that affair primarily in terms of vision and light.

Chaucer's version of this poem closely resembles Boccaccio's in its hand-ling of the basic love affair. Chaucer likewise develops the story in terms of visual encounters from the moment that Troilus mocks the type of knight that lets 'his eighen baiten/ On any womman that he koude espye' (1.192–3). This is the typical activity of would-be lovers. Ovid begins his instructions in the *Ars amatoria* by having his student imagine himself in a situation where a variety of women pass before him. These knights have learned their tuition well. Troilus uses the idea of sight in a very different way when he calls these knights 'nyce and blynde' (202). They are fools for love, lacking sense, but Troilus is blind to the ways of love. In this way he falls prey to this primary weapon of the god of love, as first his own eyes and false sense of security betray him:

> With-inne the temple he wente hym forth pleyinge,
> This Troilus, of euery wight aboute,
> On this lady, and now on that, lokynge,
> Where so she were of town or of with-oute;
> And vp-on cas bifel that thorugh a route
> His eye percede, and so depe it wente,
> Til on Criseyde it smote, and ther it stente.
>
> And sodeynly he wax ther-with astoned. (1.267–74)

His eye has met beauty, which is the beginning of love and the end of knowl-edge for every lover. But this still does not place us in the epicentre of the eyes' activity; we are not in the eye of the storm just yet. It is Criseyde's look that completely devastates the defenseless Troilus. His look has pierced the crowd, but hers pierces his heart:

> To Troilus right wonder wel with alle
> Gan forto like hire meuynge and hire chere,
> Which somdel deignous was, for she let falle
> Hire look a lite a-side in swich manere
> Ascaunces, 'what, may I nat stonden here?'
> And after that hir lokynge gan she lighte,
> That neuere thoughte hym seen so good a syghte.
>
> And of hire look in him ther gan to quyken
> So gret desire and swich affeccioun,
> That in his hertes botme gan to stiken
> Of hir his fixe and depe impressioun;

> And though he erst hadde poured vp and down,
> He was tho glad his hornes in-to shrinke;
> Unnethes wiste he how to loke or wynke. (1.288–301)

The look of the beautiful woman entirely overcomes him and makes an impression upon his heart. Chaucer has the command of the metaphor of sight to follow it through and express Troilus' transformation with the line, 'Unnethes wiste he how to loke or wynke.' The 'subtile stremes of hire yen,' are in sharp opposition to his 'konnynge' and effect his conversion to love.

Later, Chaucer describes Criseyde's initial emotional reaction to Troilus with the same emphasis on this primeval battle. That she and Pandarus implement a plan gives the impression that she is in control, that reason rules her. But as she observes Troilus riding through the town, she is effectively caught in her own scheme:

> Criseyda gan al his chere aspien,
> And leet it so softe in hire herte synke,
> That to hire self she seyde, 'who ʒaf me drynke?'
>
> ffor of hire owen thought she wex al reed,
> Remembryng hire right thus, 'lo, this is he
> Which that myn vncle swerith he moot be deed,
> But I on hym haue mercy and pitee.' (2.649–55)

Chaucer draws attention to this facet of love with a digression upon the nature of Criseyde's response:

> Now myghte som envious iangle thus:
> 'This was a sodeyn loue; how myght it be
> That she so lightly loued Troilus
> Right for the firste syghte, ʒe, parde?' (2.666–9)

Strangely, Chaucer seems to discriminate between the value of Troilus' instantaneous response and Criseyde's. He takes pains to argue that the value of her love lies in the fact that she inclined to like him first and by a process of consideration came to love Troilus. The episode stresses the importance of the visual effect upon her and this is conventional but Chaucer deconstructs the meaning. His argument creates ambivalence towards Criseyde, casting a shadow of doubt in the reader's mind regarding the authenticity of her response. That this doubt turns on the value of love at first sight is, admittedly, somewhat puzzling.

Chaucer adds to the number of visual meetings between Troilus and Criseyde with a scene where Criseyde sees Troilus parading down the street. He then follows this up with a window scene similar to the one in *Il Filostrato* but more elaborate. We shall have a closer look at these for Chaucer's changes enhance the importance of vision. It is important for us to notice, however, that these scenes have the same primary function as they do in Boccaccio – they promote the love story according to convention. Chaucer emphasizes the basic phenomenon of the way vision creates hostility between love and knowledge. The theme continues throughout the poem. Once he has brought the two lovers together at his home, Pandarus takes his candle and withdraws. His remark calls attention to the lighting of the scene, and with the importance of eye contact in love ever before us provides a pleasant inversion:

> Quod Pandarus, 'for aught I kan aspien,
> This light nor I ne seruen here of nought;
> Light is nought good for sike folkes yen.' (3.1135–7)

In other ways too, the eyes continue to play an expressive role: in the tears of the lovers, in their mournful glances, in Troilus' hopeful gaze out onto the Greek camp. Troilus mourns his loss in this way:

> 'O woful eyen two, syn ꝫoure disport
> Was al to sen Criseydes eyen brighte,
> What shal ꝫe don but, for my discomfort,
> Stonden for naught and wepen out ꝫoure sighte,
> Syn she is queynt that wont was ꝫow to lighte?' (4.309–13)

The eyes function metonymically in this passage, as they do in the entire poem; but as well as representing the total experience of love, they receive their due attention as the primary agents in love. The eye is the vulnerable window through which the banality of everyday life for Troilus is immediately and irrevocably transformed. Sight necessarily figures in the poem as ubiquitously as it does in *Il Filostrato* since it maintains love as its main concern. This is what gives sight its currency. Though Boccaccio does little to explore the implications of sight in a contemporary context, Chaucer presents a number of readings in parallel. He layers the conventional language of love with phenomenological detail that enhances our awareness of the characters' individual psychological frameworks. This psychological emphasis grows out of the prevailing interest in sight and perception as conduits to the mind. Chaucer also encourages, especially in *Troilus*, a moral or philosophical reading on the basis of vision. In the process he encourages multiple readings because of the failure of a philosophical reading to provide the poem with closure. The potentiality of sight in love literature begins with the convention of love at first sight and the ensuing hostility between love and rationality. This, however, is only the beginning. As we have now seen, sight is well placed in a number of overlapping discourses in medieval thought to point to several layers of interconnections, the possibilities of which Jean de Meun, Chaucer, and other poets are well aware. These various interconnections as they surface in medieval poetry suggest not only the inherent hostility of love and knowledge but the symbiotic compatibility of these notions. The love poet reveals his paradigmatic instincts even whilst working with such a contrary subject.

4

The Hospitality of Love and Knowledge

I

The Shared Language and Shared Ideas of Erotic Love and Spiritual Love

> La bellezza ch' io vidi si trasmoda
> non pur di là da noi, ma certo io credo
> che solo il suo fattor tutta la goda.
> . . .
> Dal primo giorno ch' i' vidi il suo viso
> in questa vita, infino a questa vista,
> non m'è il seguire al mio cantar preciso.   (Dante)

> (The beauty I saw not only surpasses our measures, but I
> surely believe that only its Maker has all the joy of it. . . .
> From the first day I saw her face in this life until this sight
> the pursuit in my song has not been cut off.)[1]

In the complex system where the language of metaphysics and that of erotic love overlaps to create registers of meaning, the convention of the simple hostility between love and knowledge acquires the quality of nonfunctioning. Hostility is complicated by symbiosis. The articulation of love in medieval literature involves considerable overlap of language used to describe either sensual or religious experience. Medieval formulations of the relationship between spiritual and sensual love are varied and complex. In the surpassing vision of his beloved Beatrice, Dante reflects on the history of his earthly love for her, a love that has found various expressions in the full range of his writings, from the *Vita Nuova* to the *Paradiso*. He uses recollection of physical experience as the basis to express the transport of what is now a thoroughly spiritual episode; sight not only provides the link but encapsulates the essence of either experience. To come to an understanding of the use of the language of vision in such shifting contexts requires that we understand the basis of this

---

[1]   Dante Alighieri, *Paradiso*, trans. John D. Sinclair, London, 1948, 30.19–21; 28–30.

complexity, and I can think of no better general guiding principles than the ones Peter Dronke sets down in his study of the rise of the European love lyric. Analyzing the language used by theologians to write about divine love, he reflects that

> It is easy to see at once to how great an extent such language is simply a transference of that used by human lovers. How could it be otherwise? How else could a transcendent love be in any way communicated? What other area of human experience would be more accessible or more relevant to it? Implicitly then, through the very need of communication, human and divine love are here in a sense reconciled. Yet this kind of reconciliation of course entails its own opposite: for here the perception and affirmation in each metaphor of an analogy between the two experiences is continually completed by an awareness of their difference. . . . Even if the Church saw marriage as a sacrament, and thus saw human love as in some measure sanctified, human love was always in the last resort bidden to make way for the love of God.[2]

Here we have both sides of the issue clearly before us. On the one hand there is a natural relationship between the language used to describe human love and that used to describe the love of God, while on the other there is a profound gap as theology articulates supreme commitment to the love of God. This exclusivity in turn refuels conceptualizations of the intensity of human love and the language folds back into itself. As Dronke amply illustrates, mystics, theologians, and poets handle this tension in different ways but share a common language.

Dante underscores the importance of language in his description of the interchange between spiritual and physical vision. The continuity of these visions lies in the fact that the pursuit in his song has not been cut off. The song, with its intention of articulating and conveying comprehension, provides the link. This formulation provides a suggestion of the potential for common ideas between the two loves; the very presence of a 'need of communication' introduces intellectual content into this tension. Expression, which immediately takes one into the realm of intellection, is one of the features that the two loves share. Indeed it is surprising how reliant the entire discourse of love is upon the theme of knowledge. This reliance gives us a clue to the perception of love as a complex subject. The shared language of religious and erotic love makes accessible to the discourse of erotic love the ideas of symbiosis that mark medieval metaphysical interest in love, knowledge, and sight.

---

2   Dronke, 58–9.

Spiritual Love and Erotic Love

The discourses of spiritual and human love share a propensity to overlap with ideas of knowledge. Perhaps the Old Testament sets the precedent in this regard with the familiar formulation of sexual intercourse as knowledge. Here these two conceptualizations, so radically opposed in medieval love poetry in one way, are actually equated. A less direct formulation that causes the two realms of love and knowledge to interpenetrate, also from the Old Testament, is that of wisdom literature. In Proverbs, for instance, wisdom is personified as a woman who satisfies those who seek her:

> I love them that love me: and they that in the morning early watch for me shall find me. With me are riches and glory, glorious riches and justice. For my fruit is better than gold and the precious stone, and my blossoms than choice silver. (Prov. 8:17–19)[3]

Her foil in these passages is the adulteress and the contrast is made in terms of love.

Dante's *Convivio* provides a good example of love language used both ambiguously and ambitiously. In the third tractate, the poet expresses his love for Lady Philosophy but at first keeps her identity a secret: his description could apply to any woman. He develops allusions to the eyes, praising her beauty:

> And since in the face the soul operates chiefly in two places, . . . I mean in the eyes and in the mouth, she adorns these most of all.[4]

He goes on to say that

> She reveals herself in the eyes so manifestly that any one who gazes intently on her may know her feeling at the moment. (3.8)[5]

To explain a short ballata in which he has called this lady disdainful and pitiless, Dante embarks upon a digression in which he carefully develops his theory of vision to explain that, just as perception of a star may be blurred under certain conditions, so too he considered this lady according to her appearance as opposed to the reality. He uses principles of physical sight in which to locate

[3]   'Ego diligentes me diligo et qui mane vigilant ad me invenient me mecum sunt divitiae et gloria opes superbae et iustitia melior est fructus meus auro et pretioso lapide et genimina mea argento electo.'
[4]   Dante Alighieri, *Convivio*, trans. W.W. Jackson, Oxford, 1909, 3.8. 'E però che ne la faccia massimamente in duo luoghi opera l'anima . . . cioè ne li occhi e ne la bocchi, quelli massimamente adoma.' Dante Alighieri, *Convivio*, in *Opere Minore 5*, ed. Cesare Vasoli and Domenico de Robertis, Milan.
[5]   'Dimostrasi ne li occhi tanto manifesta, che conoscer si può la sua presente passione, chi bene là mira.'

this discourse on beauty. Dante consistently returns to in-depth optical concepts as he develops episodes of love. This explanation has a two-fold effect. It contributes to the extended interplay between an erotic and a metaphysical theme. Additionally, it complicates what in erotic terms we might expect from convention to be the development of a simple theme – love's domination. *Parasitisme* of love and knowledge contributes to the description of what at this point could be an earthly love.

Eventually, he reveals the name of his lady as Philosophy. Love, vision, and intellection entwine and although Dante now moves away from ideas of earthly love to more spiritual conceptions, the allegory of earthly, passionate love continues to leave its impress. On the philosophical level, these three concepts continue to entwine, for the metaphor of the sun as illumination enters as a proper analogy for the activity of God; and Dante also emphasizes the inseparability of God and love. First, on the Augustinian idea of illumination, he writes,

> No object of sense in the whole world is more worthy to be made a type of God than the sun, which illumines first himself and then all other celestial and elemental bodies with sensible light. So God illumines with intellectual light first Himself and afterwards the dwellers in heaven and all other intellectual beings. (3.12)[6]

Having begun by keeping religious and sensual language as close as possible, now that he has revealed Philosophy's identity he seizes the opportunity to celebrate the intellect. Later in the same section, he draws in love:

> Philosophy is a loving converse with wisdom, which is found in God most of all, since in Him dwell highest wisdom and highest love and highest actuality. (3.12)[7]

While the system of love, knowledge, and sight is easier to describe in this metaphysical context, the germ of the idea appears in Dante's earlier inclusion of intellectual concepts.

The blending of religious and sensual concepts of vision in love that Dante achieves becomes most extensive in the beatific vision in *Paradiso*. In *Paradiso* 30 Dante has his sight redirected to Beatrice, whose beauty he describes again:

---

6   'Nullo sensibile in tutto lo mondo è più degno di farsi essemplo di Dio che 'l sole. Lo quale di sensibile luce sé prima e poi tutte le corpora celestiali e le elementali allumina: così Dio prima sé con luce intelletuale allumina, e poi le creature celestiali e l'altre intelligibili.'
7   'Filosofia è uno amoroso uso di sapienza, lo quale massimamente è in Dio, però che in lui è somma sapienza e sommo amore e sommo atto.'

Chè, come sole in viso che più trema,
   così lo rimembrar del dolce riso
   la mente mia di sè medesmo scema.
Dal primo giorno ch' i' vidi il suo viso
   in questa vita, infino a questa vista,
   non m'è il seguire al mio cantar preciso. (30.25–30)

(For, like the sun in the most wavering sight, the remembrance of the sweet smile deprives my mind of its very self.
From the first day I saw her face in this life until this sight the
pursuit in my song has not been cut off.)

This declaration emphasizes the continuity of his experience and the breadth
of his meaning as he describes her beauty and his love for her. The description
includes the sense of vision overpowering the mental faculties. John D. Sinclair
understands this continuity when he writes, '[Dante's] mind is carried back
over the stormy years to "the first day I saw her face in this life" when both
were children, just as it had been on the summit of Purgatory when he knew
her again and "felt old love's great power." So identical were Dante's life and
his vision, both of them the record of his love and the discovery of its meaning.'[8] That continuity includes his poetic sensitivity to the inadequacy of a
simple convention of opposition in the description of erotic love. Beatrice yet
again redirects his thoughts and again calls attention to the integration of light,
knowledge, and love:

   'Noi siamo usciti fore
     del maggior corpo al ciel ch'è pura luce:
   luce intellettüal, piena d'amore;
     amore di vero ben, pien di letizia;
     letizia che trascende ogni dolzore.' (30.38–42)

('We have come forth from the greatest body to the heaven
that is pure light, – light intellectual full of love, love of true
good full of joy, joy that surpasses every sweetness.')

What happens next closely resembles Dante's experience in the *Vita Nuova*:

Como subito lampo che discetti
   li spiriti visivi, sì che priva
   dall'atto l'occhio di più forti obietti,
così mi circunfulse luce viva;
   e lasciommi fasciato di tal velo
   del suo fulgor, che nulla m'appariva. (30.46–51)

8 Sinclair, 441.

> (Like sudden lightning that scatters the visual spirits and de-
> prives the eye of the action of the clearest objects, a vivid light
> shone round about me and left me so swathed in the veil of its
> effulgence that nothing was visible to me.)

The difference from the *Vita Nuova* consists in the fact that in this context light
has an obvious intellectual component as part of a metaphysical system. The
experience culminates three cantos later in the end of all desire:

> E io ch'al fine di tutt' i disii
>   appropinquava, sì com' io dovea,
>   l'ardor del desiderio in me finii. (33.46–8)

> (And I, who was drawing near to the end of all desires, ended
> perforce the ardour of my craving.)

He looks up with pure sight, fulfilling Beatrice's words that

> 'l'esser beato nell'atto che vede,
> non in quel ch'ama, che poscia seconda.' (28.110–11)

> ('The state of blessedness rests on the act of vision, not on that
> of love, which follows after.')

Love is a feeling, yet it cannot exist without vision and 'the act of conceiving'
(Canto 29). This remarkable conclusion delimits love and suggests the eleva-
tion of the intellect, though Dante leaves himself a way out by simply giving
priority to vision. Considering the integrity of Dante's experience and conception of love, his ordering of vision and love might apply to earthly love as well
as to spiritual love. In one way – love at first sight – it does. On a deeper level,
the spiritual context allows him to articulate a symbiotic relationship which he
expresses indirectly in his poetry of earthly love.

   Throughout Dante's writings we see the profound enmeshing of love and
intellection, and the concept of vision plays a crucial role in this process. Dante
shows his familiarity with spiritual applications of the idea in his understanding
of illumination and description of the beatific vision in *Paradiso*. He also exhibits fascination with the science of optics, and brings such language to bear
upon his thought in his writings, especially in the *Convivio* and *Commedia*.
Joseph Mazzeo builds a convincing thesis around the way Dante alludes to the
qualities of physical light: 'Dante's imagery of light was not conceived as more
or less adequate representation of a reality whose real nature is conceptual and
imageless, but as a literal description of that reality.'[9] For Mazzeo, understanding Dante's use of light entails a clear understanding of the existence of a

---

9   Joseph Anthony Mazzeo, 'Light Metaphysics, Dante's "Convivio" and the Letter to
Can Grande Della Scala,' *Traditio* 14 (1958), 191–2.

hierarchy of light among those who held to a metaphysics of light, but the important point here is to recognize the basic correspondence between levels. Indeed, he shows that Dante espoused the theory that corporeal light necessarily implied the existence of incorporeal light but he does not linger over the usefulness of the relationship to Dante. The 'literal description' of ultimate reality is readily adaptable to forays into vision, and Dante, fascinated by the principles of this burgeoning science, readily incorporates and builds upon such ideas.

He uses optical concepts to great effect. In the *Purgatorio* Dante organizes contrasting ideas of vision and their implications for his quest for love. As he and Virgil make their way upwards to the third terrace, Dante finds himself blinded by the light. This experience induces a brief reflection on the properties of physical light:

> Come quando dall'acqua o dallo specchio
>   salta lo raggio all'opposita parte,
>   salendo su per lo modo parecchio
> a quel che scende, e tanto si diparte
>   dal cader della pietra in igual tratta,
>   sì come mostra esperïenza ed arte;
> così mi parve da luce rifratta
>   quivi dinanzi a me esser percosso;
>   per che a fuggir la mia vista fu ratta. (15.16–24)

(As when from water or mirror the beam leaps the opposite way, rising at the same angle as it descends, and at an equal length departs as much from the fall of the stone, as is shown by science and experiment, so it seemed to me I was struck by light reflected there before me, so that my sight was quick to flee.)

Dante has entered decisively into the realm of the intellect, of science and experiments. Virgil's answer is a chastisement. It conveys the message that spiritual realities are of a higher order than physical ones, and that the viator should not try to assimilate this body of earthly knowledge into his quest for a higher love:

> 'Però che tu rificchi
>   la mente pur alle cose terrene,
>   di vera luce tenebre dispicchi.
> Quello infinito ed ineffabil bene
>   che là su è, così corre ad amore
>   com'a lucido corpo raggio vene.
> Tanto si dà quanto trova d'ardore;
>   sì che, quantunque carità si stende,

cresce sovr'essa l'etterno valore.
E quanta gente più là su s' intende,
    più v'è da bene amare, e più vi s'ama,
    e come specchio l'uno all'altro rende.' (15.64–75)

('Because thou still settest thy mind on earthly things thou
gatherest darkness from the very light. That infinite and unspeakable good which is there above speeds to love as a sun-
beam comes to a bright body; so much it gives of itself as it
finds of ardour, so that the more charity extends the more does
the eternal goodness increase upon it, and the more souls that
are enamoured there above the more there are to be rightly
loved and the more love there is and like a mirror the one
returns it to the other.')

Virgil could be Augustine. Like Augustine, for all his protestations Dante's
Virgil also relies on the physical analogy to clarify the activity of 'that infinite
and unspeakable good.' Even if Dante does believe in an actual hierarchy of
light, he never seems to take altogether seriously Virgil's remonstrance that he
gathers darkness from light. It does show his self-consciousness as he works
within the system he has created, aware of the interference generated by the
discourse of light. In the climactic vision of *Paradiso* imagery that suggests his
fascination with earthly optical principles again intrudes in Beatrice's speech:

'La prima luce, che tutta la raia,
    per tanti modi in essa si recepe,
    quanti son li splendori a ch' i' s'appaia.
Onde, però che all'atto che concepe
    segue l'affetto, d'amar la dolcezza
    diversamente in essa ferve e tepe.
Vedi l'eccelso omai e la larghezza
    dell'etterno valor, poscia che tanti
    speculi fatti s' ha in che si spezza,
uno manendo in sè come davanti.' (29.136–45)

('The primal light that irradiates them all is received by them
in as many ways as are the splendours with which it is joined,
and, therefore, since the affections follow the act of conceiving, love's sweetness glows variously in them, more and less.
See now the height and the breadth of the Eternal Goodness,
since it has made for itself so many mirrors in which it is
broken, remaining in itself one as before.')

That Dante returns to this theme reveals both his interest in this branch of
natural philosophy and the place of knowledge in his discourse of love. The

choice of imagery and the consistency with which he develops it reflect the integration of love and knowledge. The allusion here to a series of reflecting mirrors at the same time reflects the challenge in medieval thought of reconciling the relationship of the divine with the created order. If he can express the *parasitisme* of love, knowledge, and sight in a metaphysical context, the optical theme bridges this realm to an earthly one, and an earthly love. It indicates how Dante's interest in giving expression to earthly love is not satisfied by the convention of opposition.

We saw in the first chapter how the *Pearl*-poet uses the language and motifs of sensuous love to describe the involvement of the dreamer with his pearl. The poem especially makes good use of imagery from *Le Roman de la Rose*, and reveals a level of ease and facility with the *Roman's* sensuousness that has long fascinated its readers. Carefully integrating the realm of the senses, *Pearl* steadily unfolds as a religious allegory along the lines of a search for a desirable object. In the process it enmeshes love and knowledge in ways that at once grow out of and supersede their initial separation. This aporia between love and knowledge is expressed both in keeping with the agenda of the *Roman* and as the dreamer's painful bewilderment. In the development of the religious import of *Pearl*, the poet also offers a development from descriptive visual motifs and an accompanying fascination with light to a more self-aware analysis of the nature of vision, ascending qualities of sight, and a surpassing light source. This parallel development poignantly illustrates the dreamer's increasing spiritual illumination. At the same time, the lingering interest in the naturalism of sight serves to consolidate interest in the naturalism that marks the *Roman*. It preserves the reader's appreciation of the vitality of the French poem in this context; the *Pearl*-poet has not reduced it to a mere springboard.

The various visual motifs converge in a vision of the heavenly Jerusalem that the poet takes more than a hundred lines to describe, and as in the Apocalypse of John to which he continually refers, a vision of the Lamb of God. It surpasses but grows out of the splendour of the delights of earthly colour and light. As this vision unfolds, it becomes more and more intense; the whole poem constitutes one increasing effluence. It grows closer to the Augustinian idea of illumination, with an emphasis on the inner sight. Nonetheless, the poet seems to keep one foot in this world, not least in his puns. Perhaps one of the most adventurous of these occurs in his elaboration of the motif of the Lamb of God as the light of the world:

> Of sunne ne mone had þay no nede;
> Þe self God watȝ her lombe-lyȝt,
> Þe Lombe her lantyrne, wythouten drede;
> Þurȝ hym blysned þe borȝ al bryȝt. (1045–8)

The beholding of the Lamb of God fulfils the quest for a spiritual vision, yet the poet arrests the metaphysical rapture with a deft allusion to mundane light. The same tension exists in the lines that follow. The supernatural scene seems to break free of obligations to the laws of nature, since the dreamer can look through walls:

> Þur3 hym blysned þe bor3 al bry3t.
> Þur3 wo3e and won my lokyng 3ede,
> For sotyle cler no3t lette no ly3t. (1048–50)

Ultimately the vision that *Pearl* offers is a mystical one, but even at this point the dreamer offers an explanation as to why he can see through walls, as if always conscious of the physical underpinnings of this expedition into the realm of light, though celebrating the nature of sight in the non-material world. But the point surely is not that he adheres or fails to adhere strictly to known principles of light, nor that he finally concerns himself with spiritual rather than physical reality, but that he has become illumined with regards to the true source of spiritual light and that his love and knowledge have become integrated. And the poet relies almost entirely on visual imagery to achieve these aims. The support for this structure of visual effects is the love which the poet feels for his pearl. To develop the rich meaning of the love and the pearl, the poet takes advantage of the milieu in which visual motifs play an important role in love language and spiritual discernment. This great religious poem relies on that nexus of ideas.

At the same time, the poem explores an individual's doubts that arise from the painful loss of his child and records a journey into assurance. Here the knowledge is specifically religious in nature, yet the poem is directly concerned with questions of perception and how we arrive at knowledge. Thus he blends the concern over the relationship between love and knowledge on a strictly metaphysical plane with phenomenal issues of how we come to knowledge at all. The child that the poet encounters simplifies his confusion with specific answers to his intellectual doubts. The dreamer questions the child's statement that the Lamb has crowned her as queen of heaven (121–4), and later, that God could reward her the same as he would a person who has endured more of life's trials (IX–X). At times he becomes quite blunt, and he expresses more doubts in response to her explanation of the vineyard parable: ' "Me þynk þy tale vnresounable" ' (590), he says, and goes on to marshal scripture against her. In section XIII he expresses further incredulity that the Lamb would wed her above all others (771–4); and finally, he asks her rather condescendingly about the 144,000 and the city they would need as a home (925–32). Only in his own vision of the heavenly Jerusalem does he resolve all his doubts. As A.C. Cawley and J.J. Anderson say in their introduction to the poem, the spiritual crisis of the loss of a child is 'resolved by the assurance, reached after prolonged mental debate, that the child's soul is safe in heaven.'[10] The death of a

10 A.C. Cawley and J.J. Anderson, 'Introduction,' in *Pearl, Cleanness, Patience, Sir Gawain and the Green Knight*, ed. A.C. Cawley and J.J. Anderson, London, 1976, ix.

child, an emotional loss, inspires a cerebral debate that results in emotional and mental comfort. The poem directs the reader to collocate the realms of the emotions and the intellect on every level.

Pearl also turns into a poem about the dreamer's own salvation. The motif of sight becomes personally real in a limiting sense when he tries to cross over the boundary into the scene he beholds as if across a stream. His vision becomes a temporary source of deep frustration and the brusque physicality of waking up momentarily marginalizes 'þo sy3te3 so quyke and queme' (1179). Meditating on his experience, however, he comes to terms with the sovereignty of God and the consistent friendship of God:

> For I haf founden hym, boþe day and na3te,
>   A God, a Lorde, a frende ful fyin. (1203–4)

The poet reinstates the motif of sight by acknowledging the faithfulness of God both in the light and the absence of light. If that phrasing sounds like an easy gloss, the poet powerfully reinforces and extends the visual motif in his appeal to the Eucharist:

> In Krystes dere blessyng and myn,
> Þat in þe forme of bred and wyn
> Þe preste vus schewe3 vch a daye. (1208–10)

The bread and the wine literally embody the body and blood of Christ according to the doctrine of transubstantiation. The poet-dreamer can remember his experience daily in the visible signs of the host which the priest *schewe3* each day. The poem has come full-circle, returning to the idea of vision in its basic, physical dimension.

Sight in the Knight's Tale

The potential for the symbiosis of love and knowledge in metaphysical terms in the Knight's Tale depends upon the conventional importance of sight. As we have seen, sight as Chaucer uses it in the Knight's Tale heightens awareness of the conflict between love and reason. This produces an especially keen awareness of the limitations of viewpoints based in this-worldly experience. This awareness in turn leads to metaphysical considerations also in terms of sight: sight brings together particularly well physical, this-worldly experience and the possibilities of a different perspective. Love and knowledge come together in a metaphysical context out of their initial opposition. That fusion in the mtaphysical sphere, combined with the proximity of the discourses of spiritual and erotic love, points to the relevance of this symbiosis in Chaucer's conception of the description of erotic love.

The experience of the two knights exemplifies their limitations in several different ways. Although they initially observe Emily in the garden, in a world that closely resembles the *Roman's* garden of leisure, Palamon and Arcite do not share Amans' freedom to wander. As much as they desire to enter into that world of passion, they find themselves trapped in the tower of Theseus' will to order:

> The grete tour, that was so thikke and stroong,
> Which of the castel was the chief dongeoun
> (Ther as the knyghtes weren in prisoun
> Of which I tolde yow and tellen shal),
> Was evene joynant to the gardyn wal
> Ther as this Emelye hadde hir pleyynge. (I.1056–61)

Their initial vision of Emily creates unexpected conflicts. The urge to order dominates the poem from the opening scene. Ever since the groundbreaking work of William Frost and Charles Muscatine, critics have recognized the poem's central concerns.[11] If love normally conquers reason easily, here love's power is further tested and realized as reason has an active representative in the duke. The condition of being in love also creates a literal sense of imprisonment within the knights' bodies insofar as both cousins suffer from the disease of lovesickness, also caused by sight: they become increasingly confined and increasingly aware of their physical circumstances as lovesickness saps them of their energy. And since natural philosophy had tried to circumscribe love by calling love a disease and enlisting it in a rational, ordered discourse, the would-be lovers are susceptible to the diagnostic observations of others. The sight of others also potentially constrains them.

   Arcite briefly turns this condition to personal advantage and manipulates the forces of rationality in the cause of love. He does so in ways that perpetuate the importance of sight. After Mercury appears to him in a dream, a minor event that reemphasizes the relevance of various kinds of sight, he looks in a mirror and sees the disfigurement of his face. By changing his 'array,' he completely alters his appearance. Chaucer uses this to introduce in microcosm the concept of *privitee*, a term with pronounced visual connotations. This capacious term has several registers of meaning: in a spiritual sense, it can refer to the unfathomable wisdom of God, the divine sight described by Boethius; it can refer to private knowledge, such as a personal secret; the term also serves as a euphemism for genitalia; in the Miller's Tale this leads into two other registers of meaning, namely wordplay on secretive, lecherous activity and sexual (especially adulterous) knowledge. The concept of *privitee* therefore encompasses pure reason and lustful passion, a contrast that informs the Knight's Tale. Arcite

---

11   William Frost, 'An Interpretation of Chaucer's Knight's Tale,' *RES* 25 (1949), 289–304; Charles Muscatine, 'Form, Texture, and Meaning in Chaucer's *Knight's Tale*,' *PMLA* 65 (1950), 911–29.

returns to Athens alone, except for a squire 'That knew his privetee and al his cas' (1411). At the same time as he undertakes this activity, motivated by passion, Arcite acknowledges the secrecy of the ways of God or Fortune:

> 'Allas, why pleynen folk so in commune
> On purveiaunce of God, or of Fortune,
> That yeveth hem ful ofte in many a gyse
> Wel bettre than they kan hemself devyse?' (1251–4)

His love affair, initiated and guided by visual considerations, has suddenly opened up new vistas of visual involvement and application. He recognizes the gap between what humans can know and what God foresees or Fortune brings around; he also recognizes that by their plans, people often cause things to turn out for the worse. Arcite's own *privetee* fulfils this. While in Theseus' court the wheel of Fortune turns in his favour, but it eventually returns him to a state of imprisonment:

> Now wol I turne to Arcite ageyn,
> That litel wiste how ny that was his care,
> Til that Fortune had broght him in the snare. (1488–90)

That snare takes the form of a meeting in a grove with Palamon. This is ironic because of the connotations of groves, woods, and forests with secrecy and disorder, values which would seem to suit Arcite's (and Palamon's) purposes. Chaucer, however, reminds us that ' "feeld hath eyen and the wode hath eres" ' (1522). Arcite unwittingly reveals himself to his cousin and both knights soon find themselves again subject to the duke's control and certainly within a larger visual framework.

The events leading up to the discovery by Theseus escalate in their randomness but Chaucer puts them into that larger framework. Of Palamon's escape he glosses,

> Were it by aventure or destynee –
> As, whan a thyng is shapen, it shal be. (1465–6)

Both notions, 'aventure' and 'destynee,' circumscribe Palamon's actions. The word 'aventure' occurs twice more in this sequence (1506, 1516) in preparation for an exposition of destiny:

> The destinee, ministre general,
> That executeth in the world over al
> The purveiaunce that God hath seyn biforn,
> So strong it is that, though the world had sworn
> The contrarie of a thyng by ye or nay,
> Yet somtyme it shal fallen on a day

That falleth nat eft withinne a thousand yeer.
For certeinly, oure appetites heer,
Be it of werre, or pees, or hate, or love,
Al is this reuled by the sighte above. (1663–72)

Chaucer encourages an ambivalent response to this declaration. He has yoked
together destiny and 'aventure,' as well as God and Fortune (cf. 1252). But if
God has everything under control on account of his foresight, Fortune's version
of control is completely arbitrary. Chaucer purposely juxtaposes different conceptions of the universe that come together with reference to sight, the mechanism responsible for the action of the knights and the tale. The wife of
Cappaneus is the first to mention Fortune in the poem and she refers to her as
'Fortune and hire false wheel' (925). In *The Consolation of Philosophy* she is
blind; a greater force imprisons the human agent, but in a pagan world one can
know very little of the nature of that force.

The coliseum stands as a monument both to love and rationality. Theseus
has it built to host the combat between his two prisoners, who serve the god of
love. It is a magnificent place – 'The circuit a myle was aboute' (1887) – representative of a grand passion, Theseus' backhanded acknowledgement of
love. At the same time the structure contains the lovers and their passion. Theseus transforms the place where he found the knights fighting madly into a
forum for a tournament that he can oversee and control. Though built because
of love, and the site at which Theseus hosts the lovers, it represents the duke's
hostility to their enterprise. The coliseum symbolizes the parasitic host/hospi-
tality/hostility system of love and knowledge.

As with the other images in the poem that express human reason and human
passion, Chaucer expresses the importance of the amphitheatre with a physical
description. The theatre itself dominates the scene and is described in its various visual details. Chaucer draws attention to the impression of the theatre and
then of the temples in it; he employs not merely a general visual stress but an
iconographic one:

But yet hadde I foryeten to devyse
The noble kervyng and the portreitures,
The shap, the contenaunce, and the figures
That weren in thise oratories thre.
    First in the temple of Venus maystow se
Wroght on the wal, ful pitous to biholde,
The broken slepes, and the sikes colde . . . (1914–20)

The meaning of the lives of the major characters is about to be completely
bound up with the images in the amphitheatre, just as it has been shaped by the
initial experience of falling in love at first sight. We can easily imagine the
initial vision of Emily by Palamon and Arcite presented iconographically, and
in fact the event is commonly depicted in medieval illuminations. Now the

subjects have in a sense come off the wall and stare back at representations of their essences in the temples. The three temples in the amphitheatre effectively limit the freedom of Emily, Palamon, and Arcite at the same time as they give expression to the freedom that the characters desire, a dialectic achieved by appealing to vision. Chaucer has almost given us a kind of virtual reality, dominated by the interpenetration of images. On the one hand, the lives of these three characters have been reduced to iconography and each of them seeks out the deity depicted in the coliseum; on the other, they live in the immediacy of phenomenal experience, inspired by images not controlled by any *homo faber*. This is especially true of the two knights, who desire a beautiful woman; it is also true of Emily, who initially witnessed them fighting in the wood. She, however, welcomes the containment of passion and the chance to appeal to Diana. If the protagonists remain largely unindividuated, this reinforces the sense of their imprisonment. The degree of psychological development that is hinted at depends entirely on their association with the three temples. The only clues that Chaucer gives us as to their mental frameworks are visual ones, a correlation in keeping with late medieval approaches to psychology. Their energies become focused on what is immediately real, the world understood in visual terms. The Knight's Tale differs radically from the *Teseida* in this respect. Boccaccio takes advantage of existing structures scattered throughout the city. This dissipates the iconography, for there is no clearly defined controlling context which represents the whole world and therefore totally defines the options or worldview of the characters.

At this point Chaucer has fully developed the importance of physical sight. As we are beginning to recognize in his poetry, however, the motif of sight allows for some interesting oppositions. As the three protagonists approach their temples, the action of the tale goes beyond what any of the characters, including Theseus, can see: it moves into the realm of the gods. Now vision is attenuated and involves distinctions, for thanks to the author the reader can see in the mind's eye and understand, or at least attempt to interpret, details of which the characters have no knowledge. In the Second Nun's Tale, Christian theology informs the meaning of sight: the converted truly see in a way that Almachius never can; the layers of sight provide degrees of freedom. Nothing like that exists in this pagan setting. Characters hint at another level of reality, but they have no perception of it. Rather, they experience only this world, where there are no angels or garlands to be seen; and this phenomenology defines them. Almachius' attitude towards visual phenomena indicates his spiritual state; the worshippers' adherence to images here vaguely outlines their mental attitudes but tells us nothing of their spiritual condition that we do not already know. If Almachius commits a gross sin in bowing to idols, it is because he should believe differently; without that option, Chaucer's pagans are simultaneously exculpated and without a choice. They are like the inhabitants of Dante's First Circle of hell. This formulation of pagan reality integrates well with non-theological interest in sight. The world of the Knight's Tale takes its shape from the visual cues that give erotic love its impulse and from the phenomenology of sight that reinforces the sense of this life as a foul prison. In contrast with the explicitly Christian meanings overlayed onto sight, the pagan setting draws attention to the gap between sight and spiritual knowledge. None the less it hosts the *parasitisme* of sight, knowledge, and love, however restricted the operations of that system might be in a pagan context.

The closest that Palamon, Emily, and Arcite come to breaking free of the confines of this prison is in the signs that they receive from their planetary gods. Each receives insight into the future, but not the consolation that they have cosmic insight. Chaucer accentuates the act of interpretation and the limitation of the insight. In Palamon's case, Chaucer emphasizes his role as interpreter:

> But atte laste the statue of Venus shook,
> And made a signe, wherby that he took
> That his preyere accepted was that day. (2265–7)

Events are far more complicated than his expectations, of course: he leaves with a glad heart but first his loss in battle and then the death of Arcite cause him sorrow from which he never fully recovers. The limitations of his sight reappear on a larger scale in his inability to interpret adequately the events surrounding Arcite's death. Emily's sign frightens her, not because she does not like the message but because she initially does not understand it:

> For she ne wiste what it signyfied,
> But oonly for the feere thus hath she cried. (2343–4)

As it turns out, this sign as interpreted by Diana is graphically accurate. However, it offers Emily no consolation, no cosmic understanding of her place in the overall scheme of things. She takes away from this experience none of the confidence that Cecilia, who has yet a higher ability to see, exudes. The sign that Mars supplies Arcite is verbal rather than visual, a notable break from the pattern of descriptions. It could be that Chaucer is paying some attention to the order in significance of the senses, for while this sign finds fulfilment just as the others do, it has the darkest implications for the one who receives it. Medieval sign theory allows for the ambiguity of signs and makes it clear that their message is bound up with phenomenal experience. A signifier might be clearly related to a clear signified, but signifiers commonly remind medieval theoriticians of the limitations of signs and the need to place them in an epistemological context.

Chaucer underlines the limits of human knowledge as the poem reaches its climax with reference to a 'change' not seen empirically. Having focused our attention on the visual world of the amphitheatre and its temples, then intimated the limitations of the characters' vision and knowledge, Chaucer again accentuates the realm of visual stimulation with a celebration of the pageantry of the tournament:

> Ther maystow seen devisynge of harneys
> So unkouth and so riche, and wroght so weel
> Of goldsmythrye, of browdynge, and of steel;
> The sheeldes brighte, testeres, and trappures,
> Gold-hewen helmes, hauberkes, cote-armures. (2496–2500)

The tournament brings the story to a climax that has built up around sensory appeal, especially appeal to sight. Interpretation does not play a part; the plenitude of the scene satisfies. That ends abruptly with Arcite's death:

> Dusked his eyen two, and failled breeth,
> But on his lady yet caste he his ye;
> His laste word was, 'Mercy, Emelye!'
> His spirit chaunged hous and wente ther,
> As I cam nevere, I kan nat tellen wher.
> Therfore I stynte; I nam no divinistre;
> Of soules fynde I nat in this registre. (2806–12)

Arcite's present struggle began with a pleasing sight of Emily, and it ends with a bittersweet one. The celebration of life within this brief span of time drives home the sense of frustration felt by the poet over the human inability to delve empirically into realms of non-sensory experience. Arcite has moved from the realm of sensory information to one where the poet has not been. This passage closely resembles the opening of *The Legend of Good Women*, where Chaucer reserves judgement on heaven and hell and casts the empiricist's dilemma in terms of sight:

> For by assay ther may no man it preve.
> But God forbede but men shulde leve
> Wel more thing then men han seen with ye! (F9–11)

For the greatest part of the tale, Chaucer defines and explores the limited space and the limited knowledge available in this world, a world especially bounded by the pagan setting of the tale. As V.A. Kolve suggests, the scene incorporates glimpses into freedom but ultimately pagan life is like a prison: 'For a mind like Chaucer's – sophisticated, compassionate, Christian – the classical world, lacking any clear knowledge of the City of God, much less any means of access to it, must remain to the end a prison/garden/thoroughfare in which men "romen to and fro" without direction or clear purpose.'[12] Even the Christian reader, conscious of the limitations of empirical sight, can identify with the sense of frustration which the narrator articulates as Arcite dies. Chaucer provides a strong sense of imprisonment and limitation by referring to sight, in

---

[12] Kolve, 106–7.

spite of the stylization in the tale. Boccaccio does not make so strong a statement in the *Teseida*, nor does he emphasize vision. The difference between these two poems recalls the difference between *Troilus* and *Il Filostrato*. Indeed, both take as their starting point the powerful impulse of love at first sight. Chaucer has already developed aspects of love, knowledge, and sight and suggested their relevance as a system whether the context be pagan or Christian, earthbound or spiritual.

The Boethian philosophizing towards the tale's end provides an alternative perspective on this life. The strength of Chaucer's philosophical meditation derives in considerable part from the fact that he relies on sight to express the impulses, ambiguities, and limitations of experience in this life. He then sets these against a Boethian interpretation that accentuates an ability to see and participate in the good. Boethius expresses the importance of sight in this way:

> Blisful is that man that may seen the clere welle of good!
> Blisful is he that mai unbynden hym fro the boondes of the hevy erthe!
>
> (3.m12)

To see correctly is to be freed from the bonds of the heavy earth. Vision engages the human mind in questions of its own capacities in relation to other forms of life and itself encourages the cosmic self-knowledge so important to Boethius. For him, visual ability encapsulates the way God exercises his sovereignty over creation:

> 'For the devyne sighte renneth toforn and seeth alle futures, and clepith hem ayen and retorneth hem to the presence of his propre knowynge; ne he ne entrechaungith nat, so as thou wenest, the stoundes of foreknowynge, as now this, now that; but he ay duellynge cometh byforn, and enbraseth at o strook alle thi mutaciouns. And this presence to comprehenden and to seen alle thingis – God ne hath nat taken it of the bytidynge of thinges to come, but of his propre symplicite.' (5.pr6)

The Boethian solution engulfs passion. Theseus echoes these ideas when he refers to the First Mover's 'wise purveiaunce' (I.3011). Chaucer ultimately leans towards a Boethian interpretation of the events which comprise the Knight's Tale, yet his sophisticated handling of the convention of love at first sight makes it impossible to suggest that for him passion is engulfed. The convention is transformed, and the discourse of philosophical knowledge feeds off of it.

The marriage of Palamon and Emily completes the happy cycle of romance. One of the ways in which that cycle is completed is in a return to the importance of physical sight. The medieval marriage ceremony accentuates the role of vision through its celebration of pageantry and through the revelation of the bride to the husband. The beautiful woman whom Palamon saw in one idyllic setting, a sight which caused him deep pain, he now sees again, in another idyllic setting, with the implied result of a considerable measure of healing. The marriage also points, for a Christian audience familiar with the Church's stress on marriage as a sacrament, to an eschatological union of God and the soul: the beatific vision. Such a prospect transcends any of the other visions proffered in the tale, with its pagan setting, yet the intimation brings together the associations sight has in the tale both with love and knowledge. Chaucer extrapolates the principle of love at first sight in a pagan setting beyond its breaking point. He concentrates on physical circumstances by appealing to sight, then reinterprets the relationship of love and knowledge by the transference of vision from the sight of a beautiful woman to metaphysical pondering to a marriage ceremony. In the process, he explores the range of human experience common to pagan and Christian.

Vision Transformed in Troilus

In *Troilus* Chaucer effects a transformation as he manipulates vision, time, and place. As Troilus and Criseyde move closer together, they do so in a clear sequence of events where there is a pronounced emphasis on immediacy, the present tense: the window scene when Criseyde and Pandarus see Troilus, followed by the at Deiphebus' home, followed by their night together. Time, however, becomes a philosophical issue when things go wrong. Both Troilus and Criseyde reflect on their love affair and draw conclusions that include other kinds of sight. Hindsight is 20/20, though they seem to overlook how the immediacy of physical vision compelled them. Troilus turns to a Boethian contemplation of predestination and free will, but his own philosophical reflections reveal his limited ability to appreciate the nature of metaphysical sight. Various kinds of vision, shifts in time, and dramatic changes in location form a series of contraries that function symbiotically.

In *The Consolation of Philosophy*, Boethius appeals to the sense of sight to summarize his argument. This strategy is perhaps due to a combination of the metaphysical nature of his topic and to a Christian habit of mind. In book five, Boethius writes this hymn of praise to God:

> To [God], that loketh alle thinges from an hey, ne withstondeth no thinges by hevynesse of erthe, ne the nyght ne withstondeth nat to hym by the blake cloudes. Thilke God seeth in o strok of thought alle thinges that ben, or weren, or schollen comen; and thilke God, for he loketh and seeth alle thingis alone, thou maist seyn that he is the verrai sonne. (5.m2)

Troilus takes up this argument, but articulates a point of view closer to that of the still unenlightened prisoner as he argues with Lady Philosophy. Chaucer tells us that Troilus

> ... seyde he nas but lorn, so weylaway –

> 'ffor al that comth, comth by necessitee,
> Thus to ben lorn, it is my destinee.' (4.957–9)

As he ruminates upon the meaning of his experience with Criseyde, he draws attention to the role of divine sight in the entire process:

> 'ffor certeynly, this wot I wel,' he seyde,
> 'That for-sight of diuine purueyaunce
> Hath seyn alwey me to forgon Criseyde,
> Syn god seeth euery thyng, out of doutaunce.' (4.960–3)

This moralizing crystallizes around an understanding of sight which, significantly, has specific links with an emphasis placed upon physical sight by the prisoner as he argues with his tutor. Troilus echoes him when he argues for necessity using an analogy of sight:

> 'ffor it ther sitte a man ȝond on a see,
> Than by necessite bihoueth it
> That, certes, thyn opynyoun sooth be
> That wenest or coniectest that he sit;
> And further ouere now aȝeynward ȝit,
> Lo, right so its it of the part contrarie,
> As thus –' (4.1023–9)

As a lover still very much committed to his beloved, Troilus feels acutely the physical reality of his circumstances. His position shows itself in his interpretation of the nature of divine foresight, one which Lady Philosophy eventually corrects in her student.

The intensity of Troilus' metaphysical questioning here stands as the contrary to his experience thus far. Although this represents an addition on Chaucer's part to Boccaccio's story, there is nothing forced or contrived about it. Troilus' extreme emotional involvement paves the way for a violent reaction when things go wrong. Until now he has responded intuitively and been able to exist on a bare minimum of ratiocination. The impending exchange, however, presents him with an insuperable problem that spawns questions, from the immediate ones concerning the threat at hand to ones of the larger, all-embracing variety. In light of the poem's carefully organized conclusion and the opportunity the ending provides for rereading the entire poem, the temptation exists to impose a strictly cerebral intent upon his pondering. Yet the Boethian passages have a mimetic function, producing a model of the complexity of love. Given the way Boethian philosophy had permeated medieval thought, Chaucer's audience would not register surprise that Troilus, when the time comes for mental anguish and global doubts, would conceive of them in these terms. (At any rate, such human philosophizing would be possible in a pagan context.) This natural reaction is reinforced by the expectation of contrasts. For this common expression, Boethius himself had helped to establish the precedent, and early in our poem Pandarus phrases the belief in this way:

> 'If thow do so, thi wit is wel bewared;
> By his contrarie is euery thyng declared.
>
> ffor how myghte euere swetnesse han ben knowe
> To him that neuere tasted bitternesse?
> Ne no man may ben inly glad, I trowe,
> That neuere was in sorwe or som destresse;
> Eke whit by blak, by shame ek worthinesse,
> Ech set by other, more for other semeth,
> As men may se, and so the wyse it demeth.' (1.636–44)

The impulse to philosophize serves as a natural contrary to the oblivion of love and in this way 'Ech set by other, more for other semeth.'

One of the reference points that makes this contrast meaningful is sight. Within the larger contrast of consuming love and intellectual preoccupation, the eyes have obviously contrasting roles. Whereas they contributed to love's beginning and the overthrow of reason, when Troilus' speculation becomes most intense he tries to accept the dogma that he should, firstly, look to God as the source of illumination, and secondly, look upon life with God's eyes, through the smoke of changing fortune. To pit the one interpretation against the other and call for a value judgement is to impose upon Chaucer a criterion at the expense of recognizing how he makes play with one of love's most basic motifs. The sensual vies with the metaphysical with equally extensive implications. If we are going to continue to take seriously the erotic matter of the poem, however, it is helpful to consider how the ending points to the powerful host/hostility/hospitality system of love and knowledge latent in that matter. In this way the ending does encourage rereading, not for purposes of reinterpretation but for elaboration.

Criseyde introduces an idea related to Troilus' and a similar application of vision in the course of her lament over events:

> 'Prudence, allas, oon of thyne eyen thre
> Me lakked alwey er that I come here:
> On tyme y-passed wel remembred me,
> And present tyme ek koud ich wel i-se,
> But future tyme, er I was in the snare,
> Koude I nat sen; that causeth now my care.' (5.744–9)

Like Troilus, she imposes a metaphysical understanding of time upon naturalistic time, the immediate past. Of course, in hindsight both lovers can see the cause of their pain but this does not mean that they could have changed anything. The impotence matters: even as they speak, their frustration locates them squarely in the present. It draws out the tension between the immediacy of experience and the mind's proclivity to reinterpret the past. Chaucer uses vision to illustrate the interplay between these forces. He understands the tension perfectly and plays with it to elucidate human psychology. The introduction of Prudence provides Chaucer with the vehicle for introducing a symbolic understanding of place as well as of time. In *Anticlaudianus*, Alain de Lille describes the ascent of Prudence through the realms of creation to the throne of God. This voyage has an element of a naturalistic understanding of space, given the medieval 'scientific' belief in a hierarchical cosmos, but Alain relies on allegorical organization. He presents an epistemological journey. As Muscatine has observed, 'The overall character of the poem's cosmography (even granting the realism of Alain's astronomy), with its detailed descriptions of the various spheres and its heavenly garden and House of Fortune, is schematic.'[13] Chaucer similarly presents a figure who not only sees across time but has insight thanks to location, in Troilus' cosmic vision at the end of the poem. The context which we have been exploring, however, alerts us to continue to expect authorial tensions. Chaucer's concentration on vision finds greatest fulfilment here in an expression that parallels Alain de Lille's epistemology even as it denies such a straightforward schematic formulation.

The ending of the poem gives fresh impetus to vision in the poem. After he has died, Troilus ascends to 'the holughnesse of the eighthe spere' (5.1809). Such experiences are always salutary, though not necessarily religious. In the Bible, Paul reports enigmatically that he has known of a man 'caught up to the third heaven' (2 Cor.12:2) but Cicero also has Scipio the Younger view the little earth from a heavenly perspective and reconsider his priorities. Here Chaucer urges a particularly Christian response and he gradually incorporates the language of spiritual insight. From the eighth sphere, Troilus reflects upon his life by looking back to the earth:

> And down from thennes faste he gan auyse
> This litel spot of erthe. (5.1814–15)

This produces in him first a general observation:

> . . . and fully gan despise
> This wrecched world, and held al vanite
> To respect of the pleyn felicite
> That is in heuene aboue. (5.1816–19)

What he first notices is a marked contrast between what lies below and what lies above. Following this, his gaze becomes more focused:

13   Charles Muscatine, 'Locus of Action in Medieval Narrative,' *Romance Philology* 17 (1963), 118.

> . . . and at the laste,
> Ther he was slayn his lokyng down he caste. (5.1819–20)

This too evokes in him an evaluation, now of his own life and the human experience:

> And dampned al oure werk that foloweth so
> The blynde lust, the which that may nat laste,
> And sholden al oure herte on heuen caste. (5.1823–5)

The language of sight becomes increasingly spiritual in intent as Chaucer contrasts two views of the heart: the view of an impure heart is 'blynde lust' while that of a pure heart is of heaven. Although the exact idea of casting involved in the phrase 'And sholden al oure herte on heuen caste' is obscure, the later line, 'And of ȝoure herte vp casteth the visage' (5.1838) consolidates the visual context and visual contrast. Young folk should seek God, whom Chaucer suggests is recognizable because of similarity in appearance: 'thilke god that after his ymage/ ȝow made' (5.1839–40). At the same time, Chaucer casts human experience in terms of love and outlines this as another pair of contrasts bound up with contrasting visions. One can experience either earthly desire or a spiritual response to God:

> And loueth hym the which that right for loue
> Upon a Crois oure soules forto beye,
> ffirst starf and roos and sit in heuene aboue. (5.1842–4)

As others have noticed, this language of love serves as a potential touchpoint for the entire poem, though Chaucer's intention remains unclear. The motif of sight serves in attendance, developed with equal care and with as extensive application to the spiritual and sensual realms as the notion of love itself.

There is a visual allusion latent in the formulaic expression of the work of Christ, who 'ffirst starf and roos and sit in heuene aboue,' a reference to his death, resurrection, and glorification. The glorification of Christ, whereby he comes to sit at the right hand of the Father, happens with his ascension. This is the last that the disciples physically see of him. The biblical account of this event stresses the visual component:

> And when he had said these things, while they looked on, he was raised up; and a cloud received him out of their sight. And while they were beholding him going up to heaven, behold, two men stood by them in white garments. Who also said: Ye men of Galilee, why stand you loking up to heaven? This Jesus who is taken up from you into heaven shall so come as you have seen him going into heaven (Acts 1:9–11).[14]

---

[14] 'Et cum haec dixisset videntibus illis elevatus est et nubes suscepit eum ab oculis eorum cumque intuerentur in caelum eunte illo ecce duo viri adstiterunt iuxta illos in vestibus albis

Art depicting the Ascension somewhat awkwardly occasionally showed the disciples craning their necks as they looked up, with only the feet of Christ visible in the frame. The image, of a physical witness to what from then on becomes simply a spiritual hope, links two complementary expressions of vision.

Chaucer's final touch in this sermon that makes so much out of common analogies of sight comes in his benediction. He has moved away from the story of Troilus completely now, directed his book to moral Gower and philosophical Strode, and he prays for himself and his readers that the triune God 'Us from visible and in-visible foon/ Defende' (5.1866–7). Chaucer makes the most of a commonplace, which here nicely encapsulates the two levels of reality. It is perfectly in keeping with the religious tenor of the last fifty lines or so; even in a strictly religious sense one must guard against visible and invisible foes. The benediction, however, touches a raw nerve: the contrast between a naturalistic interpretation of the world and life experiences and a spiritual interpretation. It suggests the poet at play as he interweaves these possibilities and ties them up together even as he closes off his topic.

The ending of the poem is carefully wrought as an explicitly Christian text in its emphasis upon vision. The initial value of this language is the way it reinforces the Christian message and the idea that Troilus learns to value the love of God after pursuing earthly love during his lifetime: it conjoins love, knowledge, and vision. Although the references to the love of God are unambiguous in themselves, the metaphors of sight render the sermon even more grave because of their association with spiritual truths. However, the importance of sight for the poem's epilogue equally alerts the reader to Chaucer's seemingly innocuous use of this motif throughout the poem. Chaucer provides his own rereading of the theme of love. Less obvious in a first reading, sight emerges as a recurring theme also available for reading, then rereading. Chaucer suggests the importance of love, knowledge, and sight by fusing them together at the end. Sight has this potential throughout. With the information supplied by the epilogue, we can see that Chaucer's use of typical love language is much more self-conscious than Boccaccio's. Vision does not merely serve as the initiation of love, but has other values as well.

Chaucer presents a complex mixture of sensual, spiritual, and phenomenological sight. Dante likewise appeals to sight in various ways in the *Commedia*, but Chaucer is perhaps even more committed to the parasitic possibilities of sight. In *Paradiso* 21.133–59, Dante experiences a fresh perspective of the earth. As in Cicero and Boethius, he comes to appreciate the smallness and insignificance of the earth. This is, strictly speaking, phenomenological and scientific, a point which is important for both Dante and Chaucer given their accurate use of sight. Chaucer concludes *Troilus* by men-

qui et dixerunt viri galilaei quid statis aspicientes in caelum hic Iesus qui adsumptus est a vobis in caelum sic veniet quemadmodum vidistis eum euntem in caelum.'

tioning a number of scientific details: the concavity of the eighth sphere, the elements, the erratic stars, and the music of the spheres. To return to Dante, for him the vision of the earth is merely a curiosity. He is rapturously happy because he is with Beatrice and on his way upwards. Chaucer presents Troilus in quite a different set of circumstances. His initial and then more penetrating look down is in keeping with his earlier confession that he still loves Criseyde. Quite unlike Dante, he is separated from his love; and although he learns a lesson about the vanity of life, he looks down, not up. Brown writes that Chaucer replaces 'the personal sense of sight and space represented in the narrative with a thoroughly Dantean version of cosmic space and spiritual perception.'[15] This is too bold. The cosmic sense of space here does not entirely conflict with the personal sense of space elsewhere in the poem, and as Muscatine has pointed out, Dante's use of space is not strictly symbolic anyway. Furthermore, Troilus gains spiritual perception but his experience is still personal, by which I take Brown to mean phenomenological; a gap exists even between Troilus' experience at this stage and the exhortation Chaucer gives to young folk, one looking down with literal vision, the other group looking up with spiritual vision.

Although the ending of the poem crystallizes its metaphysical aspects into a thorough-going Christian exhortation, it does not satisfy as the final intention of the author. Chaucer distances it from the bulk of the poem, marginalizing the closing words, giving them the status almost of an afterthought. He achieves this deferral in several ways. First of all, he seems to close his subject by reintroducing himself. We have come to expect authorial presence as part of the story, however, so this reappearance alone only gently signals closure. Also, Chaucer provides advice to lovers with as much urgency as he then tells them to seek another love altogether. He gives no indication that this is just a ruse, and so the first set of instructions lingers in the mind along with his later remarks. Then the poet seems to have finished: he addresses his 'litel boke' as a complete product ready to go into the world and, significantly, to make its way to the place where pagan poets pace. His interests seem to be very much in this world. Admittedly, he reintroduces his subject dextrously:

> But ʒet to purpos of my rather speche –
>
> The wrath as I bigan ʒow for to seye
> Of Troilus the Grekis boughten deere. (5.1799–1801)

Chaucer, however, does nothing to deconstruct the love story before the marginalized epilogue that follows. If it is meant to serve as an exemplum, the life of Troilus does not adequately serve the moral. One could just as easily argue, I think, that the disjunction between story and exemplum parodies this homiletic practice. But I would not want to press that suggestion either, because it

15 Brown, 1.238.

seems to me that the two portions of the poem coexist in symbiosis. If we look beyond the narrow *sentence* of the conclusion, an act which its marginal status encourages, we find several registers. Indeterminacy, or at least the prospect of new formulations, results from the superabundant power of vision to fashion various readings.

A comparison with *Il Filostrato* at this point discloses a specific kind of indeterminacy. Boccaccio's *sentence* is a condescending evaluation of women:

> Giovane donna, e mobile, e vogliosa
> è negli amanti molti, e sua bellezza
> estima piú ch'allo specchio, e pompos
> ha vanagloria di sua giovinezza,
> la qual quanto piacevole e vezzosa
> è piú, cotanto piú seco l'apprezza;
> virtú non sente né conoscimento,
> volubil sempre come foglia al vento. (8.30)

> (A young woman is fickle and is desirous of many lovers, and her beauty she esteemeth more than it is in her mirror, and abounding vainglory hath she in her youth, which is all the more pleasing and attractive the more she judgeth it in her own mind. She hath no feeling for virtue or reason, inconstant ever as leaf in the wind.)

Troiolo reacts to the betrayal of Criseida harshly and vindictively. Addressing Jove, he prays:

> O vero lume, o lucidi sereni,
> pe' quai s'allegran le terreni menti,
> togliete via colei nelli cui seni
> bugie e 'nganni e tradimenti sono,
> né piú la fate degna di perdono. (8.18)

> (O true light, O bright skies by which earthly minds are cheered, put an end to her in whose bosom are lies and deceits and betrayals and deem her ever more unworthy of pardon.)

These two passages contain a pair of sharply contrasting appeals to vision. On the one hand, Boccaccio alludes to the young woman who looks proudly and overgenerously in the mirror; on the other, he has Troiolo appeal to Jove as the true light, the accurate measure, and *ipso facto* the righter of wrongs done to men. It is as if he wants ironically to quell erotic love with the harsh light of day. Boccaccio never steps back to address young folk collectively. Instead he addresses young men and advises them to choose their loves carefully, on guard against the evil woman:

conceda grazia sí d'amare accorti,
che per rea donna al fin non siate morti. (8.33)

(. . . grant you the boon of loving so wisely that ye shall not
die in the end for an evil woman.)

Chaucer's Troilus, by contrast, bears pain but no such ill will. In fact, he confesses that he still loves Criseyde:

. . . I ne kan nor may,
ffor al this world, with-inne myn herte fynde
To vnlouen ȝow a quarter of a day.
In corsed tyme I born was, weilaway,
That ȝow that doon me al this wo endure
ȝet loue I best of any creature. (5.1696–1701)

Chaucer does offer some general avuncular advice to lovers, but he directs his
comments to both sexes. If anything, he reverses Boccaccio's warning:

Ny sey nat this al oonly for thise men,
But moost for wommen that bitraised be
Thorugh false folk; god ȝeue hem sorwe, amen!
That with hire grete wit and subtilte
Bytraise ȝow; and this commeueth me
To speke, and in effect ȝow alle I preye,
Beth war of men, and herkneth what I seye. (5.1779–85)

Such a comparison with his source highlights the fact that Chaucer complicates
Boccaccio's reading of social relationships. He renders Criseyde's status more
ambiguous by portraying Troilus' enduring devotion. He refuses to endorse his
model's attitude towards women, articulating instead a view of mutual caution
in love. Additionally, Boccaccio warns young men about women as his last
word, while Chaucer offers a very different prescription for love as his last
word: one that is for both sexes, is positive, and otherworldly. Though his message does not provide a satisfying reading for the whole poem, it does clearly
offer an alternative to the ending of *Il Filostrato*.

Troilus and Criseyde from start to finish makes capital out of the language
of vision. The mimesis of vision and space has contributed to our awareness of
the individual's psychological framework, and this Chaucerian development
has direct bearing on the social values espoused here. In this context, the ending
subverts the closure of the exemplar. And though apparently not about 'the olde
daunce' of love, the epilogue indirectly speaks against an attitude in love
towards women. The poem's lack of closure has internal, philosophical implications as well. There are two reasons for this. The failure of one philosophical
system, imported to provide the sense of an ending, to effect closure

encourages further discussion along these lines. The ideal and the actual remain pitted against each other. Secondly, in the fourteenth century, the concept of vision immediately raises questions of perception and knowledge that derive from a growing zeal in natural philosophy, and the poem includes naturalistic aspects that have bearing on these questions.

Troilus' problem stems from the fact that he saw. His philosophical question should therefore address this problem; that it does not suggests the impotence of his inquiry. He has not addressed the fundamental question. In a sense, Troilus has learned nothing since the days when he ridiculed other knights but then continued to look at the women. The initial, seemingly uncomplicated phenomenon of love at first sight continues to reappear in the midst of these issues. We must bear in mind that doctors as well as poets considered the role of sight in love to be crucial and physiologically traceable. Chaucer clearly recognizes this from the way he refers to *ereos* in the Knight's Tale. References to the eyes and to sight always had substance because their influence was always physiological as well as psychological. Perhaps the difference between our attitude towards the possible role of the eyes and theirs can be compared to our attitude towards the influence of the planets and theirs, or our attitude towards the music of the spheres and theirs. The vision that inspires erotic love in this poem cannot be dismissed. It is the first instance of an interest in phenomenology that pervades the poem.

By examining sight in this poem, we become aware of its ubiquitous presence. Chaucer takes material that is at hand, namely a convention of love literature that Boccaccio has just used pervasively in *Il Filostrato*. He creates new instances when vision furthers the love affair, and he proceeds to play with vision extensively. In the context of a love story, he uses it to increase the realism of space and time, adds a layer of received theological wisdom, allows for competing philosophical meanings, and above all points to the *parasitisme* of love, knowledge, and sight. In short, he complicates our preconceptions of what sight means in keeping with the experimental and theoretical excitement associated with sight in painting, science, and philosophy; and he complicates the convention of the division between love and knowledge. His applications of the symbiosis of these concepts, in contexts that verge towards the metaphysical in the Knight's Tale and *Troilus*, benefit both from developments in Neoplatonic metaphysics and the increasingly complicated transference of language and ideas between the discourses of human and spiritual love.

Insight and Hiddenness in Fragment VIII of the Canterbury Tales

Fragment VIII of the *Canterbury Tales* furthers our awareness of his interest in the interpenetration of the realms of the spiritual and the physical and he continues to explore the *parasitisme* of love, knowledge, and sight in both, even though he departs from exploring the extended parallels and possible transferences of language and theme between erotic and religious love. The Second

Nun's Tale expresses traditional religious sentiment in the form of an exemplary saint's life, but it does so through the primary theme of sight. It portrays Chaucer's understanding of the religious connotations of sight; it also reveals his interest in the interplay of love and knowledge in this context. He develops the possibilities fully in that St Cecilia stresses the importance of spiritual insight, the ability to see with the eyes of the heart; and the Romans who undergo conversion miraculously actually see things that testify to spiritual realities. Within the clearly marked boundaries of the genre, Chaucer draws together spiritual and physical sight, a device that lends the tale some of its earnestness since religion tries to reconcile both the physical and the metaphysical. The *Pearl*-poet achieves a similar effect in the dreamer's vision of the heavenly city, which grows out of his circumstances in an earthly garden. This episode, complete with an ability to see through walls, gives priority to the dreamer's spiritual ability; but at the same time, he takes the tack that this experience does not contradict normal visual processes because of the nature of the light source and the realm in which he finds himself. The interplay of physical and spiritual layers of meaning clearly marks this investigation into sight. Though it occurs in the context of a religious tale, it has implications for Chaucer's understanding of the relationship between love and knowledge in the physical realm. The Second Nun's Tale offers themes that Chaucer develops in other ways in the Miller's Tale and Canon's Yeoman's Tale. The relationship with the Miller's Tale especially allows us to see Chaucer's awareness of the intellectual currency of love language, whether the immediate context is spiritual or sensual. Notions of sight facilitate the movement between physical and spiritual concepts, and between love and knowledge.

The collocation of the spiritual and the physical finds its most religious expression in the doctrine of the Incarnation, which Chaucer elucidates in the Prologue to the Second Nun's Tale. The mystery of the Incarnation hinges upon the paradox of the divine becoming human, God becoming flesh and taking upon himself the form of a man. Chaucer gives this concept thematic importance in the *Invocacio ad Mariam*:

> Thow Mayde and Mooder, doghter of thy Sone,
> Thow welle of mercy, synful soules cure,
> In whom that God for bountee chees to wone,
> Thow humble, and heigh over every creature,
> Thow nobledest so ferforth oure nature,
> That no desdeyn the Makere hadde of kynde
> His Sone in blood and flessh to clothe and wynde.
>
> Withinne the cloistre blisful of thy sydis
> Took mannes shap the eterneel love and pees,
> That of the tryne compas lord and gyde is,
> Whom erthe and see and hevene out of relees
> Ay heryen; and thou, Virgine wemmelees,

>   Baar of thy body – and dweltest mayden pure –
>   The Creatour of every creature. (VIII.36–49)

Bernard's canticle in Dante's *Paradiso* 33, from which Chaucer borrows this passage, occurs in the context of the consummation of love. Here, without that context, the emphasis falls on the mystery of the Incarnation itself as much as it does on Mary as the object of devotion. Chaucer returns to the paradox insistently and carefully emphasizes that God 'chees' and had 'no desdeyn' for human corporeity, even though in this act eternal verities ('eterneel love and pees') took physical form ('mannes shap'). Chaucer's emphasis on the conjunction of the physical and spiritual realms continues with his description of God as lord and guide of the 'tryne compas' of earth, sea, and heaven and later as the 'Creatour of every creature.' The images of enclosure in this passage, Mary's body as a 'cloistre blisful,' recall the idea of enclosure in *Troilus and Criseyde* in that both involve the conflation of the spiritual and the physical in terms of love.

   The connection with Dante's *Commedia* provides the first suggestion of the theme of sight. Bernard's hymn to the Virgin is part of the final crescendo of celebration of light and sight and the viator finds his travels coming to a happy end. Dante combines physical and spiritual motifs which culminate in an unambiguous spiritual sentence; Chaucer avails himself of this combination by adopting the invocation. The theme of sight in the Second Nun's Tale belongs in this larger context, where spiritual and physical aspects are consciously juxtaposed to further a spiritual truth. The *Commedia*, like the doctrine of the Incarnation itself though on a less grand scale, contributes to a sense of paradox that confronts the rational reader; that sense of paradox infuses the Second Nun's Prologue and Tale as well.

   Nonetheless, the Prologue clearly involves a defense of Christian truth on intellectual grounds; both Prologue and Tale emphasize rationality. Using Jacobus de Voragine's Life of St Cecilia as a source, the tale offers a defense that includes an etymological homily, and although the interpretations offered here are wrong, the exercise itself has a high degree of credibility in the tradition of Isidore of Seville's *Etymologies*. The act itself puts the stamp of intellectualism on the presentation as a whole. Furthermore, the exercise introduces the theme of sight into the Prologue directly, first with the appeal to colours: Cecilia's whiteness of honesty and greenness of conscience. More substantially, she is ' "the wey to blynde," ' (92) giving light to the blind by her good teaching. She is also personally

>   'Wantynge of blyndnesse,' for hir grete light
>   Of sapience and for hir thewes cleere. (100–1)

Chaucer embellishes this reading of Cecilia's name and its import in terms of sight:

For 'leos' 'peple' in Englissh is to seye,
And right as men may in the hevene see
The sonne and moone and sterres every weye,
Right so men goostly in this mayden free
Seyen of feith the magnanymytee,
And eek the cleernesse hool of sapience,
And sondry werkes, brighte of excellence. (106–12)

The references to sight here combine wisdom with morality, commensurate with both the theology of light and the generic expectations of a saint's life. The Prologue ends with an icon of burning that furthers the emphasis on sight, defines Cecilia's moral character, and foreshadows the nature of her martyrdom. The comparison here is unusual and calls attention to humanistic learning and interests:

And right so as thise philosophres write
That hevene is swift and round and eek brennynge,
Right so was faire Cecilie the white. (113–15)

Like the allusion to the 'tryne compas' and the sun, moon, and stars previously, this reference too reveals the writer's sense of marvel at the phenomena of creation. He keeps returning to them, and though they do not overpower the spiritual objective of the comparison and thus render the Prologue ironic, they do enhance the complementarity of spiritual and physical marvels. The interpretation of the name of Cecilia fundamentally shows the poet's interest in language as another such phenomenon. That a name serves as a means for introducing the primary theme of the tale suggests Chaucer's awareness of theological trends: both etymologies and analogies of sight are prevalent in theology. In late medieval thought these areas continue to overlap in ways that become increasingly independent of theology; Chaucer will integrate sight and language without a theological context in the Manciple's Tale. Even though the etymologies presented are false, there is a real connection between language and sight. The Prologue in this way prepares us for an ambitious intellectual exercise.

The Second Nun's Tale is at once the most religious of the collection and the most insistent upon a rational defence of Christianity. More than once, Cecilia presents a sound apology for her faith just as the Prologue relies on appeals to the mind. At times this cerebral quality is emblematic, as in the way Chaucer weaves a pattern of threes that runs through both Prologue and Tale: the three sections of the Prologue itself; the three natures of the Virgin; her mercy, goodness, and pity; God's guidance over earth, sea, and heaven; the three etymologies.[16] The Prologue also prepares us for the tale by introducing

[16]   Helen Cooper provides an extensive list in *Oxford Guides to Chaucer: The Canterbury Tales*, Oxford, 1989, 360.

the theme of sight, which dominates the tale. Given the appeal to reason on other grounds, the theme of sight represents a masterstroke on Chaucer's part, at once diversifying that appeal and giving the Prologue and Tale greater unity.

Sight in the tale fulfils the expectations of theology, and it does so insistently, combining the idea of the sight of the inner eye of faith with miraculous confirmation by physical sight of spiritual realities. Chaucer sets the wheels in motion through Valerius' request for empirical proof that his wife really has a guardian angel:

> Valerian, corrected as God wolde,
> Answerde agayn, 'If I shal trusten thee,
> Lat me that aungel se and hym biholde.' (162–4)

Interestingly, his attitude and request have begun to be directed by God so that religion induces his empirical request. Cecilia transforms his demand and makes it part of a religious exercise involving penance and contrition; she replaces the physical with the spiritual. Through obedience Valerius becomes an initiate and Chaucer delicately records the change with his casual observance of the angel's visit to their home. Here Chaucer reinforces the interdependency of moral rectitude and truth in terms of sight.

This development occurs in the privacy of the wedding chamber. There the themes of sight and marriage converge in the contrast between what is open to view versus what is hidden; they also overlap in the newlyweds' discussion behind closed doors. Chaucer has established the semantic range of *privitee* elsewhere in the *Tales*, notably in the Miller's Prologue and Tale; by studying them we gain a greater appreciation for the contrasting ideas Chaucer promotes here.[17] In the Miller's Prologue several notions of the term rub against each other abrasively:

> 'An housbonde shal nat been inquisityf
> Of Goddes pryvetee, nor of his wyf.
> So he may fynde Goddes foyson there,
> Of the remenant nedeth nat enquere.' (I.3163–6)

Initially the Miller issues the sober maxim that a man ought to restrain his own curiosity in the light of God's superior and impenetrable wisdom. As the context suggests, however, he quickly twists this pious meaning of the term to give it more lecherous connotations. A husband anxious about his potential status as a cuckold could find himself with unwanted knowledge if he were to pry too deeply into his wife's secrets, those registering as the first implied pun on *privitee*. He should content himself with finding 'Goddes foyson,' the second,

---

[17]   Chaucer plays with this concept extensively throughout the *Tales*. See, for instance, Paula Neuss, '*Double-Entendre* in *The Miller's Tale*,' *Essays in Criticism* 24 (1974), 329f.

physical, implied pun on this very suggestive word, and restrain himself from any further inquiries. The scintillating brevity of this passage illustrates the powerful suggestiveness of ideas that span the physical/spiritual spectrum.

In the tale Nicholas has a reputation for loving secretly:

> Of deerne love he koude and of solas;
> And therto he was sleigh and ful privee. (I.3200–1)

Chaucer plays with the concept of *privitee* in Nicholas' furtiveness with Alison:

> this hende Nicholas
> Fil with this yonge wyf to rage and pleye,
> Whil that hir housbonde was at Oseneye,
> As clerkes ben ful subtile and ful queynte;
> And prively he caughte hire by the queynte. (I.3272–6)

The Second Nun's Tale, by contrast, places the private act of sexual union in the context of marriage; while this represents a change from the fabliau-bawdiness of the Miller's Tale, *privitee* nonetheless has strong associations with what should never be revealed, especially for Cecilia. She refuses to have sex, a stance for which she has the backing of most of the Church fathers. The Sarum Missal takes a more accommodating view, but reinforces the privacy of consummation with the ritual movement from public ceremony to the blessing of the wedding chamber.[18] In this circumstance, Cecilia confronts Valerius privately. The convergence of sight and marriage echoes mystical theology. The idea of *privitee* occurs in the tale when Tiburtius accurately assesses the alternatives before him:

> 'And whil we seken thilke divinitee
> That is yhid in hevene pryvely . . .' (VIII.316–17)

This allusion to *privitee* picks up on the notion of spiritual insight and helps bind together the themes of marriage and sight; at the same time sensory and spiritual experience become more tightly interwoven as well.

Cecilia and Nicholas form another opposition in terms of music. As the patron saint of music, Cecilia sang to God in her heart 'whil the organs maden melodie' (134). Nicholas has something of a reputation as a musician himself:

> And al above ther lay a gay sautrie,
> On which he made a-nyghtes melodie. (I.3213–14)

---

18 Robert P. Miller, ed., *Chaucer: Sources and Backgrounds*, New York, 1977, 374–84.

'Making melody' has had associations with sex since the opening of the General Prologue, when Nature stirs up the 'corages' of the birds. Similarly, after procuring a promise of sexual favours from Alison, the clerk takes up his psaltery:

> He kiste hire sweete and taketh his sawtrie
> And pleyeth faste, and maketh melodie (I.3305–6)

while with Alison herself

> Withouten wordes mo they goon to bedde,
> Ther as the carpenter is wont to lye.
> Ther was the revel and the melodye. (I.3650–2)

An intricate set of oppositions takes shape involving these themes. The saint seeks the divine which is hidden and leaves the body and sex a secret, while the worldly clerk seeks out sexual opportunities and conceives of ways to avoid discovery. The sharp contrasts between these two tales depend on the permutations of sexuality and secrecy. Both tales refer to the senses, primarily sight but also sound, in ways that conjoin the sensory and the spiritual: the saint's life to reinforce theological resonances, the fabliau to promote stark physicality.

Valerius teaches Tiburtius to see correctly, again linking sight with right belief and knowledge of the truth. That Tiburtius can smell the crowns of flowers yet not see them due to his unbelief corresponds with the preeminence of sight in any context. Valerius tells his brother that if he confesses, this will be signalled by increased powers of sight:

> 'And as thou smellest hem thurgh my preyere,
> So shaltow seen hem, leeve brother deere,
> If it so be thou wolt, withouten slouthe,
> Bileve aright and knowen verray trouthe.' (VIII.256–9)

The prayer of another can improve the power of the senses somewhat, but only right belief can complete this transformation. The sub-theme of the two crowns affords Chaucer an opportunity to discuss the issue in a learned way. He draws upon St Ambrose's exposition on this miracle (270ff) and draws the miraculous together with rational discourse. Cecilia deals with another of Tiburtius' intellectual doubts by providing an apology for the Trinity (338–41). The analogy that she chooses, that of the three 'sapiences' or mental faculties, firmly places the discourse in the realm of reason. There is a natural relationship between sight and the faculties as well, for the phenomenology of sight repeatedly raised the issues of how abstractive cognition resulted from intuitive cognition. As he sees correctly, Tiburtius will undoubtedly come to terms with the mystery of the Trinity, another question of threes that furthers Chaucer's interest in that number. Maximus' conversion completes another trilogy, after which he uses his ability to see in two ways that effect spiritual results: by witnessing the brothers' martyrdom and then miraculously seeing their souls' ascent into heaven.

The debate between Almachius and Cecilia brings to a climax the question of what constitutes proper sight. Cecilia becomes quite shrewd in her arguments, and she spars with her foe before focusing on the central issue of correct vision. At the very outset of her confrontation with Almachius, she trips him up in his own rhetoric by mocking his manner of interrogation:

> 'Ye han bigonne youre questioun folily,'
> Quod she, 'that wolden two answeres conclude
> In o demande; ye axed lewedly.' (428–30)

Although this is a saint's life, and Chaucer keeps to the moral *sentence* of the tale with sufficient rigour, he imbues the saint with sharp debating skills and sophisticated rhetorical insights. Cecilia's tack takes Almachius by surprise: ' "Of whennes comth thyn answeryng so rude?" ' (432). He finds himself in a verbal joust with a tenacious opponent and admits as much when he declares,

> 'I recche nat what wrong that thou me profre,
> For I kan suffre it as a philosophre.' (489–90)

She unseats him with her exposition on sight and derision of his idols. The argument, like the whole tale, stresses the limited ability of his outer eye:

> 'Ther lakketh no thyng to thyne outter yen
> That thou n'art
> blynd; for thyng that we seen alle
> That it is stoon – that men may wel espyen –
> That ilke stoon a god thow wolt it calle.
> I rede thee, lat thyn hand upon it falle
> And taste it wel, and stoon thou shalt it fynde,
> Syn that thou seest nat with thyne eyen blynde.' (498–504)

Obviously the appeal to sight here and elsewhere in the tale involves the individual's moral and spiritual condition, but Chaucer consistently puts a great deal of weight on the seemingly varying abilities of the outer eye itself. The tale demonstrates admirably the extent to which theological applications are made based on vision and the extent to which ties are maintained with the physical sense.

Cecilia remains faithful to her incarnated Christ when Almachius commands her to worship an idol. Here again image and incarnation are brought together to form a contrast. For her disobedience, Almachius burns her in a bath of flames, but miraculously

> For al the fyr and eek the bathes heete
> She sat al coold and feelede no wo.
> It made hire nat a drope for to sweete. (520–2)

This episode reflects the situation in Daniel, where Daniel's three friends similarly undergo trial by fire. In both cases being thrown into a fire because of one's faith is the culmination of an extended exploration of the mesh of learning and religious faith. Through this combination Daniel and his three friends rise to prominence and various sorts of trouble:

> And to these children God gave knowledge and understanding in every book and wisdom: but to Daniel the understanding also of all visions and dreams. (Dan. 1:17)[19]

For Daniel in particular learning involves sight, and this ability to see exalts him to a status above that of all the wise men of Babylon. He passes into mythology as an icon of the seeing man and his book as the book of visions. The story goes on to contrast the temptation to respond to an earthly image and the spiritual ability to see and interpret another dimension. Shadrach, Meshach, and Abednego refuse to worship Nebuchadnezzar's ninety-foot-high image of gold and are therefore thrown into a fiery furnace. Like Cecilia, they too suffer no harm:

> [They] considered these men, that the fire had no power on their bodies and that not a hair of their head had been singed, nor their garments altered, nor the smell of the fire had passed on them. (Dan. 3:94)[20]

The book of Daniel portrays Jewish humanistic confidence, the confidence of a people that takes advantage of a cosmopolitan environment of learning and influence. This same attitude informs the Second Nun's Prologue and Tale.

The companion piece in the eighth fragment, the Canon's Yeoman's Tale, presents the negative ground of these values. Whereas the Second Nun concerns herself solely with spiritual themes, the Canon's Yeoman deals in archmateriality. It is a tale of legerdemain, gullibility, deceit, and self-interest. Chaucer alerts us to the alchemy he will perform upon the theme of sight with the yeoman's opening reflections, summed up in the line, 'And of my swynk yet blered is myn ye' (730). The form rather than the reality of learning, embodied in fine-sounding terminology, replaces the earnestness of the Second Nun's Tale:

---

19 'Pueris autem his dedit Deus scientiam et disciplinam in omni libro et sapientia Daniheli autem intelligentiam omnium visionum et somniorum.'
20 'Contemplabantur viros illos quoniam nihil potestatis habuisset ignis in corporibus eorum et capillus capitis eorum non esset adustus et sarabara eorum non fuissent inmutata et odor ignis non transisset per eos.'

> Whan we been there as we shul exercise
> Oure elvysshe craft, we semen wonder wise,
> Oure termes been so clergial and so queynte. (750–2)

Chaucer reproduces this language, as a glance at the extensive glosses in *The Riverside Chaucer* will confirm. In a fashion not unlike the Squire's Tale, Chaucer piles on the learning, in this case to parody a self-contained and pretentious craft that represents learning gone askew. The art of alchemy puts real learning into disrepute; Chaucer's depiction also calls attention to the potential excesses of learning. The importance of sight in this tale suggests Chaucer's interest in wider, general problems involved in learning. Sight is the metaphor for learning of various kinds and alchemy involves particular dangers for the practitioner's eyesight, physical as well as spiritual. The alchemist poses a threat to himself, using the dangerous element mercury; the potentiaɫ outcome is physical blindness, due to the harmful effects of mercury. The alchemist in this tale is also engaged in a materialistic, idolatrous search for gold. He is well on the way to total spiritual blindness, through deception, rapacity, and ultimately self-deception. The alchemist naturally also poses a threat to the gullible. The beguiled priest is complicit in a tale marked by the absence of learning, insight, or a vision for anything other than material gain. That the tale concerns a church canon and a priest also speaks of the relevance for Chaucer of the complete absence of any semblance of Christian love or pastoral care. This dark vision annihilates love from the system of love, knowledge, and sight. The system completely breaks down in a way similar to the breakdown of love, knowledge, and sight in the Merchant's Tale.

In Fragment VIII Chaucer carefully analyzes aspects of the nature and importance of learning, including its relationship to spiritual faith, potential excesses, and the dark implications of a masquerade of learning at the service of selfish interests. Peter Brown has argued that Fragment VIII presents polar opposites mediated by the 'common-sense naturalism' of the frame.[21] His observation of the stark contrast between spiritual and material realism, shared by others, is undoubtedly correct; throughout, however, Chaucer conveys a positive attitude towards learning embodied in the concept of sight. The manner in which Chaucer handles the motif of sight in the Second Nun's Prologue and Tale softens the influence of the miracle and highlights the relationship between sight, spiritual love, and a learned apologetic. The Canon's Yeoman's Prologue and Tale shows the negative effects of the separation of knowledge, sight, and love. In Fragment VIII one need not see Chaucer's religious attitudes in terms of polarity to see that he recognizes the intellectual complexity of Christianity, the discourse of love, and of the concomitant idea of sight. Of course the discourse of naturalism makes an enormous contribution to Chaucer's analysis of the symbiotic relationship between love, knowledge, and sight.

---

[21]   Brown, 1.243.

5

The Hospitality of Love and Knowledge
II
Erotic Love and Natural Philosophy Revisited

> A merveillous metels mette me thanne,
> I was ravysshed right there – for Fortune me fette
> And to the lond of longynge and love she me broughte,
> And in a mirour that highte Middelerthe she made me to
> biholde.[1]   (Langland)

Love and knowledge feed each other in the discourse of erotic love where it overlaps with naturalistic thought just as they do where the discourse overlaps with metaphysical verities. Langland's interest in visual motifs illustrates the bridge between spiritual love and earthly love. It also unites his concern about the proper form of spiritual knowledge and his clear celebration of naturalistic knowledge. In Passus XI, Will has a dream-within-a-dream that helps to emphasize the role of sight, even though it must be said that Langland generally pays scant attention to making his dream-poem visual. At the end of this dream-within-a-dream, Will meets Ymaginatif; this inner dream therefore initiates a sustained treatment of sight and psychological processes. Where Langland highlights sight, he usually draws attention to the relationship between love and knowledge. He does so here and he does the same again in Passus XV. The vision of middle-earth provides the foundation for a two-fold consideration of the relationship between love, earthly knowledge, and sight, the first negative and the second positive.

The first look at the earth in this inner vision, when Fortune seizes Will and has him look into the mirror which is middle-earth, is negative. Fortune is accompanied by two damsels, *Concupiscencia Carnis* and Coveitise of Eighes. Both of these characters are associated in the Middle Ages with *vitium curiositatis*, an unspiritual desire to acquire learning. Fortune tempts Will with the prospect of acquiring knowledge: ' "Here myghtow se wondres,/ And knowe

---

1   William Langland, *The Vision of Piers Plowman*. A Complete Edition of the B-Text, ed. A.V.C. Schmidt, London, 1978, XI.6–9.

that thow coveitest" ' (10–11). *Concupiscencia Carnis* in particular reflects a mutated form of love that is part of Fortune's offer, the lust of the flesh rather than a desire for God. Coveitise of Eighes embraces both the sensuality of letting one's eye wander and covet what is pleasing to it or what strikes it, and the intellectual component of careful and determined rational investigation. The object in question is middle-earth, which is presented as a mirror. That image of course potentially sparks associations both with love, such as the mirror of the lady's eyes, and with knowledge, intellectual reflection. The inner dream, therefore, begins with the establishment of a series of (negative) interconnections between love, knowledge, and sight in a context which is thoroughly naturalistic.

Later in the dream Kind comes to Will and also shows him middle-earth, which is now a mountain. His goal is positive, and one in which Langland emphasizes love and knowledge. Kind

> bad me nymen hede,
> And thorugh the wondres of this world wit for to take.
> And on a mountaigne that Myddelerthe highte, as me tho
>   thoughte,
> I was fet forth by ensaumples to knowe,
> Thorugh ech a creature, Kynde my creatour to lovye.
>
> (321–5)

Initially the emphasis is entirely on understanding and knowing, but Langland entwines that knowledge with love. Will grows in knowledge and love through sight: in the ensuing description (326–67) reference to sight (such as 'I seigh') is made seven times. This fusion of love and knowledge takes place in a naturalistic context; it is manifest in the creatures of middle-earth, formalized in medieval thought as the doctrine of plenitude. In *The Vision of Piers Plowman* Passus XI love, knowledge, and sight come together in the context of naturalism in ways that are either negative or positive. And although the naturalism is crucial, the interaction between the terms also feeds off of metaphysical applications of them.

The overlap between spiritual and amatory language with reference to sight creates meaning; it signals, in the midst of conventional erotic descriptions, the system of hostility/hospitality present in metaphysics. The language and concepts of natural philosophy add to the interference which is meaning where the convention of love at first sight would deny meaning. But the language of nonfunctioning contributes to functioning, the articulation of erotic love. No medieval poet does more than Jean de Meun to organize rationally the contradictions and marvels of love around the principles of vision. Like Langland, he seizes upon the doctrine of plenitude to bring together love, knowledge, and sight. Unlike Langland, of course, Jean de Meun, has a much more focused interest in the articulation of erotic love and the conventions of such love literature. He explores the doctrine of plenitude, which is based on the philosophical hierarchies of creation and explicable with reference to a chain of mirrors; and he further synthesizes the phenomenon of erotic love and knowledge of natural philosophy with a series of visual and optical allusions. Among efforts to subject the discourse of love to rationality, Jean de Meun's continuation of the *Roman de la Rose* emerges as probably the single most influential source informing Chaucer's sophisticated interest in sight. Chaucer himself organizes the physicality of sight into literary realism, an epistemological touchstone, and exploration of plenitude. His interest in this physicality is introduced by the theme of love at first sight and fleshed out through his own pervasive interest in the functions of the human eye. Like Langland, he is particularly sensitive to the ways in which, in a naturalistic context, the connections between love, knowledge, and sight also reverberate with metaphysical applications. This is nowhere more evident than in the Merchant's Tale.

Jean de Meun: Nature, Love, and Optics

The binary opposition of love and reason in medieval poetry often gives way to the rational urge to understand and control. Love literature expresses hostility for it asserts that love consumes rational inquiry; and as one literary commonplace and one order of experience it is so. But for those writing about love the philosopher-poet is not consigned to the flames. Jean de Meun reintroduces sight as a category of knowledge to manipulate the convention of vision's role in love and make a conundrum of the relationship between love and knowledge. For him the opposition of love and knowledge collapses in the face of the reasonable doctrine of plenitude.

The contest between Reason and the god of love for the soul of Amans illustrates the conflict between them. In the midst of his victory, however, the god of love dictates a course of action that caters to the intellect. He comments on the value of Jean's book for instructing lovers and keeping them away from Reason:

> «Que jamés cil qui les orront
> Des dous maus d'amer ne morront,
> Por qu'il le croient sainnement;
> Car tant en lira proprement
> Que tretuit cil qui ont a vivre
> Devroient appeler ce livre
> *Le Miroër as amoreus*,
> Tant i verront de bienz por eus,
> Mes que Raison n'i soit creüe,
> La chetive, la recreüe.» (10645–54)

> ('Then those who hear will never die of love
> And its sweet woes, for they'll believe in him;
> And, rightly read, his book shall have such worth

That all men living should give it the name
Mirror for Lovers. Reading its contents good,
They'll no more trust in Reason, recreant wretch.')

The forces of bookishness and learning normally fall under the province of
Reason, who is the enemy, yet here become part of the lover's practice. The
idea of a mirror as expressed in the book title differs considerably from that
associated with the mirror of the beloved's eyes. The attention drawn to the title
points to an interest in textuality and all its aspects. Jean is presenting the mirror
of thoughtful reflection, of reasoned argument. To look into this mirror is at
least one remove from the experience of looking into real mirrors of love. The
poet draws attention to apparently diverging pursuits and brings them together
through bookish metaphors and a title that contains a paradox.

Later Jean engages in a lengthy discussion of optical principles and further
endorses the role of the intellect. The properties of mirrors and glasses have a
consolidated place in Nature's survey of her realm. She moves into optics naturally in the course of explaining rainbows, a phenomenon that sparked interest
in optics from the time of ancient Greek scientific writings onward. Jean makes
optics the source of special knowledge and the solution to a riddle of creation.
Before long, Nature insists on the importance of knowing Alhazen's book on
optics. After a very brief description of the power of glasses, she embarks upon
a weird hypothesis of how such an instrument could have helped Mars and
Venus in the course of their adulterous relationship:

> Mars et Venus, qui ja pris furent
> Ensemble ou lit ou il se jurent
> S'il, ains que sor le lit montassent,
> En tex mirooirs se mirassent,
> Mes que les mirooirs tenissent
> Si que le lit dedens veïssent,
> Ja ne fussent pris ne liés
> Es las soutiz et deliés
> Que Vulcanus mis y avoit,
> De quoi nus d'aus rienz ne savoit. (18061–70)

(If Mars and Venus, ere they went to bed
And as they there together lay were trapped,
Had looked in such a glass, so held that they
Could in it see the bed, they had escaped
The subtle, tenuous net that Vulcan made
And set for them, of which they nothing knew.)

It would be a very circumspect lover who thought to carry an optical glass
around and use it to inspect the bed, but Genius readily joins in with Nature in
this bizarre speculation. The oddity of the 'digression' draws attention to itself.

It shows the esteem of optics in medieval thought and the readiness with which its principles are applied, even to a myth that would appear to have nothing to do with vision. Optics provides the poet with a tool he can use and in this way Jean continues to toy with the nature and uses of vision. Genius speculates that, had he known, Mars could have cut down the net, allowing the lovers to use the bed unscathed. He then imagines an entire scenario in which the lovers barely avoid discovery and Venus has to make excuses to her husband. The science of optics leads to ruminations on the subject of love, and a mythographically significant love affair comes under close scrutiny. Speculation based on scientific advances transforms the story. Genius is bent on illustrating the cleverness of women in intrigue and his imaginings culminate in a misogynistic invective:

> Tout l'eüst il neis veüe,
> Deïst ele que la veüe
> Li fust oscurcie et troblee,
> Tant eüst la langue doblee
> En diverses plicacions
> A trover excusacions.
> Car riens ne jure ne ne ment
> De fame plus hardiement. (18121–8)

> (Nay, though his very eyes had seen her sin,
> She might convince him that his sight was bad.
> She knows how to employ a double tongue,
> Twisting this way and that to find excuse;
> For there's no creature can more hardily
> Than women commit perjury and lie.)

At this point vision has become unreliable: the best of the outer wits is no match for a woman's double tongue. Vision has limited value in the processes of love, necessary as a starting point and valuable for solving certain problems, but not alone the most powerful force. Nature agrees with Genius, then promptly goes on to talk about other properties of mirrors and glasses. Jean embeds the matter of love – here adultery and cuckoldry – in a passage that keeps optical concepts as its focus.

Nature does not attempt to cover the topic at length, but instead relies on the cliché that one could unfold other details at length:

> Car trop y a longue matire,
> Et si seroit grief chose a dire
> Et mout seroit fort a entendre,
> S'il ert qui le seüst aprendre
> As genz laiz especiaument,
> Qui nel diroit generaument. (18273–8)

('Twould surely be
Too big a subject, and a grievous one
To talk about, and hard to understand,
Especially for laymen, unless I
Confined myself to generalities.)

Now this is certainly a technique for cutting off the discussion and moving on, but it still attests the widespread knowledge of the power of optics and the recognition that this discipline is integral to natural philosophy. More significantly, it binds vision and love together in Jean's presentation. It also creates a thematic link with Guillaume de Lorris' part of the *Roman*, a connection with the motif of love at first sight.

There is a connection between certain principles of light and the doctrine of plenitude which Jean espouses. The idea of the multiplication of species that grows out of Neoplatonic thought finds expression in the doctrine of the chain of being. Macrobius describes this chain alternatively as a series of mirrors reflecting light:

> Accordingly, since Mind emanates from the Supreme God and Soul from Mind, and Mind, indeed, forms and suffuses all below with life, and since this is the one splendor lighting up everything and visible in all, like a countenance reflected in many mirrors arranged in a row, and since all follow on in continuous succession, degenerating step by step in their downward course, the close observer will find that from the Supreme God even to the bottommost dregs of the universe there is one tie, binding at every link and never broken.[2]

This expression of the connectedness of life heavily influences medieval thought. As elsewhere, here it is the image of light that connects all of creation in a powerful way. The phenomenon of light has profound implications for how writers like Jean account for and celebrate sexuality. The doctrine of plenitude represents the culmination of Nature's discourse and is Jean's chief message in his continuation of the poem. Nature instructs Genius to go to Cupid with this message:

«Dites li que la vous envoi
Por touz ceus escommenier

---

[2] Macrobius, *Commentary on the Dream of Scipio*, trans. William Harris Stahl, New York and London, 1952, 1.14.15. 'Secundum haec ergo, cum ex summo de mens, ex mente anima fit, anima vero et condat et vita compleat omnia quae sequuntur cunctaque his unus fulgor illuminet et in universis appareat, ut in multis speculis per ordinem positis vultus unus, cumque omnia continuis successionibus se sequantur degenerantia per ordinem ad imum meandi, invenietur pressius intuenti, a summo deo usque ad ultimam rerum faecem, una mutuis se vinculis religans et nusquam interrupta conexio.' Macrobius, *Commentariorum in Somnium Scipionis libri duo*, ed. and trans. Luigi Scarpa, Padua, 1981.

Qui vous vuelent contrarier,
Et pour assoudre les vaillans
Qui de bon cuer sont travaillans
As regles droitement ensivre
Qui son escrites en mon livre,
Et forment a ce s'estudient
Que lor linages monteplient
Et qui pensent de bien amer.» (19378–87)

('Tell him that I
Send you to excommunicate all those
Who us withstand, and freely to absolve
The valiant hearts who labor to observe
Rightly the rules found written in my book,
And strongly strive to multiply the race,
And give themselves to love.')

Nature reflects God himself, who is the radiant source of life:

Cist est salus de cor et d'ame;
C'est li biaus mirooirs ma dame;
Ja ma dame riens ne seüst
Se cest biau mirooir n'eüst. (19899–902)

(He is the cure
Of body and of soul – the mirror He
Of Lady Nature. She had nothing known
Were it not for that mirror true and fair.

Jean employs the term 'mirror' here in a way different again from those we have already considered, one in keeping with medieval cosmology and medieval comprehension of God's interest and role in filling the universe. Optical associations here conjoin the fiction of love at first sight and an understanding of sexual creativity. As Alan Gunn points out, 'Casual and incidental as it may appear, Nature's discussion of mirrors and optical science is therefore no mere parade of curious learning, but a passage with as rich and relevant a content, and as profound implications as any in the poem.'[3] The discussion nicely ties in with the theme of plenitude. Together, the intellectual theme of light and the doctrine of plenitude point to a hospitality of love and knowledge.[4] Yet the

---

3   Alan Gunn, *The Mirror of Love*, Lubbock, 1952, 273. See also Patricia Eberle's discussion, 'The Lovers' Glass: Nature's Discourse on Optics and the Optical Design of the *Romance of the Rose*,' *University of Toronto Quarterly* 46 (1977), 241–62.
4   Pierre-Yves Badel draws a similar conclusion from his perceptive analysis of the role

sense that some 'curious learning' has been paraded persists. The learnedness of the discourse matters and as we are by now abundantly aware, it is hardly 'curious.' Jean does not merely put forward the doctrine of plenitude; the poem becomes an elaborate depiction of love as a system. Both reason and love find expression in terms of light, and both are central to the construction of Jean's continuation of the *Roman*. Intellectual complexity permeates many subsequent medieval treatments of love to the extent that it is in fact a defining feature.[5]

Jean takes advantage of this context to allude to matters of epistemology. At first, this has less to do with the effects of optical instruments than with the opacity of the lay mind to comprehend the fact that instruments could produce superior vision. But then he presses the point and refers to the capacity of the visions themselves to impart either knowledge or deception:

> Ne des visions les manieres,
> Tant sont merveilleuses et fieres,
> Ne porroient il otroier,
> Qui les lor vodroit desploier,
> Ne quex sont les decepcions
> Qui viennent pas tex visions,
> Soit en veillant soit en dormant,
> Dont maint s'esbahissent forment. (18287–94)

> (Indeed, the vulgar could not give belief
> To demonstrations one might make for them,
> So grand and wonderful the visions are.
> Nor the deceptions could they realize
> That from such visions come, and much amaze
> Many a man while sleeping or awake.)

The instruments of optics, developed through knowledge of Alhazen's book, make possible visions that affect the mind, that have some power in their own right. Nature then moves immediately into a discussion of dreams and frenzies, picking up precisely where she has just left off:

---

of Genius: 'Toujours est-il que, dans la procréation, sont réconciliés le désir et la rationalité. Ce que Raison était incapable de faire – importer l'adhésion – l'éloquence chaleureuse de Genius l'obtient, parce que, dans le domaine borné qui est le sien, il met au service de l'ordre rationnel de Nature le désir qui n'est pas moins natural.' Pierre-Yves Badel, Le Roman de la Rose *au XIVe Siècle: étude de la réception de l'œvre*, Geneva, 1980, 51. I will develop the importance of eloquence in the following chapter.

5   As Badel writes, 'Avec Jean de Meun tous les domaines de la connaissance et de l'action sont envisagés à la lumière d'une réflexion sur l'amour' (85). Badel has shown the importance of this tendency of the dit in fourteenth-century writers such as Machaut and Froissart (85f).

Tant en vuel dire a ceste fois
Que maint en sont si deceü
Que de lor liz se sont meü
Et se chaucent neïs et vestent
Et de tout lor harnois s'aprestent
Si cum li sen commun someillent
Et tuit li particulier veillent. (18304–10)

(Many a man is so deceived by dreams
That, jumping from his bed, he dons his clothes
And shoes, and gathers all his other gear,
As if his common sense were still asleep
While all his other senses were awake.)

Jean's reference to the common sense is part of his technical discussion of human psychology and mental operations. He moves from one variety of visions to another with an ease and facility that reflects a close relationship between the two in his construction. The last point made about mirrors raises questions of how we know what we know, as does the first point made about dreams. In the latter case, of course, the vision occurs strictly inside the dreamer's head, while in the first the processes of actual sight produce a vision which can induce knowledge or deception. The easy transition reveals the importance of both types of seeing as well as the underlying questions of epistemological significance. This collocation in Jean's poem also provides a clue for interpreting Chaucer's dream-poetry and his preoccupation with physical principles there.

The intricate use of visual motifs reveals the hand of a master craftsman. Lewis' erroneous blanket condemnation of the long excursions into scholastic learning is relevant here. Lewis complains that Jean's addition is a 'huge, dishevelled, violent poem' so that 'We never know, at one page, what we shall be reading about on the next.'[6] He goes on to say that 'The meandering in Jean de Meun's work is therefore a fault, and a fault fatal to his poem.'[7] In Jean's development of optical concepts, though, we see the significant integration of vision in two registers. First, Jean takes this specific field of learning and applies it to a scenario of love. The example is plausible given that visual concepts play an extraordinarily important role in medieval love poetry and in the unfinished poem of Guillaume itself. Jean makes an elegant generalization based on a theory of vision and applies the rigour of optical discourse to his own analysis of love. He chooses the work of a leading theorist, whom he duly notes, and in that way puts his optical allusion in love on the most firm footing possible. Jean's tendency to blend scholastic learning with a straightforward allegory of

---

6   Lewis, 137.
7   Lewis, 142.

love, so reprehensible to Lewis' sensibilities, is indicative of the desire and ability of some medieval poets to blend love discourse with intellectual concepts. This is the second, more fundamental way in which Jean integrates sight. Guillaume's poem hints at the contradiction in the notion of a self-contained analysis of love, and Jean's pushes out the boundaries. Guillaume treats the visual concepts beautifully, but conventionally; Jean seizes upon this convention and alters it. He does so in an historic intellectual climate of discovery, and at a time when optics is reemerging as an important sub-discipline, perhaps the specialization without peer. His approach highlights the relationship between love and knowledge where these two terms exhibit an indeterminable host/guest relationship as well as hostility.

Forms of Vision, Knowledge, and Love in the Merchant's Tale
Throughout his *oeuvre* and in the Merchant's Tale in particular Chaucer follows Jean's lead in using the principles of the essential conflict between love and knowledge in other ways, ones that complicate the basic opposition. He appeals to various aspects of physical sight, or at least to phenomena of 'seeing' interpreted in relation to a physical basis. By doing so he raises questions of epistemology and foregrounds the construction and the interpretation of reality. Finally, he does this in the context of love. Jean's purpose in reconstituting the parts of this opposition is to promote the doctrine of plenitude; in the Merchant's Tale Chaucer overburdens the associations possible with sight to draw attention to the connections between love and knowledge. Of course January mangles the system, but the very brutality of his approach serves for Chaucer to highlight the terms with which even he must deal as a would-be lover.

The Merchant's Tale seems to have the basic conflict of love and reason intact: January is in love, at least as in love as he is likely to get; he is single-minded about achieving his delight with May; and the sense of sight is appealed to, especially in the description of the garden to lend the aura of convention to this situation. In this tale, however, Chaucer offers a gross mutation in which love never really develops, reason becomes a monster, and quality of sight becomes a measure of much more than quality of love. Rather than demolishing the realm of reason, the tale foregrounds rational issues *per se* in expansive rhetoric. The prominence of debatable issues in the tale stands as a generic anomaly, since the tale has the markings of a fabliau. Certainly, the *senex amans*, the young wife, and the plot of adultery together belong in that tradition, in which details of realism play an important role. Here details especially related to the sense of sight, such as the garden setting, reinforce Chaucer's play with physical sight. January's moral blindness is revealed in the various topics tabled for discussion. In his own words or in his exchanges with his friends, January repeatedly reveals his decrepitude: blindness of the inner eye becomes collocated with an abundance of words. It fulfils the warning of the *Fasciculus morum* on the nature of lechery: 'it shuns the light, seeks darkness, and entirely plunders man's mind.'[8] And of course according to the preacher's handbook sight is the first occasion for lechery. Expressions of tortured logic, however, finally meet their match in the woman's ready response. May's explanation of events fully discloses January's moral condition and the categories of love, reason, and sight ultimately converge in the inversion of what should happen in love. Chaucer's parody accentuates the elements of the parasitic system.

In multiplying rhetorical forms, the Merchant's Tale raises issues that require depth of insight. The speaker of the introductory lines for the marriage encomium I take to be the Merchant, incapable of not telling us more of his 'owene soore' (1243).[9] Nonetheless the voice of the old knight, whom we know from the outset to have radically different ideas, registers simultaneously. The Merchant states his own position in clear but ironic terms:

> And certeinly, as sooth as God is kyng,
> To take a wyf it is a glorious thyng. (1267–8)

These introductory remarks go on for twenty-odd lines, but the speaker is not naive about the problems of his position. A thriving tradition in clerical literature held strongly and vociferously that marriage held few benefits. This tradition found its most eloquent spokesman in the Church father, Jerome, whose polemical tract *Adversus Jovinianum* established the tone of anti-matrimonial invective for a millenium. Theophrastus' tract, the *Golden Book on Marriage*, survives in Jerome, and our speaker makes the wise debating gesture of alluding to an opponent's possible counterpoint:

> And yet somme clerkes seyn it nys nat so,
> Of whiche he Theofraste is oon of tho. (1293–4)

His style underscores the intellectual tenor of the discussion. On the surface, he marshals one of Theophrastus' main points only to dismiss it:

> This sentence, and an hundred thynges worse,
> Writeth this man, ther God his bones corse!
> But take no kep of al swich vanytee;
> Deffie Theofraste, and herke me. (1307–10)

The bitterness of his own brief experience in marriage seeps through in such moments as the aside,

---

8   *Fasciculus morum*, 649. 'Lucem odit, tenebras appetit, totam hominis depredatur mentem' (648).
9   Donald R. Benson has an excellent discussion of how critics have interpreted this passage in 'The Marriage "Encomium" in the Merchant's Tale: A Chaucerian Crux,' *Chaucer Review* 14 (1979), 48–60, though I find his own conclusion that the passage is 'a tantalizing anomaly' (59) unsatisfying.

> A wyf wol laste, and in thyn hous endure,
> Wel lenger than thee list, paraventure. (1318–19)

He has raised an openly debated concept and done so with the rhetorical flourish that establishes tension between the language used and the ideas conveyed.
The presence of this tension contributes to the devolution of any possible interest in the discourse of *fin' amor*. The accent on debate parodies this latent force
of the language of *fin' amor*.

The speaker of this prolegomenon presents another difficulty when he cata-
logues a number of women to illustrate the idea that a man can let down his
guard in marriage, unafraid of deception:

> For thanne his lyf is set in sikernesse;
> He may nat be deceyved, as I gesse,
> So that he werke after his wyves reed. (1355–7)

The members of this list include Rebecca, Judith, Abigail, and Esther, all undoubtedly heroic women in medieval biblical interpretation, but all, ironically,
famous for some act of deception. The manner in which they achieved their
fame does nothing to reinforce the argument that a husband need not fear deception by his wife. At the very least, the exempla raise as many questions as
they purport to answer.[10]

When the marriage encomium gives way to January's personal story, the
speaker introduces a dialogue between January and his friends similar to that
of Job and his three friends:

> For which this Januarie, of whom I tolde,
> Considered hath, inwith his dayes olde,
> The lusty lyf, the vertuous quyete,
> That is in mariage hony-sweete,
> And for his freendes on a day he sente,
> To tellen hem th'effect of his entente. (1393–8)

January essentially has his mind made up on the subject of marriage, and yet
he does invite his friends to add their thoughts, if only obsequiously:

---

[10] The critical row over their meaning serves as a litmus test. See, for instance, Emerson
Brown, jr., 'Biblical Women in the Merchant's Tale: Feminism, Antifeminism, and Beyond,' *Viator* 5 (1974), 387–412; Charlotte F. Otten, 'Proserpina: *Libiatrix Suae Gentis*,'
Chaucer Review 5 (1971), 277–87. Both of these take preceding opposing arguments into
account and so provide both good examples of opposing readings and summaries of their
developments.

> 'And syn that ye han herd al myn entente,
> I prey yow to my wyl ye wole assente.' (1467–8)

In the story of Job, Job eventually turns away from all of his counsellors to seek an answer from God himself. Here, January gives no indication of seeking such a perspective. Placebo willingly falls in line, but Justinus does not, and their difference of opinion mirrors the general conflict between his friends, a reasonable debate over a very open question:

> Diverse men diversely hym tolde
> Of mariage manye ensamples olde.
> Somme blamed it, somme preysed it, certeyn,
> But atte laste, shortly for to seyn,
> As al day falleth altercacioun
> Bitwixen freendes in disputisoun,
> Ther fil a stryf bitwixe his bretheren two. (1469–75)

This sequence of question, debate, and strife singularly unfolds an aspect of love's power that clearly is not operative in this tale: its domination of reason.

What takes place within the realm of reason is, however, marred. January holds a view of sex within marriage that at first seems plausible, although he does not greatly disguise his lecherous inclinations:

> 'If he ne may nat lyven chaast his lyf,
> Take hym a wyf with greet devocioun,
> By cause of leveful procreacioun
> Of children to th'onour of God above
> And nat oonly for paramour or love;
> And for they sholde leccherye eschue,
> And yelde hir dette whan that it is due;
> Or for that ech of hem sholde helpen oother
> In meschief, as a suster shal the brother,
> And lyve in chastitee ful holily.' (1446–55)

Chaucer continues to emphasize the intellect by injecting theological terms like 'procreacioun,' 'leccherye,' and 'dette.' By using these terms, January raises the theological issue of the degree of sin involved in marital intercourse, although he misunderstands or refuses to see the teachings of the Church. In Justinus' second attempt to help January see the error of his ways, he picks up on an allusion to sex which January himself made. Justinus warns him that a wife may be his purgatory and goes on to advise him to exercise discretion in his sex life so as not to risk losing his eternal salvation:

> 'I hope to God, herafter shul ye knowe
> That ther nys no so greet felicitee

In mariage, ne nevere mo shal bee,
That yow shal lette of youre savacion,
So that ye use, as skile is and reson,
The lustes of youre wyf attemprely,
And that ye plese hir nat to amorously,
And that ye kepe yow eek from oother synne.' (1674–81)

His allusion is to the sinful taint of sex, even in marriage, a common teaching of the Church. Jerome had outlined a very severe position against women generally; in the context of a theology of marriage, a similarly stern body of opinion held that all marital intercourse not strictly for procreation was mortally sinful, a view promulgated by severe commentary on Gratian.[11] True, Augustine and others outlined a more positive view. Partly in response to Jerome, Augustine displayed a softer attitude towards marriage itself, and an attitude towards sex in marriage less severe than that of some rigorists.[12] Either way, however, January's ambitions do not align with prevalent teachings of sex in marriage. His view is lax and reveals his heterodoxy, a failure to see with the inner eye.[13]

In between visits from his friends, Chaucer gives us another glimpse into the workings of January's mind which collocates a vivid description of mental operations with the theme of love. As part of his search for a marriage partner, January reflects at night upon the various women he has seen:

Many fair shap and many a fair visage
Ther passeth thurgh his herte nyght by nyght,
As whoso tooke a mirour, polisshed bryght,
And sette it in a commune market-place,
Thanne sholde he se ful many a figure pace
By his mirour; and in the same wyse
Gan Januarie inwith his thoght devyse
Of maydens whiche that dwelten hym bisyde. (1580–7)

The mirror is a powerful image in this context. It serves as an analogy for the process of inner reflection, a mental operation that is going on in January's 'herte' (1581). It also represents a beautiful object available in the market-

---

[11] Joseph Morgan, 'Chaucer and the *Bona Matrimonii*,' *Chaucer Review* 4 (1970), 125–6.
[12] This view consists of the following gradations: sin does not taint sex for the sake of procreation; sex for the sake of satisfying the debt to preserve fidelity or simply for pleasure, without the intention of procreation, constitutes venial sin; adultery and fornication are mortal sins. Peter Lombard later reinforced the gradation of venial sin in the *Sentences*.
[13] P.J.C. Field has noted that Justinus' reference to 'oother synne' may well be a discreet allusion to what the Church considered to be sins against nature, seen to be even more serious than adultery and fornication. P.J.C. Field, 'Chaucer's Merchant and the Sin Against Nature,' *N&Q* n.s. 17 (1970), 85.

place, so that the analogy for the heart's contemplation becomes transformed into one for the women themselves. The idea of the polished mirror now reflects his unsavoury attitude towards women as potential love-objects, to be obtained for a price. The image of the mirror brings together a conceptualization of reflective processes and an attitude towards women and love.

The perverseness of January's attitudes is fully revealed in the idea of the *hortus deliciarum*. For January wedlock means paradise, a return to Eden:

> 'For wedlok is so esy and so clene,
> That in this world it is a paradys.'(1264–5)

After the wedding and the blessing of the bedchamber by the priest, Chaucer relates that

> Januarie hath faste in armes take
> His fresshe May, his paradys, his make. (1821–2)

This reference to paradise is more specific, with January locating it not simply in the state of wedlock but in the person of his wife. In his study of the image of paradise in this tale, Michael Cherniss points out that the paradisal garden which January claims to have entered is theologically inaccessible to mankind.[14] The medieval Christian pined for the earthly paradise as for a distant homeland, but understood that with the Fall God had barred mankind from returning there. In the context here, the same restrictions definitely held true for the possibilities of sexual freedom. For his own part, January reveals his bad theology more explicitly once he has bedded May:

> 'And blessed be the yok that we been inne,
> For in oure actes we mowe do no synne.
> A man may do no synne with his wyf,
> Ne hurte hymselven with his owene knyf,
> For we han leve to pleye us by the lawe.' (1837–41)

Fully disclosed, his theological position is ridiculous. As Field has pointed out, in the tradition of the thirteenth-century manual of moral theology *Somme le Roi*, one could indeed hurt himself with one's own knife, either in the form of excessive enjoyment of one's own wife or in the form of sins against nature.[15] Chaucer's Parson himself refers to the potential for sin in marital relations in his disquisition on lechery:

---

14   Michael D. Cherniss, 'The *Clerk's Tale* and *Envoy*, the Wife of Bath's *Prologue*, and the *Merchant's Tale*,' *Chaucer Review* 6 (1971–2), 246–7.
15   Field, 85.

And for that many man weneth that he may nat synne for no likerousnesse
that he dooth with his wyf, certes, that opinion is fals. God woot, a man
may sleen hymself with his owene knyf, and make hymselve dronken of
his owene tonne. (X.858)

January's idea of marriage is foolish and self-deceptive at best and indicative
of his secular and spiritual ignorance. January expresses himself *ad nauseam*
on this topic in some of the most inappropriate of situations and in doing so
reveals his spiritual blindness.

The bulk of the first section of the Merchant's Tale suggests a rational presentation of issues for careful, reasonably objective consideration. It works
against the simple impulse of love and the principles of paradise and bliss
which guide the knight. The deliberations on marriage (1245–1688) incorporate material from a number of scholarly sources, including the *Liber de amore
Dei* and *Liber consolationis et consilii* of Albertanus of Brescia. This latter
work constitutes the Tale of Melibee, and just as that tale sees Prudence put
forward a rational and objective case, the several difficult issues raised through
rhetorical style of deliberation suggest similar possibilities for this tale. The
value of marriage, the reliability of women, the place of sex in marriage: these
are all extraordinarily complex issues with a variety of opposing attitudes
brought to bear on each of them. That they should be raised at all, let alone in
a generic style that lends an aura of dialogue, implies that an objective and
stimulating analysis will unfold openly. The remainder of the tale, however,
confounds this expectation. The activity of reason, such as it is, has already
deferred the account of January's experience of paradise, such as it is. Chaucer
now juxtaposes that intellectual realm with the realm of love, equally mis-
shapen, a mixture of elements of courtly romance and fabliau where vision runs
wild. The romance-fabliau of the second half of the tale undermines the more
respectable discourse of the first part of the tale and the sermon rhetoric of the
so-called encomium. It undermines the more elevated clerical forms of discourse, and since clerical writings often provided a bastion for anti-feminist
sentiment it undermines that as well. The contrast between these two genres
serves as an encompassing example of polarized discourses brought together;
the discourses of the sermon and romance-fabliau in a way represent knowledge and love respectively, which together function as a parasitic system here
about as effectively as January's rational processes or love-making techniques.

While Chaucer is preparing us for an image of the *senex amans* as a blind
man caught in words, he diversifies the theme of sight with a strong appeal to
visual images. The idea of the garden provides the poem with a visual image
that has associations with sight in keeping with an ideal of love, however ab-
surd for January to contemplate in his mind's eye. As in the Knight's Tale, the
garden motif perpetuates interest in physical images and is in turn collocated
with a tradition of lovely eroticism in which the eyes play an important role. In
the Knight's Tale the two prisoners fall in love with Emily, who is 'fressher than

the May,' when they see her in the garden; in *Le Roman de la Rose* the god of love pierces the lover's heart with an arrow of Beauty through his eye. Chaucer goes to some length to make a similar courtly impression here by drawing a comparison between January's garden and that of the *Roman*:

> He made a gardyn, walled al with stoon;
> So fair a gardyn woot I nowher noon.
> For, out of doute, I verraily suppose
> That he that wroot the Romance of the Rose
> Ne koude of it the beautee wel devyse. (2029–33)

It no longer really matters whether or not January should be seeking paradise in a mate, or if his theology is shaky. Chaucer has smoothly reclaimed the garden as a courtly symbol of love. The *Roman*, it will be recalled, incorporates a strong appeal to the sense of sight and a marked iconography of the dream landscape. Ironically, not long after he has built this garden January goes blind. He cannot fully enjoy his physical surroundings and he is now even less of a candidate to participate in the eroticism associated with gardens. The spiritual language with which January later addresses May reinforces the visual motif associated with the garden at the same time as it reveals his enfeebled carnal desires:

> 'Rys up, my wyf, my love, my lady free!
> The turtles voys is herd, my dowve sweete;
> The wynter is goon with alle his reynes weete.
> Com forth now, with thyne eyen columbyn!
> How fairer been thy brestes than is wyn!
> The gardyn is enclosed al aboute;
> Com forth, my white spouse! Out of doute
> Thou hast me wounded in myn herte, O wyf!
> No spot of thee ne knew I al my lyf.
> Com forth, and lat us taken oure disport;
> I chees thee for my wyf and my confort.' (2138–48)

The allusion evokes striking visual images: the beloved as the 'white spouse' with her 'eyen columbyn' and without spot; it also evokes the attending images of the enclosed garden developed throughout the Song of Songs. The order of events in Chaucer's narrative is equally striking. The movement from allusion to the *Roman* to the revelation of January's blindness draws together different concepts of vision, each with differing valuations of knowledge, and potentially conflicting notions of love. Chaucer moves back and forth between them, doubly indicating January's confusion as well as the proximity of the terms.

In January's mouth the poetry of the Song of Songs is reduced to mere words, 'olde lewed wordes' (2149). Chaucer separates the signifiers from the signifieds so that they produce only the impression of a man blinded by his desires, with bad theology and bad taste. The invitation to go into the garden is the pivotal juncture of the plot, and everything rests on signs and their various and conflicting significations. At this point, January uses old words that are revealed as just that, words without power or meaning; at the same time, May employs her own language to direct Damian, a language that her husband cannot understand because he cannot see. The way Chaucer collocates sight with language enhances the serious philosophical possibilities of the motif of sight in his poetry. Not only does he associate it with traditional concepts of spiritual understanding and with the eroticism of love literature but with the role of language as well. In the Merchant's Tale the relationship between sight and language is complicated. At the outset the genre privileges discourse but the moral insight of both the Merchant and January is suspect; January's moral obtuseness becomes increasingly obvious as his speeches multiply. Now, in his recitation of a passage from the Song of Songs, he invokes more words that are inappropriate to the condition of his inner and outer eye. The mystical ideas in this passage certainly lack their resonance given his spiritual condition; and the quotation is simply inappropriate given his vulgarity and his blindness. Sight reveals the controvertible role of language by contrast, a point Chaucer reemphasizes in the Manciple's Tale. Here May will provide a working illustration of the possibilities for manipulating sight rhetorically.

In the climax to the plot Chaucer reveals sight as the illustration that encapsulates January's moral condition as he collocates love, reason, and sight. Chaucer continues to foreground the problem of language through the Merchant's apology to the ladies:

'I kan nat glose, I am a rude man.' (2351)

Through the story-telling merchant he draws attention to the involvement of the author in relating deeds of love. Befitting a situation that involves January, the problem is not that of conveying a sense of inexpressible rapture but of reconciling the listeners to what they are about to hear. In this gross mutation of *fyn lovynge*, putting it into words continues to be a crucial issue. The danger of words has already become evident in the exchange between Pluto and Proserpina. When Pluto sees May and Damian in the tree, he restores January his sight, but with some reluctance. His wife has already bested him in argument and he goes through with his promise to restore January's sight only because he has already sworn an oath:

'I yeve it up! But sith I swoor myn ooth
That I wolde graunten hym his sighte ageyn,
My word shal stonde, I warne yow certeyn.
I am a kyng; it sit me noght to lye.'
    'And I,' quod she, 'a queene of Fayerye!
Hir answere shal she have, I undertake.' (2312–17)

He knows that his action will result in more words, since Proserpina promised to supply May with a ready answer, and that the knowledge associated with sight probably will be meaningless. January regains his sight and sees what the narrator, not wanting to 'speke uncurteisly' (2363) belatedly becomes reticent about. The merchant's own mixed messages contribute to the relativization of values that puts considerable strain on the motif of blindness. We do not know, from one line to the next, if we should value plain speech, polite reticence, clarity of vision, insight, or quick thinking.

In response to her husband's exclamations and unfortunate question ' "O stronge lady stoore, what dostow?" ' (2367), May launches into a well- constructed argument defending her actions on the basis that she acted for his sake. In the Venus and Mars scene of the *Roman,* Genius reflects on a woman's ability to have a ready answer for a husband who has seen her commit a misdeed. Chaucer here builds on that passage and gives an example of such an answer. Like Jean, he works within the context of concepts of vision related to kinds of knowing. May's answer involves an extended foray into the realm of medical and physiological knowledge that begins with the dubious claim that she was trying to heal him:

> 'As me was taught, to heele with youre eyen,
> Was no thyng bet, to make yow to see,
> Than strugle with a man upon a tree.' (2372–4)

January wants to keep it simple:

> 'Strugle?' quod he, 'Ye, algate in it wente!
> God yeve yow bothe on shames deth to dyen!
> He swyved thee; I saugh it with myne yen,
> And elles be I hanged by the hals!' (2376–9)

What he has seen with his eyes he declares with his lips. Although May tries to convince him otherwise, we know that January has seen clearly because of what the Merchant has just narrated. Briefly in the old knight's experience language and sight become synchronized; but Chaucer gives us no framework in which to evaluate whether or not he considers this to be an ideal situation. With his statement, the *senex amans* has just admitted to being blind to his wife's designs; and he knows that should word get out he would be seen by his peers to be lacking in judgement, an opinion he may have already sensed in some. His insistence on the efficacy of his vision, despite May's reasonable claim that in the circumstances he could expect 'no parfit sighte' (2383), leaves him no way out. For once January sees clearly and it undoes him. Of course he does not see at all clearly in any sense other than the physical one. The implication of this clarity of sight only slowly dawns on him; and he in fact is merely acting in his usual 'unenlightened' way. The clarity of his sight has no corresponding moral dimension. Sight becomes his punishment, January relents, and his moral blindness becomes complete. Chaucer invokes the concept of sight, so familiar and useful as a homiletic analogy, to illustrate the *senex amans'* utterly hopeless state. His worst vision of life as a married man has come to be and he wilfully turns away from that knowledge.

After May has scored her victory and elicited an apology from her husband, she goes on to insist that January should not expect to be able to see properly immediately after a period of blindness:

> 'But, sire, a man that waketh out of his sleep,
> He may nat sodeynly wel taken keep
> Upon a thyng, ne seen it parfitly,
> Til that he be adawed verraily.
> Right so a man that longe hath blynd ybe,
> Ne may nat sodeynly so wel yse.' (2397–2402)

May's reasoning echoes the scientific explanations of what can happen when sight is restored as offered by Alhazen and others and summarized by the encyclopedist Bartholomaeus Anglicus:

> Þe siȝt most haue tyme, as it is iproued in *Perspectiue.* Þey a þing come sodeinliche tofore þe siȝt it is noȝt knowen rediliche wiþoute auisement and þerto nediþ tyme. And [þer]for it nedith also þat þe soule take hede.
> (110)

The sustained cleverness of May's response parodies both the conventional appeal to sight in love literature and the homiletic practice of making analogies based on sight.[16] Homiletic treatises often draw attention to the danger of sight, and of the woman's eye in particular. Here it is this woman's ability to use the basis of physiological sight to confound both the would-be lover January and a straightforward homiletical exemplum. At this point the knowledge of the natural philosopher is seconded by the adulteress.

Knowledge weighs heavily on the tale and especially on the ending, where it is concentrated in the concept of sight. Chaucer uses it to encumber even the sophisticated homiletical analogy of outer/inner sight, so that visual knowledge produces no clear spiritual moral. Knowledge as sight also weighs down the convention of love at first sight and contributes to the twisted form of *fyn lovynge* which is January's experience. The language of *fyn lovynge* makes it possible for him to bring these elements together. The parasitic system of love, knowledge, and sight allows him to produce this kind of monstrosity. That

---

16   For further discussion of the allusions to optical concepts which Chaucer has May make see Peter Brown, 'An Optical Theme in *The Merchant's Tale*,' in *Studies in the Age of Chaucer*, Proceedings 1, 1984: Reconstructing Chaucer, ed. Paul Strohm and Thomas J. Heffernan, Knoxville, 1985, 231–43.

system also makes it easier to understand Chaucer's purpose in bringing together the genres he uses in this tale. Chaucer plays extensively with traditional
and recent interest in sight as a metaphor and physiological fact. He acts upon
Jean's suggestion that language and sight overlap in the context of the traditional opposition of love and reason. Both Jean and Chaucer create a spectrum
of ways in which the dialectic of love and knowledge can be expressed in terms
of sight.

Hospitality in The Parliament of Fowls

The conflict of love and reason as expressed in terms of vision is a complex in
which the terms can be pulled apart from one another. The ideas of love, knowledge, and vision are grotesquely reintegrated in the Merchant's Tale to produce
a study in lechery. In the dream-poetry, Chaucer manipulates the themes of
love, knowledge, and vision much as Jean does in Nature's confession, where
they are ultimately folded into his mirror for lovers. For his part, Chaucer displays considerable interest in the self-reflexiveness of this system as experi-
enced by the poet. In the dream-poetry, this agenda is most clear in *The House
of Fame* and the Prologue to *The Legend of Good Women*, and I shall explore
this self-reflexiveness in the last chapter. In *The Book of the Duchess*, as we
have seen, he uses visual principles to reflect upon love in a context of pain.
The Chaucerian piece that most closely resembles Jean's in its central concerns
and its admixture of love, knowledge, and sight is *The Parliament of Fowls*.
With its concern for common profit and procreative interpretation of what this
means, *The Parliament of Fowls* makes a natural companion piece to Jean's
continuation of the *Roman*. As in Nature's disquisition in the *Roman*, Chaucer's
interest in sight embraces many possibilities, many of them on display here.
Both Jean and Chaucer show a marked interest in various sorts of vision.
Nature goes from a discussion of optics to an incident involving discovery back
to optics and then to a consideration of dreams without blinking. Chaucer's
own approach to dreams shows a similar interest in the link between natural
experience and vision and the variety of ways in which that link can be defined.
This philosophical interest then introduces the subject of love, the complexity
of which outstrips a facile opposition between love and reason.

The Parliament of Fowls is perhaps the most deeply indebted to the tradition
of dream-visions of Chaucer's four vision poems. Its central theme of common
profit is organized around two pivotal pieces of such literature, Cicero's *Somnium Scipionis* and Alain de Lille's *De planctu Naturae*. Both of these firmly
establish the philosophical tenor of Chaucer's interest in love in this poem, and
the use of sight here initially belongs in that tradition. Along with that leading
idea, the poem develops other aspects of sight in keeping with the visual experience of erotic love in the literary tradition, including the idea of the dreamer
as an observer. The influence of the *Roman* is evident in the nature of the visual
experiences in the poem and in the overarching appeal to sight to integrate its

thematic concerns. Unsurprisingly, this broad appeal to sight contributes to Chaucer's ability to consider many different aspects of love.

The theme of common profit first appears when the narrator recounts his reading from Cicero. He first summarizes how Africanus tells his grandson, Scipio the Younger, the destiny of those who work for the common profit: this itself takes the form of a vision, invented as a way of communicating insight. He then concludes his summary of the work by returning to this idea and quoting the grandfather's words:

> Thanne preyede hym Scipion to telle hym al
> The wey to come into that hevene blisse.
> And he seyde, 'Know thyself first immortal,
> And loke ay besyly thow werche and wysse
> To commune profit.' (71–5)

This double-edged wisdom reveals a tension between meditating on the heavenly realm and concentrating on earthly duties central to the *Somnium Scipionis*. It is a tension reflected in Scipio's attitudes that he cannot hide even as he dreams, for although both his grandfather and his father attest to the supremacy of the afterlife (*vita mors est*) his gaze keeps returning to the earth. Chaucer's narrator reports Africanus' estimation of the value of this life:

> And Affrican seyde, 'Ye, withouten drede,'
> And that oure present worldes lyves space
> Nis but a maner deth, what wey we trace. (52–4)

Interestingly, he passes over the fixity of Scipio's interest in the earth; but the dream that he has as a result of this reading reveals a similar earthward vision on his part. The *Somnium Scipionis* serves to introduce the theme of common profit as well as a philosophical dialectic between objects of vision.

Alain's *De planctu Naturae* sustains this tension in the figure of Nature. The twelfth-century poet bases his description of her on the figure of Philosophy in Boethius' *Consolation of Philosophy*, like whom Nature is a tall, prepossessing figure. The first thing the narrator notices about her is her radiance:

> Her hair shone with no borrowed sheen but with one special to itself and presenting an image of light-rays, not by mere resemblance but by a native lustre surpassing the natural, it made the maiden's head image a star-cluster.[17]

---

[17] Alan of Lille, *Plaint of Nature*, trans. James J. Sheridan, Toronto, 1980, 73. *De planctu Naturae*, ed. Nikolaus M. Häring, *Studi Medievali* 3rd ser., 19 (1978), 806–79. 'Cuius crinis, non mendicata luce sed propria scintillans, non similitudinarie radiorum representans

Chaucer, who essentially imports Alain's Nature, describes her this way:

> That, as of lyght the somer sonne shene
> Passeth the sterre, right so over mesure
> She fayrer was than any creature. (299–301)

Nature extends the aura of brilliance associated with Lady Philosophy, who illuminates the mind. Both Boethius' and Alain's female figures wear a tunic that has been torn: Philosophy's has the symbols for practical and theoretical philosophy and has been torn by the differences between the various schools of philosophy; Nature's tunic depicts the parliament of creation but has been torn because of sexual perversion. Alain's figures therefore recalls the philosophical preoccupations and interest in a cosmic vision of the *Consolation* and approaches this aspect of nature philosophically; but his orientation is more earthbound, his concern with sexual conduct and procreation. For Chaucer, Nature sets up a parliament in order to oversee the engendering of species:

> Ne there nas foul that cometh of engendrure
> That they ne were prest in here presence
> To take hire dom and yeve hire audyence. (306–8)

The idea of 'commune profyt' becomes more specific in the doctrine of plenitude. The dream-vision, which provides the overarching context for the poem, contains the seeds of a change in interest from the philosophical and abstract to the natural and the concrete. We remain, however, in the realm of 'the derke nyght' (85) that 'Berafte me my bok for lak of lyght' (87), where the dreamer sees only by inner sight.

The poem incorporates other aspects of vision that have associations with erotic literature. The dream-vision accommodates the impetus of beauty and the motif of the eyes as active agents in love. *The Book of the Duchess* and *The House of Fame* both call into question the dreamer's experience in love in contrast with what he knows secondhand. In the former poem he plays an almost voyeuristic role, a role much more pronounced in Machaut's version; in the latter he has bookish knowledge, as well as what he hears through tidings. In *The Parliament of Fowls* Chaucer pursues this separation of experience and secondhand knowledge through the idea of sight. As the dreamer stands indecisively in the gateway to the park of love, Africanus pushes him in with this consolation:

> 'But natheles, although that thow be dul,
> Yit that thow canst not do, yit mayst thow se.' (162–3)

effigiem sed eorum claritate natiua naturam preueniens, in stellare corpus caput effigiabat puelle' (2.3–5).

Given the fundamental importance of the role of sight in love, this is an ironic possibility. This sort of observation has nothing to do with love directly and in some way signals that the would-be observer is not subject to love. In contrast, Troilus makes the mistake of thinking himself impervious to love and finds himself smitten because he observes too much. The vision that the dreamer does not receive is that of the rose or the beautiful lady whose eyes send rays like darts, whereas Troilus does encounter such a vision.

What the dreamer does see is highly stylized and iconographic, in many ways reminiscent of the *Roman de la Rose*. The dominant image is that of a garden:

> A gardyn saw I ful of blosmy bowes
> Upon a ryver, in a grene mede,
> There as swetnesse everemore inow is,
> With floures white, blewe, yelwe, and rede,
> And colde welle-stremes, nothyng dede,
> That swymmen ful of smale fishes lighte,
> With fynnes rede and skales sylver bryghte. (183–9)

As in *The Book of the Duchess*, Chaucer describes the scene in terms of both sights and sounds. His appeal to the eye is traditional yet also delicate, as in the description of the fish; it is also subtle, with a pun on 'lighte' that unfolds with the rhyming word 'bryghte.' What the dreamer sees here prepares us for the figures of Cupid and Will, Plesaunce, Aray, Lust, Curteysie, and many others so much like those encountered by Amans. Some of the images are startling, such as those of Priapus and Venus in the temple. The scene of Dame Pacience sitting 'upon an hil of sond' (243) largely interprets the activity in this first setting as that of sterility and frustrated purpose. By contrast, when he comes out of the temple of Venus he walks onward to a place 'sote and grene' (296) where he meets Nature, who sits 'upon an hil of floures' (302). The two contrasting scenes are both part of the park of love and form a continuum of images as the dreamer explores this landscape. Finally, the representation of the birds in parliament before Nature is one of hierarchy, with the birds positioned in the park according to their status. This series of images provides us with a landscape of love not unlike that of the *Roman* with intimations of the real power of sight that eludes the dreamer.

The closest that Chaucer comes to developing the role of sight in love here is in the presentation of the formel. The courtly language used emphasizes her physical beauty: 'of shap the gentilleste' (373). Nature herself enjoys looking at her:

> So ferforth that Nature hireself hadde blysse
> To loke on hire, and ofte hire bek to kysse. (377–8)

The narrator does not describe the gaze of the beloved or the process of the eagles' beholding and being struck by Beauty, but the effects upon the first eagle's heart closely resembles what happened to Amans when the god of love pierced his heart with the arrow of Beauty through the eye:

> For certes, longe may I nat lyve in payne,
> For in myn herte is korven every veyne. (424–5)

The formel's reaction to the eagle's declaration of love makes the comparison with how *fin' amor* unfolds in the *Roman* still more relevant:

> Ryght as the freshe, rede rose newe
> Ayeyn the somer sonne coloured is,
> Ryght so for shame al wexen gan the hewe
> Of this formel, whan she herde al this. (442–5)

In this courtly episode with which the parliament opens, Chaucer includes the language of love inspired by Guillaume de Lorris' dream-vision. Perhaps he does not make explicit reference to the activity of the eyes because that normally isolates the lover and the beloved in their private world and, especially for the lover, his own private pain. Here Chaucer gives priority to the orderly proceedings of love under the control of Nature. The noisy debate that arises in the parliament out of the conflict between the eagles gains some of its poignancy in the contrast of the senses. The courtliness of the scene has a strong visual component, with the formel on display and the language expressive of what happens when love occurs at first sight; this devolves into the clamour of competing voices as romance gives way to sexual urgency. Just as the dream-vision of the *Roman* frames other aspects of vision that have importance in their own right, especially in Jean de Meun's continuation, so too in Chaucer's dream poetry vision becomes a complex theme that moves some distance from its mooring in the generic context.

The Visually Conceived Realities of Troilus

In *Troilus*, having firmly established the typical importance of vision in the processes of love, Chaucer uses vision in a variety of ways to accentuate the physicality of the lovers' circumstances as a means of expressing their psychological conditions. The sensitivity he creates towards colour, location, and therefore individual physical perspective enhances the love story, for it creates a greater awareness of the main characters' alienation, their progress towards unity, and the final rupture. By using these details extensively, Chaucer adds to the mimetic effect of his poem and this effect complements rather than subverts the simpler idea of love at first sight. He builds upon the ideas put in place by the convention of the opposition of love and reason to create a fiction far more complex, allusive, and historically relevant than the opposition itself suggests.

In his doctoral dissertation, Peter Brown introduces the important relationship between vision and space into a reading of Chaucer's poetry.[18] One of his chief objectives being to explore Chaucer's realism in these terms, he makes use of Muscatine's insights into the nature of Chaucer's realism. In his brief article on the locus of action, Muscatine explores some categories of literary space by taking advantage of the 'provocative start' given by art historians.[19] He sees in late medieval literature a 'Gothic tension' between the use of space to produce a 'rationalized pattern' and moral relationships on the one hand and 'an irregular, humane, naturalized setting to represent psychological and emotional experience.'[20] Elsewhere, Daniel Poirion has pursued a similar line of argument, insisting that the poetry of Machaut reflects the mimesis of painting.[21] The collocation of vision and space in *Troilus* follows in that vein: and the contemporary influences include others besides the pictorial. One receives a strong impression of the subject as perceiver and a sense of the complexity of what this means. This episode combines the act of seeing, as an important component in its own right, with psychological processing. Ockham would describe this as a combination of intuitive and abstractive cognition and he would use the example of sight to describe those two cognitive processes. Others would have different ideas about what is happening internally, but they would almost certainly appeal to the sense of sight to describe these psychological processes.

Some of the basic material of the story of Troy helps Chaucer bring out the importance of location in a visual way. The fact that Troy is a city under siege immediately establishes the reality of a boundary wall separating the protagonists inside from outside forces, and the city itself as an enclosed, limited space. Chaucer does not give us a map, but one can easily imagine a medieval map of a city, with the area within the walls carefully labelled and the wilderness beyond uncharted (here be Greeks). Further adding to the importance of location is the initial movement of Calkas, with which both *Il Filostrato* and *Troilus and Criseyde* open. His leaving makes the contrast of places very tangible, and establishes the inside/outside opposition. These two locations ultimately provide the crisis of action as well, with the exchange of Criseyde for Antenor, her passage from being accessible and visible in the city to being hidden and faithless outside it. The historical setting for these poets' exploration of human emotions provides foundational material.

Chaucer adds to the sense of localization by establishing additional barriers and movement within Troy itself. Where Boccaccio hastens towards the union

---

[18] This relationship is central to the thesis and developed productively also in his article 'The Containment of Symkyn: The Function of Space in the *Reeve's Tale*,' *Chaucer Review* 14 (1979–80), 225–36.
[19] Muscatine, 115.
[20] Muscatine, 119.
[21] Daniel Poirion, 'The Imaginary Universe of Guillaume de Machaut,' in *Machaut's World*, ed. M.P. Cosman, New York, 1978, 199–206. I discuss Poirion's ideas in more detail in chapter six.

of the lovers, Chaucer lingers over their movements as they sedulously grow closer together, making it increasingly possible to visualize the drama. This includes the tactic of drawing attention to their separate dwellings. In *Il Filostrato* the emphasis is on the lovers, of course, and on Pandarus carrying their messages to one another. In *Troilus*, the action in their homes is amplified. This especially happens at Criseyde's. When Pandarus first visits her on Troilus' behalf, Chaucer takes pains to paint the scene of the three women listening to a maiden read of the siege of Thebes, and of how Pandarus settles in. Boccaccio spends no time at all on such details.

Of greater significance is the episode that Chaucer inserts after this visit. In addition to conveying Criseyde's thoughts, with which Boccaccio satisfies himself, Chaucer has Criseyde see Troilus by chance. Troilus is riding through the streets on his way to the palace, and in anticipation Criseyde's servants throw open the gates to catch a glimpse of him:

> 'A, go we se, cast vp the ʒates wyde,
> ffor thorwgh this strete he moot to paleys ride.' (2.615–16)

Criseyde, who had withdrawn to the privacy of her own bedroom, has the chance to see Troilus from the security of her own home. Chaucer contrasts her isolation with the pageantry of his ride, and emphasizes her perspective in this moment in physical as well as psychological terms. Chaucer devotes four stanzas to describing the scene as she sees it. One can almost imagine a painting with gates framing a scene of frozen movement.

Chaucer continues to emphasize realism in the garden scene at Criseyde's home. Undoubtedly, the garden reinforces the theme of love in the tradition of the Song of Songs and the *Roman de la Rose*. It also provides Chaucer with the opportunity to add realistic detail:

> Adown the steyre anon right tho she wente
> In-to the gardyn with hire neces thre . . .
>
> This ʒerd was large, and rayled alle thaleyes,
> And shadewed wel with blosmy bowes grene,
> And benched newe, and sonded alle the weyes.
> (2.813–14; 20–2)

This attention to detail for its own sake differs from that of the *Roman de la Rose*, which holds closely to an allegorical presentation. Here Chaucer expresses genuine interest in Criseyde's physical surroundings without suggesting symbolic meanings and he consistently places her in that context.

The second trip that Pandarus makes on Troilus' behalf closely parallels the first, with a similar development of movement and sense of space within her home, followed by a frozen image. If we trace their movements, after Pandarus arrives with the letter, he and Criseyde go from her chamber to the garden. They

talk for awhile and he thrusts the letter down her bosom, then they go into the
hall to dine. Criseyde disengages herself, however, to return to her chamber to
read the letter. She then finds Pandarus in a contemplative mood, takes him 'by
the hood,' and together they go back to the hall. After lunch, Pandarus leads
her to the window in anticipation of the scene he has arranged with Troilus.
Making small-talk, he soon has Criseyde sitting with him in the window looking out onto the street:

> And fillen forth in speche of thynges smale,
> And seten in the windowe bothe tweye. (2.1191–2)

Already Chaucer has deferred the basic action by adding considerable dramatic
detail and presented the scene realistically. As the conversation turns to the
subject of the letter, Criseyde leaves the window to go pen her response. Eventually she returns, and sits by Pandarus on a stone of jasper, 'vp-on a quysshyn
gold y-bete' (2.1229). Only then does Troilus appear, the climax to a scene of
elaborately choreographed movement that ends in a still. And throughout,
Chaucer appeals to the senses in his description, especially the sense of sight:
the gold-embroidered cushion, Criseyde's rosy hue, Troilus' array.

Once again, Chaucer employs a frame, the window, giving the scene a strong
pictorial quality for both lovers. At the same time, this frame emphasizes their
separate locations and their discrete viewpoints. The episode is all the more
remarkable when contrasted with the way Boccaccio handles it. Boccaccio devotes only one stanza to the entire window scene, the only scene in *Il Filostrato*
where he could express the contrasting perspectives of the lovers visually:

> Ella si stava ad una sua finestra,
> e forse quel ch'avvenne ella aspettava;
> né si mostrò selvaggia né alpestra
> verso di Troiol che la riguardava,
> ma tutta volta in su la poppa destra,
> onestamente verso lui mirava.
> Di che allegro Troiol se ne gìo,
> grazie rendendo a Pandaro ed a Dio. (2.82)[22]

He separates the window scene from the letters, and in both cases concerns
himself only with how they facilitate the communication of the lovers. He has
none of the detail of Criseyde's home or of the long series of movements that

---

[22] 'She was standing at one of her windows and was perchance expecting what happened.
Not harsh nor forbidding did she show herself toward Troilus as he looked at her, but at all
times cast toward him modest glances over her right shoulder. Troilus departed, delighted
thereat, giving thanks to Pandarus and to the gods' (literally: to God).

Chaucer lingers over; he does nothing to develop the possibilities of this arranged meeting.

At the home of Deiphebus the space between Troilus and Criseyde begins to contract. Chaucer, having raised his audience's level of consciousness of visual love from a distance as well as the attendant individuality of their psychological positions, takes full advantage of localizing factors here. He supplies two images from sport of relentless movement towards enclosure that foreshadow the tryst in Pandarus' 'littel closet.' The first comes from deer hunting, an allusion to the technique commonly employed by hunters of closing the circle on the deer and driving the game towards the place where the bowmen lay in wait. Pandarus uses this image when he reveals his plan to Troilus:

> 'Lo, hold the at thi triste cloos, and I
> Shal wel the deer vnto thi bowe dryue.' (2.1534–5)

In the prologue to book three, Chaucer uses a similar image as he ponders the reasons why people fall in love:

> Whan they kan nought construe how it may jo
> She loueth hym, or whi he loueth here,
> As whi this fissh, and naught that, comth to were. (3.33–5)

The *were* is a trap for fish, another image of confinement. These two representations of what happens in love simply augment the typical idea of love at first sight. The prologue in which the second such image occurs in fact addresses Venus as the 'blisful light':

> O blisful light, of which the bemes clere
> Adorneth al the thridde heuen faire. (3.1–2)

The idea of confinement fits well in the immediate context Chaucer has established as well as in the overall design of the work. Awareness of visual circumstances includes spatial concreteness.

As at Criseyde's home, and in keeping with the hunting images, the scene at Deiphebus' home relies on movement and the judicious use of locations, culminating in their meeting face to face. The circle begins to tighten with Troilus and Criseyde in the same home. This initial step actually accentuates their separation as the locations become more precisely related and integral to the plot. The characters gathered for dinner speak of Troilus as someone other, removed from their company. Then Helen and Deiphebus go in and see Troilus in his small chamber. Chaucer follows their movements afterwards, again to establish firmly the blocking of his drama:

> Downward a steire, in-to an herber greene,
> This ilke thing they redden hem bitwene;

> And largely, the mountance of an houre,
> Thei gonne on it to reden and to poure. (2.1705–8)

This sets the scene for Pandarus first to peek in on Troilus at the curtain (3.60), announce Criseyde's arrival, to which Troilus responds, 'I se nought trewely' (3.67), and then lead Criseyde into Troilus' chamber, so that the circle continues to close in on their union. To use a motif from Dante, this is like the passage to another level upwards to the place where the poet sees his beloved. Chaucer will offer a vision similar to Dante's from a point beyond the earth, but will change to context in some vital respects.

Visual localization in *Troilus and Criseyde* continues with the shift in locus for the bedroom scene. Whereas Boccaccio uses the least number of locations possible, Chaucer multiplies them so that they represent various stages in psychological development. In the little closet their vision will be fulfilled and their perspectives melded as they reach the absolute centre of their love. As we have now come to expect, Chaucer complicates the secretive meeting. Criseyde's ladies-in-waiting sleep just outside the room; Pandarus appears at a trap-door and passes through the room to close the main door; finally Troilus appears at the trap-door. In this confined space Chaucer creates a small bustle of activity. Before long, Troilus faints and the movement towards the very centre, the bed, requires one last dramatic push from Pandarus. With this, the inexorable movement from temple to bed dissolves and such staging in the poem never again acquires the same importance. Pandarus leaves with his candle, all distractions are forgotten, and Troilus finds the paradise standing in Criseyde's eyes. Afterwards, Chaucer will maintain this complex of ideas by including the activity and searching, reflective gazing of Troilus, but he turns his attention to the philosophical inquiry that depends upon another understanding of sight. This leads us to consider the hospitality of love and knowledge in the context of metaphysical visions.

The phenomenon of physical sight as understood and applied in medieval thought and poetry, especially after Jean de Meun, allows for and results in the considerable interpenetration of love and knowledge. Chaucer portrays this overlap in numerous ways, calling attention to language, to sexual politics, to community and plenitude, to psychological circumstances. They variously constitute part of the real complexity of love as he perceives it.

6

The Interference of Self-reflexiveness
The Poet and the *Parasitisme* of
Love and Knowledge

> But whenever the sentence 'I see the tree' is so uttered that
> it no longer tells of a relation between the man – I – and
> the tree – Thou –, but establishes the perception of the tree
> as object by the human consciousness, the barrier between
> subject and object has been set up. The primary word I-It,
> the word of separation, has been spoken.[1]
>
> (Martin Buber)

> Love itself cannot persist in the immediacy of relation;
> love endures, but in the interchange of actual and potential
> being.[2]   (Martin Buber)

> For he hath toold of loveris up and doun
> Mo than Ovide made of mencioun.[3]   (Chaucer)

The relationship between love and knowledge in medieval poetry is a parasitic
system comprising elements of hostility and hospitality. The poet's self- conscious awareness that in broaching the subject of love he somehow denies its
essence contributes to the system. Martin Buber offers a helpful perspective on
the functioning of relation and nonrelation when he appeals to the phenomenal
epistemology of vision and integrates that into an analysis of what happens in
other relationships, including those of love. Buber's theological philosophy
ostensibly focuses on a problem of relation based on knowing, yet his epistemology finds application in the discourse of love: he transforms epistemology
into a discourse rooted in social as well as cerebral reality.[4] In doing so, he

---

1   Martin Buber, *I and Thou*, trans. R.G. Smith, Edinburgh, 1959, 23.
2   Buber, 99.
3   *Canterbury Tales*, II.53–4.
4   This refreshing direction has also been taken recently in philosophy by Alasdair MacIntyre in *After Virtue: A Study in Moral Theory*, London, 1985. In terms specifically of her-
meneutics, Tom Wright has argued persuasively for a relational epistemology. N.T. Wright,

restates a late medieval concern: the tension between the immediacy of relation and the articulation of that relation. For Buber, sight easily allows for the immediacy of relation, what he calls an I-Thou relation: 'There is nothing from which I would have to turn my eyes away in order to see, and no knowledge that I would have to forget. Rather is everything, picture and movement, species and type, law and number, indivisibly united in this event.'[5] Buber's language recalls the principles of medieval aesthetics. Indeed, his choice of sight as a means to express the potential for indivisible unity and the paradox inherent in this situation reflects the various ways in which love, knowledge, and sight function as a system.

Medieval poetry approximates this situation in the overlap of spiritual and physical discourses of sight. Its language closely resembles that of late medieval thought, with the emphasis on law and number, species, speed, and pain. The narrator, like the medieval practitioner who diagnoses lovesickness, for example, is clearly often in the position of describing a relationship that disallows analysis *and* of making an utterance that establishes perception by human consciousness and sets up the barrier. Buber, like Serres, and, I submit, like the best medieval love poets, does not rue this situation or choose (in vain) to pass over it silently, because he recognizes that love cannot persist in the immediacy of relation. For Chaucer, his position combines the pleasure of narration with the freedom, and the challenge, to enter into the situation as self-conscious narrator, as voyeur, as analyst of epistemological complexity. Love poetry consequently endures in the interchange of actual and potential being.

The participation of the poet/narrator in the system of love and knowledge receives extensive treatment on the basis of sight in medieval literature, especially in Chaucer's poetry. A link exists between the role played by sight in medieval accounts of love and the role of sight as a means by which, as one critic has written, 'the private activities of lovers can be brought to public knowledge, and as actions which may themselves become sexually charged.'[6] Telling such a story well, so that an awareness of its essentially private nature remains, is a part of the literary achievement. This process binds the narrator/audience in the processes of I-Thou/I-It. Medieval poetry often reveals an internal contradiction in its disclosure of what it means to hide, especially sexual knowledge. A.C. Spearing identifies this disclosure as voyeurism, which

The New Testament and the People of God, London, 1992, 32–46. Like Buber, both of these current thinkers collocate the issues of epistemology with some form of the discourse of love. See also Vincent Brümmer, *The Model of Love: A Study in Philosophical Theology*, Cambridge, 1993.

5   Buber, 7.

6   A.C. Spearing, 'The Medieval Poet as Voyeur,' in *The Olde Daunce: Love, Friendship, Sex, and Marriage in the Medieval World*, ed. Robert R. Edwards and Stephen Spector, New York, 1991, 57. Spearing has followed up this article with a book-length study, *The Medieval Poet as Voyeur: Looking and Listening in Medieval Love-Narratives*, Cambridge, 1993. The following references are to his 1991 article.

implicates the narrator and, by extension, the audience, both of whom see the ostensibly private act, whatever that may be, performed before them. In one of the poems that he uses to exemplify this voyeurism, a maiden relates how a knight ravished her with only a nightingale looking on, a witness that will not betray her. The speaker has betrayed her own shame and effectively put the reader in the place of the nightingale. For Spearing, this exemplifies the 'self-consciousness or reflexivity' of the medieval poet and emerges especially when the subject is love, that 'essentially private experience,'[7] where knowledge is severely circumscribed. To narrate about love is to break its privacy: the narrator and, subsequently, the audience are, by implication, secret onlookers. Instances abound in which the privacy of love, or the separation of love and knowledge, gives way to narration. One might conclude that 'the element of voyeurism in a narrative about love is brought to our attention, so that it functions not as a silent necessity for that favorite kind of medieval narrative, but as something in which we as readers are knowingly implicated, so that the excitement and the shame of voyeurism become parts of the narrative effect.'[8] Medieval poets often do bring this element of self-consciousness to bear upon their narratives, but voyeurism is only one manifestation of something more basic that is going on here.

What, you may ask, could be more basic than sex? For a starter, Spearing himself points out that voyeurism represents a perversion of natural sexuality; it is therefore already tangential.[9] This is not to say that allusions to perversion are irrelevant to a discourse of love: Chaucer and other writers happily get what mileage they can out of various manifestations of love. We can and will stay within the realm of sex and love: but voyeurism is simply one aspect of the medieval poets' exploration of the multifarious ways in which love and knowledge interpenetrate. Spearing's understanding of what happens when a narrator raises the subject of love in this way is thoroughly Freudian. The methodology is not to be dismissed as anachronistic (Freudian situations could and did arise in characters antedating the psychoanalyst) but it makes light of some of the material in its late medieval context. The position of the poet overlaps with the tension between love and knowledge as understood by medieval culture. He becomes implicated in this dialectic, and furthers the narrative effect through the excitement and paradox of extending the dialectic between love and knowledge, a phenomenon that is both intellectual and sexual. Because it inevitably

---

7   Spearing, 62.
8   Spearing, 62–3.
9   He quotes a popularizer of Freud: 'Perversions are forms of incomplete maturity of sexual object and aim, which prevent full union of any kind with another individual. Among them may be included voyeurism, where looking at other people of the same or opposite sex naked, watching others having sexual intercourse, seeking to see the genitalia of others, or watching them in the act of urination or defecation, takes the place of a more complete sexual aim.' David Stafford-Clark, *What Freud Really Said*, Harmondsworth, 1967, 99, quoted by Spearing, 60.

draws attention to their position as articulators of love, what Spearing calls voyeurism draws attention to the system as such. It is a manifestation of *parasitisme* or interference. The poet and the audience participate in the immediacy of relation and the undoing of that relation. Love itself cannot exist in the immediacy of relation. The relation becomes a perception by human consciousness on the part of the narrator that nonetheless interferes with the actuality of the I-Thou relation.

The position of the narrator and the audience is one of participation in the process of love: that process incorporates love and reason and the onlooker participates in this dialectic. The fact that this involvement normally hinges upon the act of seeing simply confirms the onlooker's entanglement. When Beroul's Tristan discovers Godoïne spying on him and Iseult, he shoots him with an arrow through the eye, an interesting variation on love at first sight. Spearing adeptly points out that the story contains many episodes that indicate that it concerns an act of voyeurism and he encourages us to see the narrator and ourselves as voyeurs.[10] The same terms that dominate the discourse of love in its purity and appear in efforts to create hospitality between love and reason also appear when the emphasis rests on the onlooker. This persisting collocation of motifs – love, knowledge, vision (including the arrow) – suggests rather strongly that the poet has drawn attention to his own and the audience's participation in this complex of ideas. That participation is unavoidable, one manifestation of a paradox that can find diminished expression in manifestations such as voyeurism but which provokes considerable intellectual, artistic, and metaphysical expression in the Middle Ages.

A brief example from a poet who influenced Chaucer considerably may serve well to orient our minds further towards the ways in which poetic self-reflexiveness operates in terms of love, knowledge, and sight in Chaucer's works. In Machaut's poetry, visual concepts have an important function in working self-reflexively. His many visual allusions naturally provide extensive examples of the medieval interest in light and colour. In *Le Jugement dou Roy de Behaingne*, Machaut quickly calls attention to a viewing subject, a wanderer familiar to us in dream-poetry such as this; he calls attention as well to the subject's reaction to the dazzling light, preparing the ground for an exploration of visual phenomena. As the poem unfolds, Machaut calls increasing attention not merely to visual effects but to the relationship between the viewing subject and the viewed object. In order to enjoy the day and the singing birds without being seen, the day dreamer had concealed himself beneath the trees. From this vantage point, he sees a lady deep in thought and a knight approaching each other. Thinking they are lovers, our onlooker hides himself further, and suddenly his experience becomes voyeuristic. The narrator's perception of the physical scene is of some importance to Machaut. The theme of beauty and the way love penetrates the heart through the eyes produce an interpretive crux in

10 Spearing, 65–9.

Machaut's poetry. The idea of beauty, its perception, and the role of the eyes as agents together lead to physical issues. As Daniel Poirion has observed, 'The abstract idea of beauty, the principle of love, leads to a more concrete vision. With the theme of vision, or "the look," of the eye through which desire penetrates the heart, the vision of physical nature reorganizes the poetry. . . . The poetic language gets closer to the art of painting.'[11] Poirion points out that Machaut's poetry focuses attention of the role of the Ego, on the Ego's perspective, and that this for him represents a developing interest in realistic, earthbound perspective: 'the scenes of life are no longer perceived and interpreted from God's point of view, at least not without referring to the human situation of the poet which defines the appearance and the meaning of things.'[12] Although Poirion overstates Machaut's intellectual position, the French poet certainly participates in a movement in which attention becomes focused on observers with an increasingly developed naturalistic perspective. And the Ego in question is predominantly the author. The human situation of the poet includes his situation as self-conscious observer.[13]

If we turn again to Chaucer's poetry, we find throughout his work clear examples of his self-consciousness as a love poet, his awareness that he paradoxically interferes with yet sustains love: that through him the interchange of actual and potential being persists. When Chaucer draws attention to himself, as he does in the Introduction to the Man of Law's Tale, he puts himself in a tradition of writers that 'hath toold of loveris,' breaking their secrets, relating what defies expression.[14] He accentuates the paradoxicality of his position. He tells us he 'kan but lewedly/On metres and on rymyng craftily' (1147–8),

---

[11]   Poirion, 200–1.

[12]   Poirion, 204. Kevin Brownlee elaborates upon the importance in this poem of narrative perspective, highlighted in part by radical shifts in perspective from a first-person narrative voice apparently as lover to narrator as witness to reappearance as character and then 'retransformation' into witness. Kevin Brownlee, *Poetic Identity in Guillaume de Machaut*, Madison, 1984, 158–71. He argues that the shifts in the narrator's stance help emphasize the subordinate relationship of narrator to poet and affirm the primacy of the poet/text relationship (see esp. 167).

[13]   Badel argues that Machaut is the first poet in French 'à réfléchir sur la poésie, à la contempler, à en faire la théorie' (93). He sees French literature moving from 'un état spontané' to an 'état réflexif' (93). Hult's thesis on the reasons for the 'unfinished' state of Guillaume's part of *Le Roman de la Rose* offers a counterbalance to these claims for the novelty of Machaut's achievement. Nonetheless, Machaut's poetry signals important developments in a literature which Chaucer knew well.

[14]   Dryden comments in his preface to *Fables Ancient and Modern* that both Ovid and Chaucer have a painterly manner: 'I see Baucis and Philemon as perfectly before me as if some ancient painter had drawn them; and all the pilgrims in the *Canterbury Tales*, their humours, their features, and the very dress as distinctly as if I had supped with them at the Tabard in Southwark' (558). This is a useful insight as a comment on the powerful role of the Chaucerian 'I' as observer: Chaucer presents both perceiving subjects and perceived objects. But he recognizes that his involvement goes beyond simply the presentation of pictures or images.

apparently incapable of putting tales of love into proper form, and that he 'hath toold of loveris up and doun,' suggesting that the sublime has become, in his hands, pedestrian, merely the useful subject matter of an author churning out one tale after another. Of course we easily recognize Chaucer's self-deprecating ironic wit but he has drawn attention to the relationship between the author and the subject of love. *The House of Fame*, the Prologue to *The Legend of Good Women*, *Troilus*, and the last fragments of the *Canterbury Tales* all consider the possible roles of the observer/linguistic reporter, putting the establishment of perception in visual terms. Chaucer also clearly and repeatedly establishes the difference between lovers and himself as one who writes but does not experience love firsthand. This self-reflexiveness contributes incalculably to the paradoxical relationship between love and knowledge which we have traced throughout Chaucer's poetry in visual terms.

Fame, the Daisy, and the Author

The development of our understanding of Chaucer's self-reflexiveness as a love poet begins with the close relationship between language and vision. The Neoplatonic viewpoint on language which Chaucer undoubtedly encounters finds clear endorsement in Boethius, where it is interwoven with the themes of love, reason, and sight. His explication of the battle between reason and passion and the accompanying illustration from the myth of Orpheus has proved particularly useful and pertinent. Lady Philosophy dismisses her subject's accusation that she has been deceiving him with labyrinthine arguments and introduces that final metre of book 3 with an appeal to Plato which surely stays in Chaucer's mind:

> But natheles, yif I have styred resouns that ne ben nat taken from withouten the compas of the thing of whiche we treten, but resouns that ben bystowyd withinne that compas, ther nys nat why that thou schuldest merveillen, sith thow hast lernyd by the sentence of Plato that nedes the wordis moot be cosynes to the thinges of whiche thei speken. (3.pr12)

Here we have Boethius' philosophy of language; he follows it up with the vivid metrical analogy of sight we considered as part of the hostility of love and knowledge. Chaucer may or may not share Boethius' view of language, but the *Consolation* sets a useful precedent for incorporating the problem of communicating knowledge into the set of concerns we have already examined. Epistemology provides a suitable environment for the various activities of *parasitisme*, especially the interference of self-reflexiveness.

The conflict between passion and reason is front and centre in the *Consolation of Philosophy*. If the book ends with a clarification and consolidation of the value of knowledge in the cosmic scheme of things, it is born in the turmoil of passion opposing knowledge. The way in which Boethius expresses the malevolent power of passion is especially pertinent to Chaucer's concerns as a poet. When Lady Philosophy appears at the prisoner's bedside, the first thing she does is to drive away the muses:

> And whan she saughe thise poetical muses aprochen about my bed and enditynge wordes to my wepynges, sche was a litel amoeved, and glowede with cruel eighen. 'Who,' quat sche, 'hath suffred aprochen to this sike man thise comune strompettis of swich a place that men clepen the theatre? The whiche nat oonly ne asswagen noght his sorwes with none remedies, but thei wolden fedyn and noryssen hym with sweete venym. Forsothe thise ben tho that with thornes and prikkynges of talentz or affeccions, whiche that ne bien nothyng fructifyenge nor profitable, destroyen the corn plenyvous of fruytes of resoun.' (1.pr1)

Lady Philosophy makes a clear distinction between reason and passion and banishes both passion and the muses of poetry that feed it. For Boethius, reason and passion are in exact opposition, and the banishment of passion is the first step on the road to recovery. Full health entails self-knowledge in the cosmic sense, or correct vision. At the end of the first book, Lady Philosophy delivers her diagnosis, and it focuses on her patient's lack of knowledge:

> 'Now woot I,' quod sche, 'other cause of thi maladye, and that ryght greet: thow hast left for to knowen thyselve what thou art. . . . But I thanke the auctour and the makere of hele, that nature hath nat al forleten the. I have gret noryssynges of thyn hele, and that is, the sothe sentence of governance of the werld, that thou bylevest that the governynge of it nis nat subgit ne underput to the folye of thise happes aventurous, but to the resoun of God.' (1.pr6)

The patient needs to build upon his not-quite-lost awareness of the power of divine reason to regain a proper understanding of his own true nature and place in the cosmos. Ultimately this knowledge takes the form of an acceptance of divine foresight and oversight. Apparently these abilities are lost when one pays attention to the muses. The activities of reading and writing perpetuate the struggle between love and reason. Chaucer clearly does not banish the muses but rather lives in the tension of love and reason that draws attention to the function of the poet.

Augustine cries the tears that Boethius' prisoner cries when the muses surround him. His analysis of the effect of poetry further defines the existing tension between reason and passion as it applies to the reader and poet. In *Confessions* 1, discussing aspects of his education and early attitude towards learning, he speaks of the value of his early lessons in reading and writing:

> For these elementary lessons were far more valuable than those which followed, because the subjects were practical. They gave me the power,

which I still have, of reading whatever is set before me and writing whatever I wish to write.[15]

He contrasts the practical value of these early lessons with the study of literature that followed. Augustine draws together a number of strands, discriminating between aspects of his secular education, commenting on the poverty of his spiritual education, and casting his spiritual immaturity in the form of thought:

> But in the later lessons I was obliged to memorize the wanderings of a hero named Aeneas, while in the meantime I failed to remember my own erratic ways. I learned to lament the death of Dido, who killed herself for love, while all the time, in the midst of these things, I was dying, separated from you, my God and my life, and I shed no tears for my own plight.
>
> What can be more pitiful than an unhappy wretch unaware of his own sorry state, bewailing the fate of Dido, who died for love of Aeneas, yet shedding no tears for himself as he dies for want of loving you? O God, you are the Light of my heart, the Bread of my inmost soul, and the Power that weds my mind and the thoughts of my heart. (1.13)[16]

Like Boethius, Augustine sees a fundamental contradiction between the role of poetry and other forms of knowledge. He is like the ailing prisoner in that he too responds to the muses and weeps over poetry. And his diagnosis of this phenomenon is essentially the same as Lady Philosophy's. He suffers from a lack of self-awareness, from both a divorce betweeen his mind and the thoughts of his heart and ignorance of his place in God's creation. If for Boethius the conflict is between passion and reason, for Augustine it is similarly between love and understanding. The example he chooses to elaborate upon the effects of poetry is the love affair between Dido and Aeneas. It is the fate of Dido, that she 'killed herself for love,' that directly causes his tears. Augustine cites this incident to express his understanding of a proper education and his own intellectual weakness. Ironically, love literature helps him to gauge his intellectual development, even though for Augustine true knowledge ought to exclude the

---

[15] *Conf.* 1.13. 'Nam utique meliores, quia certiores, erant primae illae litterae, quibus fiebat in me et factum est et habeo illud, ut et legam, si quid scriptum invenio, et scribam ipse, si quid volo.'

[16] '. . . quibus tenere cogebar Aeneae nescio cuius errores oblitus errorum meorum et plorare Didonem mortuam, quia se occidit ab amore, cum interea me ipsum in his a te morientem, deus, vita mea, siccis oculis ferrem miserrimus.

Quid enim miserius misero non miserante se ipsum et flente Didonis mortem, quae fiebat amando Aenean, non flente autem mortem suam, quae fiebat non amando te, deus, lumen cordis mei et panis oris intus animae meae et virtus maritans mentem meam et sinum cogitationis meae?'

affections. Even the wedding that occurs between the mind and heart is between knowledge and thoughts; it is not a marriage of reason and passion.

Like Augustine, Chaucer encounters the story of Dido and Aeneas, and he reports his reaction to it in *The House of Fame*. He too shows every sign of being swept away by the current of the poetry. He too recognizes that the poetry is a force and that he can analyze its effects, trying to put its power into perspective. The foregoing passage from the *Confessions* helps us to appreciate that the act of reading does provoke general questions about the nature of learning. In *The House of Fame* Chaucer learns in a number of ways besides reading. Reading, then, is one part of a larger undertaking, the acquisition of knowledge. Unlike Augustine, Chaucer does not offer the same evaluation of reading poetry. Whereas for the Church father such reading is affective and contrasts with the certainty of acquiring basic skills or essential spiritual knowledge, for Chaucer it provokes positive questions of his relationship as poet to *auctoritas*. He is conscious of the role of the individual in negotiating the past, hearsay, truth. His is a humanistic response, where knowledge in whatever form has become interesting *per se*. In the character of the garrulous eagle, Chaucer effectively makes knowledge less sacrosanct, more accessible. The eagle is therefore his backhanded compliment to the subject. Critics have pointed out that with the eagle Chaucer takes on Dante and parodies his device of a spiritual guide. Dante himself participates in the quest for knowledge, and it is not this that Chaucer goes after. Dante interleaves naturalistic learning with spiritual certainty and thereby continues to encourage the elevated treatment of learning. Chaucer changes the context, so that even though a teaching eagle may be a fabulous idea it is not charged with notions of religious dogma – the sort of truth having the stamp of authenticity that comes from revelation and is beyond proving.

Chaucer's way into this complex of problems is to address the subject of dreams, which allows him to draw attention to issues of authority and connect them with the idea of sight as knowledge. The medieval dream-vision has its sources in philosophical visions such as Cicero's *Somnium Scipionis*, preserved by Macrobius, and Boethius' *Consolation of Philosophy*, as well as a thriving tradition of religious visions, inspired by the Old and New Testaments, especially the Apocalypse, and the mysticism of Dionysius. The issue of authority is prominent whenever dreams are discussed, as suggested by Macrobius' initial division of dreams into those which are substantial and those which are meaningless. With the thirteenth-century *Roman de la Rose*, the dream-vision is lastingly transformed into a powerful form of love literature. By the time that Chaucer is writing, the dream-vision combines several elements: interest in authoritative sources of knowledge (which have some connection with seeing); the theme of love; literary realism.[17] Although the

---

17   A.C. Spearing points out that by the fourteenth century there was a movement towards realism: 'This movement towards a kind of realism, at least of surface, is typical of the later

dream-vision is a subject in itself, as a number of studies have shown, a cursory examination reveals how Chaucer links the themes of love, knowledge, and the phenomenon of sight.

Chaucer's concern over the value of dreams is pronounced in the proem to *The House of Fame*. Chaucer is clearly familiar with Macrobius' analysis of the various kinds of dreams. The speaker of the proem apparently finds the whole enterprise inscrutable and makes that point repeatedly: 'For hyt is wonder, be the roode,/ To my wyt' (2–3); 'Why this a fantome, why these oracles,/ I not; but whoso of these miracles/ The causes knoweth bet then I,/ Devyne he, for I certeinly/ Ne kan hem noght' (11–15); 'But why the cause is, noght wot I' (52). Part of the problem also is the unreliability of dreams:

> And why th'effect folweth of somme,
> And of somme hit shal never come. (5–6)

The speaker's reaction to the ambiguity surrounding dreams is to invoke spiritual comfort, but it sounds more like a pipe-dream than a considered hope:

> God turne us every drem to goode!
> For hyt is wonder, be the roode . . . . (1–2)

The repetition of calling on the cross at the end of the proem increases the resonance of this phrasing as well as the writer's admission of futility:

> For I of noon opinion
> Nyl as now make mensyon,
> But oonly that the holy roode
> Turne us every drem to goode! (55–8)

He places this discourse further in the realm of the religious by referring to dreams as 'these miracles' (12). The demonstrative would seem to apply to the entire list of different dreams, the effect of which follows some, some of which have various causes, *et cetera*. Chaucer implies that the phenomenon of the dream is itself a miracle, a marvel for its built-in ambiguity. The implication of this language is that one needs special insight to understand dreams; in the language of the Church, one needs illumination. But for Chaucer illumination does not mean that one will understand the message of various dreams but rather, fundamentally, that dreams present a plethora of interpretive possibilities, many of which are viable at a given time. Even as he couches his pro-

medieval arts in general, and it is of great importance for the development of the dream-poem, involving a new interest in the realities of sleep and dreaming, in the poet-dreamer's real life, and in his personality and social status.' A.C. Spearing, *Medieval Dream-Poetry*, Cambridge, 1976, 42.

legomenon in religious language he shifts attention away from metaphysical
types of vision to a kind of vision rooted in natural experience.

What follows is a dream but the subject matter has much more to do with
secular poetic interests than it does with spiritual truth. We have already
pointed out the conflict between poetry and divine wisdom as expressed by
Augustine and Boethius. Here Chaucer pursues the concept of vision *à propos*
spiritual literature but applies it to the mental operations of a reader. Inside the
temple of Venus, the dreamer finds the opening lines of the *Aeneid* inscribed in
a table of brass. After quoting six lines, however, he switches from the strict
idea of reading to that of seeing:

> And tho began the story anoon,
> As I shal telle yow echon.
>   First sawgh I the destruction . . . . (149–51)

'Sawgh I' or some variation thereof becomes a rubric for the recounting of the
story over the course of the following 300-odd lines. After the opening quotation the brass table contains carved images rather than words, a sort of Bayeux
tablet. As he finishes recounting the story the dreamer marvels,

> Yet sawgh I never such noblesse
> Of ymages, ne such richesse,
> As I saugh graven in this chirche. (471–3)

This ambiguity mirrors the proximity of reading and the inner process of visu-
alization; in a dream they are both inward, doubling the proximity. The emphasis on sight also highlights the physical basis for this metaphor. Although the
dream frames the dreamer's activity in the temple, the act of perception involved in the physical act of reading becomes interwoven with the physicality
of dreaming as well as the strictly internal kinds of sight. Chaucer alludes to
this physical aspect of dreaming in the proem:

> As yf folkys complexions
> Make hem dreme of reflexions. (21–2)

Pertelote's rationalization of dreams in the Nun's Priest's Tale also depends on
such a basis; so too, in another way, does *The Book of the Duchess'* dreamer's
melancholy make him dream of a man in black.

With the act of reading completed, the dreamer tries to orient himself in his
mental landscape and again the motif of vision becomes integral to the act:

> When I out at the dores cam,
> I faste aboute me beheld.
> Then sawgh I but a large feld,

> As fer as that I myghte see,
> Withouten toun, or hous, or tree
> . . .
> Ne no maner creature
> That ys yformed be Nature
> Ne sawgh I, me to rede or wisse.
> 'O Crist,' thoughte I, 'that art in blysse,
> Fro fantome and illusion
> Me save!' And with devocion
> Myn eyen to the hevene I caste. (480–4; 489–95)

Within the context of a dream, the viator tries to come to terms with his surroundings in a phenomenal way, seeking the sure ground of personal experience. This is the same kind of attitude that he exhibits outside the dream. He
finds this basis, however, to offer no comfort and spontaneously prays to be
saved 'Fro fantome and illusion,' though of course he has no awareness of
being in a dream. Chaucer uses the situation to combine the sight of reading, a
hoped for phenomenal basis, and the vision of some sort of devotion; he builds
upon the admixture of ideas with which he began the poem.

Book 2 of *The House of Fame* consolidates the place of this dream as being
in the tradition of famous dreams. Once again Chaucer draws on the *Somnium
Scipionis* as the eagle gives him an alternative perspective on the earth. The
eagle himself points out that

> 'half so high as this
> Nas Alixandre Macedo;
> Ne the kyng, Daun Scipio,
> That saw in drem, at poynt devys,
> Helle and erthe and paradys.' (914–18)

The journey with the garrulous eagle is an adventure in learning for the
dreamer, in which the metaphor of sight serves as a thematic focal point. The
most reliable of the outer wits is integral to this discussion of natural philosophy, cold hard facts; while the subordinate wit of hearing plays a prominent role
in book 3, at the house of Fame. As he listens, the dreamer looks down and at
first sees his world laid out like a map. Soon his perspective changes:

> But thus sone in a while he
> Was flowen fro the ground so hye
> That al the world, as to myn yë,
> No more semed than a prikke. (904–7)

Looking up he sees the Milky Way and the 'ayerissh bestes' and this experience
induces a meditation on Boethius and the weakness of unfettered thought. The

dreamer sensibly stops looking around him but his guide takes exception, arguing that this has implications for his ability to read poetry. But the dreamer has two excuses: he bows to the authorities and he claims that the constellations are so bright that the light could blind him.

The first line of book 3 encapsulates the terms with which Chaucer plays throughout the entire poem:

> O God of science and of lyght. (1091)

He is at play even here for the god he apostrophizes is Apollo, not the Christian God. Nonetheless, the religious idea of God as the Father of lights and source of all knowledge, the divine illumination that is shed upon our minds, stands behind all his play with dream theory, reading, experience, and the acquisition of knowledge from authority. The playfulness continues with a pun on light that takes us to the heart of his concerns as a maker of poetry:

> Nat that I wilne, for maistrye,
> Here art poetical be shewed,
> But for the rym ys lyght and lewed,
> Yit make hyt sumwhat agreable,
> Though som vers fayle in a sillable;
> And that I do no diligence
> To shewe craft, but o sentence. (1094–1100)

From brilliance we move to unsophisticated rhyme. Apparently. Light has strong associations with effective rhetoric. In the Prologue to the Clerk's Tale Harry Bailey asks the Clerk to tell a tale of adventure and to keep his terms, colours, and figures in storage. The Clerk responds with a reference to Petrarch,

> 'whos rethorike sweete
> Enlumyned al Ytaille of poetrie,
> As Lynyan dide of philosophie.' (IV.32–4)

The use of light imagery to convey the sense of effective rhetoric closely resembles the way light means intellectual insight. Chaucer wants Apollo to shed this kind of light on his poetry: to assist in the meter even though it will fail in the occasional syllable; and ostensibly to help him communicate the *sentence* above all. His insistence that 'I do no diligence/ To shewe craft, but o sentence' reveals a contradiction in his objectives. The tentativeness with which Chaucer treats knowledge in this poem, which the multiple meanings of sight and light reflect, deconstructs the intention of communicating 'o sentence.' The whole of the artistic creation which is *The House of Fame* is a kind of dream, subject to the baffling criticisms and cautions voiced in the opening proem. The poetic act is a dream, a kind of naming similar to Macrobius' fiction of naming dreams.[18] Chaucer embeds his entire discussion of the poetic enterprise, including the act of reading, receiving literary tradition, understanding and communicating knowledge, within a dream. All along he causes the poem to shimmer, reflecting the light of rhetoric and indeed of science; all of this amounts to a *sentence* on medieval poetics, but not the sort implied by the self-effacing request to Apollo.

In the Prologue to *The Legend of Good Women* this self-reflexiveness again manifests itself. Chaucer's abiding interest in the dream-poetry in the relationship between authority and experience, the operations of the mind, the nature and place of reading, and the language of love once again find expression here. Chaucer does not completely work out any one of these concerns, but the image of the daisy presents possibilities that suggest continued interest and play on the poet's part rather than misguided amibition. The dream-vision itself again adds an extra dimension to his achievement in working with visual motifs in a quasi-intellectual framework; it eventually helps tie in other ideas of vision with more familiar ones associated with love, since dream-visions are often about love.

The Prologue opens with a contrast of experience and authority that invokes the most reliable of the outer wits. Speculating on the nature of heaven and hell, the narrator raises the spectre of uncertainty and then dispels it:

> For by assay ther may no man it preve.
> But God forbede but men shulde leve
> Wel more thing then men han seen with ye! (F.9–11)[19]

His contemplation of the realm of experience is brief, and having retreated from it he goes further and further into the realm of the mind. We have already seen Chaucer's illustration of the activity of the mind in reading in *The House of Fame*, in which the activity of the eye connects with authority rather than personal assay. Here he focuses on an internal mental process, the act of remembering, closely associated with reading:

> And yf that olde bokes were aweye,
> Yloren were of remembraunce the keye. (25–6)

Although the narrator claims to reverence books, his passion for May quickly

---

[18] Steven Kruger has an excellent discussion of the self-reflexivity of the dream-vision and the parallel complexity of oneiric and literary realms (130–40). With a similar interest in the relationship between dreaming and writing, in his analysis of Chaucer's authorial concerns in his early poetry Robert R. Edwards writes that Chaucer 'suggests that poetry assimilates in a strange sense to the operations of the mind. Consequently, poetry is not an analogue or product of perception but an essential element.' Robert R. Edwards, *The Dream of Chaucer: Representation and Reflection in the Early Narratives*, Durham and London, 1989, 9.
[19] All of this discussion pertains to the F version.

distracts him and keeps him distracted for the remainder of the Prologue. Two things happen at once: on the one hand, his passion draws him into the realm of love literature with the typical landscape of May and the importance of vision in love; on the other, he moves back into the realm of experience, though not for certain knowledge of anything, only for the enjoyment of his love. A. Blamires asserts that Chaucer 'is prepared to flirt with an empirically nuanced first person amatory mode in the *Prologue* only as a conspicuous truancy, from which he has prearranged an escape.'[20] Blamires strikes the right tone with the notion of flirting. Chaucer certainly could escape to the realm of books, especially as he insists on his own lack of experience. We gain insight into the complexity of the presence of the author, however, by the potentiality of both poles, potentiality that finds expression in visual terms in both cases.

The dreamer loves a flower, and not the symbolic rose either, but he wants to use the language of lovers to express his feelings:

> But helpeth, ye that han konnyng and myght,
> Ye lovers that kan make of sentement. (68–9)

The language incorporates the idea of light. Speaking of the daisy, he remarks,

> She is the clernesse and the verray lyght. (84)

There is something quintessential about this use of language, for where once the flowers used to be part of the typical scene of May into which the beloved would be introduced, here the beloved is part of that backdrop. Even in the *Roman*, the rose is introduced only after the scene has been painted. The language here has an immediacy that is most apparent when the narrator pulls apart the word 'daisy':

> That wel by reson men it calle may
> The 'dayesye,' or elles the 'ye of day.' (183–4)

The narrator loves an eye, and one cannot be certain whether Chaucer is employing metonymy here or not. In contrast to and perhaps in parody of the *Roman*, he gives us love for a flower *per se* using familiar, suggestive language. If this scenario has only so many possibilities, he makes a way for himself by transforming the flower into a person through the mechanism of a dream. Now he has more of the conventions of love literature at his disposal, though the god of love and his queen are dressed primarily in green, reminding us of the altogether natural basis of the dream. Significantly, the god of love has two fiery darts like the dart with which he pierced Amans' heart; in this and other ways Chaucer perpetuates the role of sight in the love vision. One of Chaucer's goals

---

20   A. Blamires, 'A Chaucer Manifesto,' *Chaucer Review* 24 (1989), 38.

in the Prologue appears to be to play with the motif of sight in love in a literal way. This effort results in some striking passages on the beauty of the daisy: Chaucer shows the resilience of love language, especially the motif of sight, in an unusual context.

Chaucer's dream-poetry gives us a composite picture of his concern for veracity and his recognition of how often truth involves factors other than simple experience. The poems begin with the narrator in a state of anxiety that produces a liminal experience. In his initial state he alludes to an indeterminable problem or to the conundrum of dreaming itself; once he has introduced the problem of knowledge and passed over into the dream proper, the subject matter of love usually gains the ascendancy. As in Jean de Meun's handling of the love vision, rationality can intrude and shape the dreamer's experience of the love scenario. To extend Poirion's idea of the emphasis placed on the Ego, the turmoil surrounding the dreamer calls attention to the role of the Ego. The abstract idea of beauty contributes to a more concrete vision; in Chaucer's poetry this is bound up with questions of the way the self knows and, in particular, with the way the poet, self-conscious as a knower, interacts with the love matter. In the Prologue, Chaucer is the author/lover who negotiates the immediacy of sense experience, dreaming process, and the authority of texts, all in the context of love. It is a process that produces no resolution: Chaucer can affirm elements of both authority and experience in the complex intellectual climate of his day, and both can be treated extensively and accurately in visual terms. But the poem does draw attention to the interference of the poet, who complicates the telling or retelling of a love story, regardless of the source of his knowledge.

Comic Interference in Troilus and Criseyde

Interference plays a crucial role in *Troilus*. From the outset Chaucer establishes a series of doubles which provide the structure for oscillation, exchange, and complication. The opening line

> The double sorwe of Troilus to tellen (1.1)

points to a two-pronged sorrow, and the exact nature of that two-pronged sorrow is open to some interpretation. It could mean the woe Troilus initially feels when he sees Criseyde in the temple, followed by the woe of losing her to Diomede; it could refer to his twofold loss of love and life; it could simply be an intensifier. The phrasing at least sets up a structure of doubleness that soon finds application in quite another way: the relationship of the author to his subject matter. That interaction has a counterpart in the story itself, in the relationship between Pandarus and the lovers. Both of these doubles complicate the basic idea the medieval love story as we have considered it, the attraction of lovers and the banishment of reason. *Troilus* undoubtedly provides that basic situation, but not only does it complicate such a scenario with a variety of intellectual and metaphysical possibilities, it complicates the essence of a love story with first the telling of the love story and the third-party manipulation of the love story. In the forms of the narrator and Pandarus, Chaucer gives us in this poem the interference of the self-conscious author.

Chaucer takes pains to differentiate between the state of lovers in general and himself as the author or servant to the god of love's servants. He does this with such regularity as to render the digression a feature of his love poetry. The strategy can readily be understood as one of endearment, for the self-deprecation is both humorous and disarming. The tactic, however, also reveals something of Chaucer's attitude towards the subject of love poetry and the relationship between the writer and his subject. The author distinguishes between the lover who truly has lost his mind to love and the poet writing about the lover's condition; yet Chaucer also includes himself in the formula of the love story. He includes a comment on his own condition so regularly as to raise the serious doubt as to whether or not he believes he could tell such a story without some such self-reference. It is not the lover in the story but the third party who is primarily responsible for the paradoxical relationship between love and reason . A lover such as Troilus, as we have seen, does wring his hands and think too much, yet the paradox of love and reason has other, deeper roots in the relationship of any outside commentator to such matter, a paradox rooted in the enduring presence of such a commentator. In *Troilus* the poet calls himself a servant to the god of love's servants, a title that describes the papal office and serves here to validate the poetic self-reflexiveness if only by associating his position with one of obvious authority, though he himself is 'fer . . . from his help in derknesse' (1.18). This brief description of his role accentuates the poet's awareness of his own participation in the system of love. Chaucer very clearly separates himself from the activity of true lovers; he is shrouded in darkness. Yet he helps lovers, stating their conditions, and recording their affairs.

Having insinuated himself into the system of love yet again, the narrator here has portentous knowledge of the outcome of the affair, knowledge which might be expected to work against the normal visceral effects of love. In spite of this opposition love blossoms and the story entrances the reader. Chaucer has such thorough control of the conventions of *fyn lovynge* that he invites the audience to forget what he makes known and instead to become like the prisoner with the muses at his side, before Lady Philosophy arrives. The poem raises love up out of the ashes of certain foreknowledge and in spite of the teller's own apparent lack of qualifications or experience in the suppression of reason by love. The knowledge that the narrator and his audience possess nonetheless recedes into the background as the love affair takes shape. By the time that Troilus sees Criseyde in the temple, the knowledge of the poet, the audience, and Troilus is replaced by the emotions of the moment, a testimony both to the power of love and the power of the poet who listens to the muses. This power is unremitting until the lovers are joined. Only then does the poet invite his audience to remember that

> But al to litel, weylaway the whyle,
> Lasteth swich ioie, y-thonked be fortune. (4.1–2)

Only then does knowledge reassert itself and the narrator's role in fostering the tension between love and knowledge again become the focal point. Chaucer shifts between the two situations, between the reality of love and knowledge in all its complexity and his self-consciousness in manipulating this system.

As Troilus and Criseyde in their own ways draw attention to divine foresight and the three eyes of Prudence, and as Troilus goes on an epistemological journey in which he has his eyes opened to various kinds of sight, the ideas at issue draw attention to the godlike control of the author at the same time as they deal with the very real medieval questions of insight and foresight.[21] Chaucer includes himself in the large questions that the poem raises in terms of sight. By posing as a historian, he locates the events of the poem in the past; through close attention to detail and a shift in emphasis, he creates a strong sense of the present; and by reminding his audience of the outcome in advance he supplies the future. The poet has an eye on all three aspects of time; he manipulates time and the nature of sight and presents himself as doing so. When he has Troilus repeat Boethius' allusion to seeing a man on a seat and then pursues metaphysical implications, he effectively makes it possible to conceive of references to ordinary physical sight as indicative of profound issues, including the issue of his own power and position as storyteller.

Troilus and Criseyde presents the inclusion of the third-party manipulator on a second level. Not only does the narrator form an integral part of the system, along with the lovers; within the story, Pandarus embodies that role again, mirroring the narrator in his knowledge, his involvement with lovers, and his own exclusion from such experience. In the character of this parasite, Chaucer develops the role of the poet-manipulator. The system of love and knowledge has a comic aspect to it, and is amenable to the implied comparison with

---

21   Edward Peter Nolan argues that the inclination towards the prudential derives from the act of beholding the self in the Other, the quality of looking in a mirror which is part of the convention of love at first sight, most famously in the pool of Narcissus scene in the *Roman de la Rose*. He points out that, in general, 'The new and providential self-knowledge may not accrue to the Lover; more often than not the image of the Lover beholding the Beloved acts as a speculum of possibility for the reader.' Edward Peter Nolan, *Now Through a Glass Darkly: Specular Images of Being and Knowing From Virgil to Chaucer*, Ann Arbor, 1990, 161. The prudential lesson draws the reader into the relationship between love and knowledge involving the two lovers. Douglas Kelly similarly pursues the idea in this context that the *reader* is aware of the distance separating him from his own perfection. In talking about the reader he goes on to say that 'Imagination as Memory is thus linked to Prudence' (37). He combines the courtly scenario with epistemology and involves the reader.

juggling: Pandarus keeps the balls in the air for the two lovers. The system of love and knowledge contributes incalculably to an atmosphere of entrancement. Part of the magic consists of not quite understanding the role of the manipulator. The third participant, either Pandarus or Chaucer, is at crucial times relegated to the role of observer, at which times his participation in the system becomes voyeuristic. His view of love provides him with tainted knowledge, from which in the poet's case he does not turn away before sharing his vision with the reader.

For the most part, Pandarus simply remains on the outside. Knowledgeable in the ways of love though without personal success, he juggles affairs for the lovers and brings them together. His helpful efforts, however, become more charged when he arranges for the lovers to meet in his home. In the beautifully erotic scene at his place, Pandarus becomes more than simply a go-between. He becomes entangled in the love affair, helping Criseyde get the faint Troilus into bed and undress him:

> But certeyn, at the laste,
> ffor this or that, he in-to bed hym caste,
> And seyde, 'O thef, is this a mannes herte?'
> And of he rente al to his bare sherte. (3.1096–9)

Eventually, Pandarus retreats with his lantern, though even as he does so he seems chagrined that he cannot see better:

> Quod Pandarus, 'for aught I kan aspien,
> This light nor I ne seruen here of nought.' (3.1135–6)

It is unclear whether or not he ever leaves the room. He appears suddenly again before retreating for good, at hand 'with a ful good entente' (3.1188) to lay the swooning Troilus to sleep, then is unheard from until the next day, when he bounces up to his niece's bed and comes to an understanding with Criseyde. Chaucer incorporates the ambiguity of Pandarus' role or motives to great effect, drawing attention to the third party in the void of failing to assign to him a place either inside or outside the room. A heightened awareness of the role of the observer, if not Pandarus than at least Chaucer and the reader, sharpens the senses and contributes to an appreciation of the love scene.[22] The onlooker has only knowledge in a situation where passion is overwhelming reason: self-consciousness interferes with the system and draws attention to it.

---

22   Linda Holley suggests that Chaucer uses visual cues to create the effect of spaces and borders, and the sense that we move into interior spaces through Chaucer's narrative telling: 'These nested spaces are presided over by Pandarus or the narrator or Chaucer and, ultimately, by the reader.' Linda Tarte Holley, *Chaucer's Measuring Eye,* Houston, 1990, 75. Her analysis of visual cues emphasizes the involvement of the author or reader in the telling of the love story.

The inclusion of a third party contributes to the achievement of eroticism in this passage and the story as a whole. Pandarus undoubtedly facilitates events, but he does much more than that. His presence, especially in the 'litel closet,' lays bare the complexity of presenting in art the essential tension of erotic love. This long poem gives us the twofold achievement of drawing attention to the poet as an observer who implicates himself in a great story, as well as the dramatization of the role of the third party.

Self-reflexiveness in the Canterbury Tales

Chaucer raises the problem of communication with reference to his role as a poet vis-à-vis the subject matter of love at several junctures in the *Canterbury Tales*. He first broaches the subject of communication in a general way in the General Prologue where he has already taken upon himself the role of observer. Having recorded his initial observations, he assumes a posture of weakness and in the process calls attention to the problematic work of the poet:

> But first I pray yow, of youre curteisye,
> That ye n'arette it nat my vileynye,
> Thogh that I pleynly speke in this mateere,
> To telle yow hir wordes and hir cheere,
> Ne thogh I speke hir wordes proprely. (I.725–29)

Words play a vital role in the transmission of knowledge, and Chaucer under-lines the importance of his concern by drawing attention to the language of Christ. In its immediate context, the reference signals how the pilgrim Chaucer wants divine sanction for whatever will follow. However lightly we may take his appeal, Chaucer realizes that issues of language have the broadest of poten-tial applications. The basic approach to the problem that he proffers, at least here, derives from the Platonic theory of correspondence that appears in Book 3 of the *Consolation*:

> Eek Plato seith, whoso kan hym rede,
> The wordes moote be cosyn to the dede. (I.741–2)

We can ill-afford to take this dictum on board as a clear indicator of Chaucer's opinion since, as Julian Wasserman reminds us, Chaucer often produces the exposition of a problem rather than the articulation of his own viewpoint.[23] Nonetheless, the question involves the relationship between words, communi-cation, or insight, and has pertinence for the subject matter of love, which more often than not is the 'dede' in question.

---

[23]   Julian N. Wasserman, 'The Ideal and the Actual: The Philosophical Unity of *Canterbury Tales*, MS. Group III,' *Allegorica* 7 (1982), 65.

The Wife of Bath's Prologue provides a useful indication of some of the issues of interference faced in communicating when the subject is love. Admittedly, the motif of sight does not enter into her Prologue, but the way Chaucer foregrounds and weds issues of philosophy and love in a relationship as twisted as any of Alice's marriages serves as a closely related study. The Wife of Bath certainly does tread on the territory of philosophy, going boldly there with a reference in her first breath to the two ways of acquiring knowledge: experience and authority. The Friar afterwards acknowledges the tenor of her discourse:

> Ye han heer touched, also moot I thee,
> In scole-matere greet difficultee. (III.1271–2)

One of the scholastic issues that the Wife of Bath addresses consistently emerges in the context of Chaucer's interest in sight as well: the problem of communicating what is known. She alludes to experience and authority, and aligns herself with empiricists, in the context of establishing her right 'to speke of wo that is in mariage' (III.3). As Wasserman has pointed out in his useful article on philosophy in Fragment III, Alice is 'a self-conscious narrator of her own life's story.'[24] This self-consciousness is a posture for claiming knowledge and the way to communicate it. Alice herself has no difficulty with epistemological questions or the problem of communication; her creator, however, seems more interested in the complex of problems associated with her prologue, especially that of narration, than in certain solutions.

Alice's self-conscious narration draws together the categories of knowledge and love. The woe that is in her marriage stands as a gnarled mutation of the ideal of love in marriage. In fact, however, she incarnates another discourse on love and knowledge, that of clerical antifeminism. Chaucer effectively transforms an existing discourse that assumes reason's authority to speak into matters of love; he places it in the realm of epistemology by focusing on the problem of authority *per se*; and he heightens awareness of the role of communication with a mock-sermon engaging this complex of issues. The case of the Wife of Bath involves current tensions of prevailing notions of wisdom and who administers it. Alice is a creation of clerical anti-feminist and anti-matrimonial sentiment, flourishing in the strange ground where rationality has been foisted upon love. Jerome's polemical tract *Adversus Jovinianum*, in which he countered Jovinian's claim that virginity was not necessarily a state superior to marriage, set the tone for future misogynistic rhetoric. Augmenting biblical references with personal disparaging remarks against women, Jerome's argument becomes increasingly aggressive. He goes on a tirade against the love of a woman and claims that a wife ranks among the greatest of evils: 'For he who marries a wife is uncertain whether he is marrying an odious

---

24 Wasserman, 67.

woman or one worthy of his love. If she be odious, she is intolerable. If worthy of love, her love is compared to the grave, to the parched earth and to fire.'[25] He abandons all pretensions of a carefully constructed scriptural rebuttal when he quotes at length from Theophrastus' anti-feminist tract, *On Marriage*. His rebuttal is excessive and hateful, leaving women and the institution of marriage without honour or dignity. Alice's fifth husband, Jankyn, has a volume of anti-feminist writings, including the pieces by Jerome, Theophrastus, and a third key medieval source, Walter Map's *Dissuasio Valerii ad Ruffinum ne uxorem ducat*.[26] The battle lines in the Prologue are clearly drawn.

The character of the Wife of Bath, inspired by clerical misogyny masquerading as wisdom, deconstructs typical love conventions. Out of that conflict he creates the Wife of Bath, a self-conscious narrator who transforms an existing clerical discourse that itself denies the power and prerogatives of love over reason. The Wife of Bath's Prologue enhances our understanding of Chaucer's awareness of the role of the narrator in the relationship between love and knowledge. Here that relationship is especially bizarre. Alice participates in and extends the parasitic relationship of these two categories simply by articulating her ideas on love; and she does that in a grand form, the mock-sermon; furthermore, she raises the subject of epistemology specifically in the context of love. The self-consciousness of her position as narrator fosters the awareness of the system of love and knowledge as handled by the communicator. Focusing on the narrator is the interference that completes the *parasitisme*.

Chaucer returns to linguistic issues in the penultimate fragment of the collection. In the Manciple's Tale, which has far-reaching implications for the project of the *Tales*, he collocates issues of communication with the fact of observation: seeing, knowing and communicating are all related here as they are in Chaucer's poetic. It starts with knowledge, through the reintroduction of Phebus, that character of science and light to whom Chaucer alludes in *The House of Fame*. There Phebus is a lofty figure, and the poet calls upon him to help him in his poetic work. Here, the god's circumstances are much more

---

[25] Jerome, 'Adversus Jovinianum,' PL 23, 211ff. Trans W.H. Fremantle. In The Library of Nicene and post-Nicene Christian Fathers 2nd ser., vol. 6, Oxford, 1893, 367–8.

[26] Robert Pratt has attempted to resuscitate Jankyn's book and further investigate the tradition of propaganda in the universities. He carefully marshalls manuscript evidence to show that, from about 1180–1280, there exist seven manuscripts containing both *Valerii ad Ruffinum* and *On Marriage* and three containing those two plus *Against Jovinian*. He concludes that to a fourteenth-century observer such as Chaucer, that combination may have seemed like a tradition (13). Examining other more obscure anti-matrimonial tracts that appear with excerpts or whole copies of these three pieces, he identifies connections with both Paris and Oxford. Pratt reaches two conclusions: that Chaucer's audience must have known something of the propaganda behind the Wife of Bath's Prologue, and that the struggle for celibacy brought about 'a sort of fourteenth-century Oxford movement' (27). Robert A. Pratt, 'Jankyn's Book of Wikked Wyves: Medieval Anti-matrimonial Propaganda in the Universities,' *Annuale Mediaevale* 3 (1962), 5–28.

pedestrian, and his science and light pale in his situation on earth. Chaucer establishes the context in the opening words of the tale:

> Whan Phebus dwelled heere in this erthe adoun . . . . (IX.1)

His domestic situation reveals the limitations of his famed abilities, both in his wife's ability to cheat on him secretly and his crow's greater awareness of what happens in his own home. Phebus and what he represents come into contact with love and the vision of the crow.

The crow brings the power of language to the heart of this situation. He speaks of what he has seen. He beholds the work of Phebus' wife and when Phebus comes home tells him so in language that recalls the straightforward manner of the Merchant, who 'kan nat glose, I am a rude man' (IV.2351):

> '. . . Blered is thyn ye
> With oon of litel reputacioun,
> Noght worth to thee, as in comparisoun,
> The montance of a gnat, so moote I thryve!
> For on thy bed thy wyf I saugh hym swyve.' (IV.252–6)

As the Manciple tells us, the crow compounds his error with 'sadde tokenes' and 'wordes bolde' (258), and by impressing upon Phebus the fact that 'ofte he saugh it with his yen' (261). The crow's entire communication mingles clear language with clear sight. He insists upon the empirical validity of his information and supplies Phebus with visual evidence, the 'sadde tokenes.' The evidence of sight provides incontrovertible knowledge which the crow injudiciously communicates to his master. Phebus' response confirms the human propensity for framing apparently simple conceptualizations with larger fictions; these naturally have profound implications for the way we value such clarity. January found a way to reinterpret or deny events in his own experience. The clear language and clear sight, at least initially, were his own; May, however, managed to manipulate language in such a way as to gain the upper hand. For Chaucer, the simplicity of language and the simplicity of facts become absorbed into further, complicating possibilities.

Chaucer invites us to consider carefully the question of clarity and insight by embedding complex issues of language and signification in the tale. Chaucer reintroduces the wisdom of Plato with which he concluded the General Prologue:

> The wise Plato seith, as ye may rede,
> The word moot nede accorde with the dede.
> If men shal telle proprely a thyng,
> The word moot cosyn be to the werkyng.
> I am a boystous man, right thus seye I:
> Ther nys no difference, trewely,

Bitwixe a wyf that is of heigh degree,
If of hir body dishonest she bee,
And a povre wenche, oother than this –
If it so be they werke bothe amys –
But that the gentile, in estaat above,
She shal be cleped his lady, as in love;
And for that oother is a povre womman,
She shal be cleped his wenche or his lemman. (IX.207–20)

The Manciple, a 'boystous' or plain man, tries to speak plainly of this manipulation of language, but as his story of the crow illustrates, such plain-speaking
is fraught with its own difficulties and internal contradictions. The Manciple
has identified a social reality and he apparently intends to reveal a social fiction
but his complaint has no more power than mere boisterousness. His language
in turn reveals how social discourse does not always reflect Plato's *sentence*.
Language creates realities that complicate the Manciple's insistence that 'ther
nys no difference, trewely. . . .' The moral itself emphasizes the Platonic line
by negation, apparently saying that to speak is necessarily to be brutally frank;
some of the other tales confirm this sentiment, but by no means all.

The Manciple's Tale reestablishes a rhetorical emphasis for evaluating
Chaucer's achievement throughout the *Tales*. It raises contemporary questions
of the nature of observed reality and does so by drawing into question the phenomenon of articulating those observations. It also incorporates the notion of
the authority of texts, as the Manciple draws upon Solomon, David, and Seneca
for much of his wisdom. In the case at hand, the onlooking crow puts the mysteries of love into words just as the poet does. But if he draws attention to the
phenomena of love, he also draws attention to himself: for the crow this is
ruinous; for Chaucer, such interference keeps the system of love, knowledge,
and poetic observation functioning. A white/black sign that returns us sugges-
tively to the realm of sight, the crow himself is another signifier with apparently
one clear signified, either white and unsullied by (revealed) knowledge or black
and tainted by independent knowledge. Phebus' vindictive power over the bird,
however, does not encapsulate the significance of the bird in Chaucer's overall
design for the tale. With its suggestiveness of the complex role of the author as
voyeur, knower, and reporter, the bird is already out of the cage regardless of
the punishment Phebus thinks he is imposing. The Manciple, when he declares,
'Kepe wel thy tonge and thenk upon the crowe' (362; cf. 315, 333, 346), has
not seen the nature of language and sign theory in their complexity. One viable
alternative is to be cautious about the correspondence between signifiers and
their signifieds and to question the truth value of vision but to continue to play
with signs and sight.

The Manciple's Tale ultimately condemns a reductive denial of human fictions. The clear message of the crow creates confusion and violence and
Chaucer suggests both in the 'boystous' words of the Manciple and of the crow

the subversive possibilities of plain speech. Furthermore, as the tale takes its place with all the others as part of an ambitious project, we see the implications of the poet's allusion to Plato in the General Prologue: some of the tales have been subversive because of plain talking. But silence could be more subversive yet. In the immediate context, if everyone listened to the sententious moral, the Parson would not take his turn. He exercises his right as part of the tale-telling fellowship by telling a meditation, entering into a very common form of medieval discourse. If we were to apply the Manciple's advice more broadly, the enterprise of the *Tales* would collapse. Chaucer affirms the great if sometimes destructive power of words. He does so here by integrating that theme with his stress on the centrality of sight, which has almost the same fundamental value and the same contemporary versatility and relevance as language. The Manciple's Tale reemphasizes the extent of his interest in visual motifs and his awareness of their complexity, a complexity that has profound relevance for himself as poet and articulator of the deeds of love.

The pilgrims make it at least as far as Bobbe-up-and-doun, under the Blee. They are close to Canterbury, but they never see it. They pass within sight of Deptford (I.3906) and Rochester (VII.1926), but a vision of Canterbury would put too much strain on the motif. Chaucer would have to declare certain priorities and the visual possibilities would narrow, as they necessarily finally do in *Pearl*. Without that vision, the other pressing issues of sight, beauty, knowledge, and the author's self-reflexive involvement, remain in sharp focus. The concepts of love and knowledge overlap to produce an area rich in paradox and in profound interconnection.

Conclusion

This study began with the consideration of aspects of love, knowledge, and sight in the metaphysical tradition that informs late medieval thought, and showed how those three terms form a complex system of *parasitisme*. It is in the metaphysical tradition that the relationship and tensions between love and knowledge are most evident and the development of which are easiest to trace; the motif of sight gives metaphysical writers perhaps their greatest access to these terms. Metaphysics informs later medieval natural philosophy and epistemology. The discourse of light and sight in these other disciplines ensures the viability of an extended consideration of the relationship between love and knowledge. This *parasitisme* is extensive and enters love literature at several points. It does so where literary convention accentuates the role of the eyes and draws upon natural philosophy and psychology to emphasize the nature and extent of their power; it does so also where love and knowledge represent a conventional bipolar opposition. The system of *parasitisme*, however, both confirms and confounds the anticipated hostility between love and knowledge. This situation is recognized, explored, and exploited by Chaucer and other medieval love poets with wide-ranging intellectual interests, among which are questions of the poet's position and what is involved in artistic expression. The functioning of love, knowledge, and sight stimulates Chaucer's discursive intellect; it proffers him both an opportunity and a model to explore his role as poet.

Chaucer is by no means the only English author to combine interest in physical science with metaphysical precepts and the phenomenon of love, especially erotic love, nor the only one to do so with an engaging appeal to visual motifs. The relationship between love and knowledge is a recurring feature in English poetry which lends itself to interdisciplinary treatment in the writings of a number of literary figures. The development of the tensions and intricacies involving these two concepts depends upon a healthy regard for the achievements of other fields and a confidence in the capacity of literature, especially love poetry, to accommodate a range of bracing ideas.

It is not surprising, therefore, to find that the next poet after Chaucer who shows the same intensity of interest in the complex of love, knowledge, and sight should be John Donne. He too complicates the conventional binary opposition of love and knowledge to intricate and stimulating effect. 'The Ecstasy' threads together many of the ideas we have been considering:

> Our hands were firmly cemented
> With a fast balm, which thence did spring,

> Our eye-beams twisted, and did thread
>   Our eyes, upon one double string;
> So to' intergraft our hands, as yet
>   Was all the means to make us one,
> And pictures in our eyes to get
>   Was all our propagation.[1]

Donne appeals to the eyes to convey a sense of the lovers' quiet rapture, the immediacy of their experience, and their unity, practically a physical union already but simultaneously definitely not such a union. The emphasis upon the eyes helps him achieve this effect. It also leads one readily into the realm of the mind, and Donne follows this possibility. Significantly, in doing so he postulates the presence of a third-party onlooker, who participates in the visual and mental activity:

> If any, so by love refined,
>   That he soul's language understood,
> And by good love were grown all mind,
>   Within convenient distance stood,
>
> He (though he know not which soul spake
>   Because both meant, both spake the same)
> Might thence a new concoction take,
>   And part far purer than he came. (21–28)

The union leads naturally to physical consummation and the ecstasies of the mind become those of the body, again observable to the onlooker who in one sense is integral to the complete drama of the poem:

> To our bodies turn we then, that so
>   Weak men on love revealed may look;
> Love's mysteries in souls do grow,
>   But yet the body is his book. (69–72)

For Donne, the processes of erotic love involve the same array of issues – love, knowledge, sight, self-reflexiveness – as those raised by Chaucer.

The Holy Sonnet 'What if this present were the world's last night?' makes a similar broad appeal to vision and light. It draws spiritual contemplation and insight together with more corporeal considerations in love:

> What if this present were the world's last night?
> Mark in my heart, O soul, where thou dost dwell,

---

1   *John Donne*, ed. John Carey, Oxford, 1990, 5–12.

The picture of Christ crucified, and tell
Whether that countenance can thee affright,
Tears in his eyes quench the amazing light,
Blood fills his frowns, which from his pierced head fell,
And can that tongue adjudge thee unto hell,
Which prayed forgiveness for his foes' fierce spite?
No, no; but as in my idolatry
I said to all my profane mistresses,
Beauty, of pity, foulness only is
A sign of rigour: so I say to thee,
To wicked spirits are horrid shapes assigned,
This beauteous form assures a piteous mind.

The octave is reminiscent of Julian's showings, with its focus on 'The picture of Christ crucified' and consciousness of an 'amazing light.' Probably the speaker only holds this picture in his mind's eye, but it has a solidity that suggests a physical presence. Certainly the sextet conjures up only a memory, but the recollection of idolatry and beauty furthers the appeal to vision in the sonnet and brings together contrasting experiences which find some kind of resolution in 'This beauteous form [that] assures a piteous mind.'

One effect of the confidence in the capacity of poetry evinced by both Chaucer and Donne is an enlarged vision of the nature of love, its resilience, suppleness, and potential to penetrate into every aspect of human endeavor. Where the writer in question incorporates Christian and spiritual ideas of love, as Chaucer and, more explicitly, Donne do, then that vision of a complex and permeating love acquires an additional dimension. Far from simplifying our reading of such poetry, or making it reductive, the inclusion of a spiritual dimension at best explains the source of confidence for engaging with such a far-reaching tension as that between love and knowledge. The tension, along with its various possibilities, remains. As Buber writes, love remains in the tension between actual and potential being. This is Chaucer's achievement. He draws us into a world of actualization and possibility as he works with a convention that will persist in love poetry, and to which he brings the vitality of his widespread learning.

Bibliography

Primary Sources

Adelard of Bath. *Die Quaestiones Naturales Des Adelardus Von Bath*. Ed. Martin Müller. Münster, 1934.

Alan of Lille. *Anticlaudianus*. Ed. R. Bossuat. Paris, 1955.

———. *Anticlaudianus, or The Good and Perfect Man*, Trans. James J. Sheridan. Toronto, 1973.

———. *De planctu Naturae*. Ed. Nikolaus M. Häring. *Studi Medievali* 3rd ser., 19 (1978), 806–79.

———. *Plaint of Nature*. Trans. James J. Sheridan. Toronto, 1980.

Alhazen. *Opticae thesaurus Alhazeni Arabis libri septem, nunc primum editi a Federico Risnero*. Basel, 1572.

Arabian Nights. Ed. and trans. Richard F. Burton. Repr. Beirut, 1966.

Aristotle. *De anima*. Trans. J.A. Smith. In *The Works of Aristotle*. Vol. 3. Ed. W.D. Ross. Oxford, 1931.

Augustine. *Confessiones*. Ed. Martin Skutella with corrections by H. Juergens and W. Schaub. Stuttgart, 1981.

———. *Confessions*. Trans. R.S. Pine-Coffin. London, 1961.

———. *De civitate Dei*. PL 41.

———. *De Genesi ad litteram*. PL 34.

———. *De musica*. PL 32.

———. *De Trinitate*. PL 42.

———. *Epistolae*. PL 33.

———. *In Joannis evangelium (Tractatus CXXIV)*. PL 35.

———. *Letters*. Trans. Wilfrid Parsons. FC 20. New York, 1953.

———. *The Literal Meaning of Genesis*. Trans. J.H. Taylor. ACW 41–2. New York, 1982.

———. *On Music*. Trans. Robert C. Taliaferro. FC 4. New York, 1947.

———. *Tractates on the Gospel of John* 1–27. Trans. John W. Rettig. FC 78–79. Washington, 1988.

———. *The Trinity*. Trans. Stephen McKenna. FC 45. Washington, D.C., 1963.

Bacon, Roger. *The* Opus Majus *of Roger Bacon*. Ed. J.H. Bridges. London, 1900.

———. *Un fragment inédit de l'*Opus Tertium *de Roger Bacon*. Ed. Pierre Duhem. Quaracchi, 1909.

Bartholomaeus Anglicus. *On the Properties of Things: John Trevisa's Translation of Bartholomaeus Anglicus*, De proprietatibus rerum. 3 vols. Ed. M.C. Seymour et al. Oxford, 1975.

Bernard of Clairvaux. *The Life and Works of St Bernard*. Vol. 4. Trans. Samuel J. Eales. London, 1896.

———. *On the Song of Songs*. Trans. Kilian Walsh and Irene Edmonds. Cistercian Fathers. Vols 4, 7, 31, and 40. Kalamazoo, 1971–80.

———. *Opera*. Ed. J. Leclercq et al. Vols 1–3. Rome, 1957.

Biblia sacra iuxta vulgatam. Ed. Robert Weber. Stuttgart, 1969.

Boccaccio, Giovanni. *Il Filostrato.* Ed. and trans. Nathaniel Edward Green and Arthur Beckwith Myrick. Philadelphia, 1929.

Boethius. *The Consolation of Philosophy.* Ed. and trans. S.J. Tester. London, 1973.

Bonaventure. *Opera omnia.* Ed. Berdard a Portu Romatino et al. 10 vols. Quaracchi, 1882–1902.

The Cambridge History of Later Medieval Philosophy. Ed. N. Kretzmann et al. Cambridge, 1982.

Chalcidius. *Timaeus. A Calcidio translatus commentarioque instructus.* Ed. J.H. Waszink. London, 1962.

Chaucer, Geoffrey. *The Riverside Chaucer.* Ed. Larry Benson et al. Oxford, 1987.

———. *Troilus and Criseyde: A New Edition of 'The Book of Troilus.'* Ed. B.A. Windeatt. London, 1984.

Chrétien de Troyes. *Arthurian Romances.* Trans. D.D.R. Owen. London, 1987.

———. *Cligés.* Ed. Alexandre Micha. Les Classiques Français du Moyen Âge. Paris, 1957.

Cicero. *De re publica.* Ed. and trans. C.W. Keyes. London, 1928.

The Cloud of Unknowing. Ed. Phyllis Hodgson. EETS os 218. Oxford, 1944.

Dante Alighieri. *Commedia.* Ed. and trans. John D. Sinclair. Oxford, 1948.

———. *Convivio.* Opere Minore 5. Ed. Cesare Vasoli and Domenico de Robertis. Milan.

———. *Convivio.* Trans. W.W. Jackson. Oxford, 1909.

———. *Vita Nuova.* Ed. Marcello Ciccuto. Milan, 1984.

———. *La Vita Nuova.* Trans. Barbara Reynolds. Harmondsworth, 1969.

Davies, R.T., ed. *Middle English Lyrics.* London, 1963.

Donne, John. *John Donne.* Ed. John Carey. Oxford, 1990.

Dryden, John. *John Dryden.* Ed. Keith Walker. Oxford, 1987.

The English Text of the Ancrene Riwle: Ancrene Wisse, edited from MS Corpus Christi College, Cambridge, 402. Ed. J.R.R. Tolkien. EETS os 249. London, 1962.

Fasciculus morum: A Fourteenth-Century Preacher's Handbook. Ed. and trans. Siegfried Wenzel. University Park, Penn. and London, 1989.

Glossa ordinaria. PL 113.

Grant, Edward, ed. *A Source Book in Medieval Science.* Cambridge, Mass., 1974.

Grosseteste, Robert. *Die philosophischen werke des Robert Grosseteste, bischofs von Lincoln.* Ed. Ludwig Baur. Münster, 1912.

———. *On Light.* Trans. C. Riedl. Milwaukee, 1940.

Guillaume de Lorris and Jean de Meun. *Le Roman de la Rose.* Ed. Daniel Poirion. Paris, 1974.

———. *The Romance of the Rose.* Trans. Harry W. Robbins. New York, 1962.

Guillaume de Deguileville. *Le Pèlerinage de la Vie Humaine.* Ed. J.J. Stürzinger. Roxburghe Club 124. London, 1893.

Guillaume de Machaut. *Jugement dou Roy de Behaingne.* Oeuvres de Guillaume de Machaut. Vol.1. Ed. Ernest Hoepffner. Paris, 1908.

Hali Meiðhad. Ed. Bella Millett. EETS os 284. London, 1982.

The Harley Lyrics: The Middle English Lyrics of MS. Harley 2253. Ed. G.L. Brook. Manchester, 1968.

The Holy Bible. Douay version. London, 1956.

Jerome. 'Adversus Jovinianum.' PL 23.

————. 'Against Jovinian.' Trans. W.H. Fremantle. The Library of Nicene and post-Nicene Christian Fathers. 2nd ser., vol. 6. Oxford, 1893.

Julian of Norwich. *A Book of Showings to the Anchoress Julian of Norwich*. Ed. Edmund Colledge and James Walsh. Toronto, 1978.

Langland, William. *The Vision of Piers Plowman*. A Complete Edition of the B-Text. Ed. A.V.C. Schmidt. London, 1978.

Leonardo da Vinci. *The Notebooks of Leonardo da Vinci*. Ed. E. MacCurdy. London, 1938.

Leon Battista Alberti. *On Painting*. Ed. J.R. Spencer. New Haven, 1966.

Liber de intelligentiis. In *Witelo: Ein Philosoph und Naturforscher des XIII Jahrhunderts*. Ed. Clemens Baeumker. Munster, 1908.

Lucretius. *De rerum natura*. Ed. and trans. W.H.D. Rouse and Martin Ferguson Smith. London and Cambridge, Mass., 1975.

Lydgate, John. *The Pilgrimage of the Life of Man*. Ed. F.J. Furnivall. EETS es 77, 83, and 92. London, 1899–1904.

Macrobius. *Commentariorum in Somnium Scipionis libri duo*. Ed. and trans. Luigi Scarpa. Padua, 1981.

————. *Commentary on the Dream of Scipio*. Trans. William Harris Stahl. New York and London, 1952.

Middle English Dictionary. Ed. Hans Kurath, Sherman M. Kuhn, et al. Ann Arbor, 1956–.

Middle English Sermons from MS Royal 18.B.23. Ed. Woodburn O. Ross. EETS os 209. London, 1940.

Miller, Robert P., ed. *Chaucer: Sources and Backgrounds*. New York, 1977.

Milton, John. *John Milton*. Ed. Stephen Orgel and Jonathan Goldberg. Oxford, 1991.

O'Donoghue, Bernard, ed. *The Courtly Love Tradition*. Oxford, 1982.

Ovid. *The Amores*. Ed. and trans. Grant Showerman. London and Cambridge, Mass., 1947.

Pearl. Ed. E.V. Gordon. Oxford, 1953.

[Peter of Limoges.] *Johannis Pithsani archiepiscopi Canthuariensis liber de oculo morali foeliciter incipit*. Augsburg, 1475.

Plato. *Phaedrus*. Ed. and trans. Harold North Fowler. London, 1953.

————. *Timaeus*. Ed. and trans. R.G. Bury. London, 1961.

Plotinus. *The Enneads*. Ed. and trans. A.H. Armstrong. London, 1984.

Pseudo-Dionysius. *The Complete Works*. Trans. Colm Luibheid. London, 1987.

Raby, F.J.E., ed. *The Oxford Book of Medieval Latin Verse*. Oxford, 1959.

Rolle, Richard. *English Writings of Richard Rolle, Hermit of Hampole*. Ed. Hope Emily Allen. Oxford, 1931.

Thomas Aquinas. *Summa theologiae*. In *Opera omnia*. Ed. Robert Busa et al. Stuttgart, 1980.

————. *The 'Summa theologica' of St. Thomas Aquinas*. Trans. Fathers of the English Dominican Province. London, 1914.

Vincent of Beauvais. *Speculum quadruplex sive Speculum maius*. Graz, Austria, 1964 (Douai, 1624).

Wack, Mary Frances. *Lovesickness in the Middle Ages: The* Viaticum *and its Commentaries*. Pennsylvania, 1990.

William of Ockham. *Opera philosophica et theologica ad fidem codicum manuscriptorum edita*. Ed. Gedeon Gál et al. St. Bonaventure, 1967–85.

William of St Thierry. *Epistola ad fratres de Monte-Dei*. Ed. M.-M. Davy. Paris, 1940.
———. *The Golden Epistle*. Trans. Walter Shewring. London, 1980 (first published 1930).
Windeatt, Barry, ed. *Chaucer's Dream Poetry: Sources and Analogues*. Cambridge, 1982.
Witelo. *Witelo: Ein Philosoph und Naturforscher des XIII Jahrhunderts*. Ed. Clemens Baeumker. Munster, 1908.
Wyclif, John. *Tractatus de benedicta incarnacione*. Ed. Edward Harris. London, 1886.

Secondary Sources
Badel, Pierre-Yves. Le Roman de la Rose *au XIVe Siècle: étude de la réception de l' œvre*. Geneva, 1980.
Bennett, J.A.W. *Chaucer at Oxford and at Cambridge*. Oxford, 1974.
Benson, Donald R. 'The Marriage "Encomium" in the Merchant's Tale: A Chaucerian Crux,' *Chaucer Review* 14 (1979), 48–60.
Blamires, A. 'A Chaucer Manifesto,' *Chaucer Review* 24 (1989), 29–44.
Bloomfield, Morton. 'Chaucer's Realism.' In *The Cambridge Chaucer Companion*. Ed. Pietro Boitani and Jill Mann. Cambridge, 1986, 179–93.
Boase, Roger. *The Origin and Meaning of Courtly Love: a critical study of European scholarship*. Manchester, 1977.
Brown, Emerson jr. 'Biblical Women in the Merchant's Tale: Feminism, Antifeminism, and Beyond,' *Viator* 5 (1974), 387–412.
Brown, Peter. 'An Optical Theme in *The Merchant's Tale.*' In *Studies in the Age of Chaucer*, Proceedings 1, 1984: Reconstructing Chaucer. Ed. Paul Strohm and Thomas J. Heffernan. Knoxville, 1985, 231–43.
———. 'Chaucer's Visual World: A Study of His Poetry and the Medieval Optical Tradition.' Doctoral dissertation. York University, York, England, 1981.
———. 'The Containment of Symkyn: The Function of Space in the *Reeve's Tale*,' *Chaucer Review* 14 (1979–80), 225–36.
Brownlee, Kevin. *Poetic Identity in Guillaume de Machaut*. Madison, 1984.
Brümmer, Vincent. *The Model of Love: A Study in Philosophical Theology*. Cambridge, 1993.
Buber, Martin. *I and Thou*. Trans. R.G. Smith. Edinburgh, 1959.
Burnley, J.D. '*Fine Amor*: Its Meaning and Context,' *Review of English Studies* n.s. 3 (1980), 129–48.
Carruthers, Mary J. *The Book of Memory: A Study of Memory in Medieval Culture*. Cambridge, 1990.
Cawley, A.C. and J.J. Anderson. 'Introduction.' In *Pearl, Cleanness, Patience, Sir Gawain and the Green Knight*. Ed. A.C. Cawley and J.J. Anderson. London, 1976, vii–xxviii.
Chenu, Marie-Dominique. *Nature, Man, and Society in the Twelfth Century*. Ed. and trans. Jerome Taylor and Lester Little. Chicago, 1968.
Cherniss, Michael D. 'The *Clerk's Tale* and Envoy, the Wife of Bath's *Prologue*, and the *Merchant's Tale*,' *Chaucer Review* 6 (1971–2), 235–54.
Clagett, Marshall. *The Science of Mechanics in the Middle Ages*. Wisconsin, 1961.
Clark, David L. 'Optics for Preachers: the *De oculo morali* by Peter of Limoges,' *The Michigan Academician* 9 (1977), 329–43.

Cline, Ruth H. 'Heart and Eyes,' *Romance Philology* 25 (1972), 263–97.

Coleman, Janet. *Ancient and Medieval Memories: Studies in the Reconstruction of the Past.* Cambridge, 1992.

Constable, Giles. 'The Popularity of Twelfth-Century Spiritual Writers in the Late Middle Ages.' In *Renaissance Studies in Honor of Hans Baron.* Ed. Anthony Molho and John A. Tedeschi. De Kalb, Ill., 1971, 3–28.

Cooper, Helen. *Oxford Guides to Chaucer: The Canterbury Tales.* Oxford, 1989.

Courtenay, William. '*Antiqui* and *Moderni* in Late Medieval Thought,' *Journal of the History of Ideas* 48 (1987), 3–10.

———. 'Between Despair and Love. Some Late Medieval Modifications of Augustine's Teaching on Fruition and Psychic States.' In *Augustine, the Harvest, and Theology (1300–1650).* Ed. Kenneth Hagen. Leiden, 1990, 5–20.

———. 'Nominalism and Late Medieval Religion.' In *The Pursuit of Holiness in Late Medieval and Renaissance Religion.* Ed. Charles Trinkaus with Heiko Oberman. Leiden, 1974, 26–58.

———. *Schools and Scholars in Fourteenth-Century England.* Princeton, 1987.

Crombie, A.C. *Robert Grosseteste and the Origins of Experimental Science 1100–1700.* Oxford, 1953.

Curry, Walter Clyde. *Chaucer and the Mediaeval Sciences.* New York, 1926.

Davis, Charles T. 'Ockham and the Zeitgeist.' In *The Pursuit of Holiness in Late Medieval and Renaissance Religion.* Ed. Charles Trinkaus with Heiko Oberman. Leiden, 1974, 59–65.

Davis, Norman. 'Review of J.A.W. Bennett, *Chaucer at Oxford and at Cambridge,*' *The Review of English Studies* ns 27 (1976), 336–7.

De Bruyne, Edgar. *Études d'Esthétique médiévale.* 3 vols. Bruges, 1946.

Delany, Sheila. *Chaucer's* House of Fame*: The Poetics of Skeptical Fideism.* Chicago, 1972.

Donaldson-Evans, Lance K. 'Love's Fatal Glance: Eye Imagery and Maurice Scève's Délie,' *Neophilologus* 62 (1978), 202–11.

Dronke, Peter. *Medieval Latin and the Rise of the European Love Lyric.* 2 vols. Oxford, 1965.

Eastwood, Bruce. 'Medieval Empiricism: The Case of Grosseteste's Optics,' *Speculum* 43 (1968), 306–21.

Eberle, Patricia J. 'The Lovers' Glass: Nature's Discourse on Optics and the Optical Design of the *Romance of the Rose,*' *University of Toronto Quarterly* 46 (1977), 241–62.

Eco, Umberto. *The Aesthetics of Thomas Aquinas.* Trans. Hugh Bredin. Cambridge, Mass., 1988.

———. *Art and Beauty in the Middle Ages.* Trans. Hugh Bredin. New Haven, 1986.

Edwards, Robert R. *The Dream of Chaucer: Representation and Reflection in the Early Narratives.* Durham and London, 1989.

Eldredge, Laurence. 'Chaucer's *Hous of Fame* and the Via Moderna,' *Neuphilologische Mitteilungen* 71 (1970), 105–19.

Ferrante, Joan M. and G.D. Economou, ed. *In Pursuit of Perfection.* Port Washington, 1975.

Field, P.J.C. 'Chaucer's Merchant and the Sin Against Nature,' *N&Q* n.s. 17 (1970), 84–6.

Frost, William. 'An Interpretation of Chaucer's Knight's Tale,' *RES* 25 (1949), 289–304.

Grabes, Herbert. *The Mutable Glass: Mirror imagery in titles and texts of the Middle Ages and English Renaissance*. Trans. Gordon Collier. Cambridge, 1982.

Grant, Edward. 'The Condemnation of 1277, God's Absolute Power, and Physical Thought in the Late Middle Ages,' *Viator* 10 (1979), 211–44.

———. 'Science and Theology in the Middle Ages.' In *God and Nature*. Ed. David C. Lindberg et al. Berkeley, 1986, 49–75.

Gray, Douglas. '*Of Sunne Ne Mone Had Thay No Nede*: Notes on the Imagery of Light in a Middle English Text.' In *Essays in Honor of Edward B. King*. Ed. R.G. Benson and E.W. Naylor. Sewanee, 1991, 85–108.

Gunn, Alan. *The Mirror of Love*. Lubbock, 1952.

Hagen, Susan K. *Allegorical Remembrance: A Study of* The Pilgrimage of the Life of Man *as a Medieval Treatise on Seeing and Remembering*. Athens, Ga., 1990.

Hahm, David. 'Early Hellenistic Theories of Vision and the Perception of Color.' In *Studies in Perception*. Ed. Peter K. Machamer and Robert G. Turnbull. Columbus, 1978, 60–95.

Holley, Linda Tarte. *Chaucer's Measuring Eye*. Houston, 1990.

Huizinga, J. *The Waning of the Middle Ages*. Trans. F. Hopman. Harmondsworth, 1924.

Hult, David F. *Self-fulfilling Prophecies: Readership and Authority in the First* Roman de la Rose. Cambridge, 1986.

Hunt, Tony. 'Irony and the Rise of Courtly Romance,' *German Life and Letters* n.s. 35 (1981), 98–104.

Jonas, Hans. 'The Nobility of Sight: A Study in the Phenomenology of the Senses,' *Philosophy and Phenomenological Research* 14 (1954), 507–19.

Kaulbach, Ernest N. *Imaginative Prophecy in the B-Text of* Piers Plowman. Cambridge, 1993.

Kelly, Douglas. *Medieval Imagination: Rhetoric and the Poetry of Courtly Love*. Madison, 1978.

Kelly, Henry. 'Gaston Paris's Courteous and Horsely Love.' In *The Spirit of the Court*. Ed. G.S. Burgess and R.A. Taylor. Cambridge, 1985, 217–23.

Klassen, Norman. 'Optical Allusions and Chaucerian Realism: Aspects of Sight in Late Medieval Thought and *Troilus and Criseyde*,' *Stanford Humanities Review* 2 (1992), 129–46.

Kolve, V.A. *Chaucer and the Imagery of Narrative: The First Five* Canterbury Tales. London, 1984.

Kretzmann, N. et al., ed. *The Cambridge History of Later Medieval Philosophy*. Cambridge, 1982.

Krier, Theresa M. *Gazing on Secret Sights: Spenser, Classical Imitation, and the Decorums of Vision*. Ithaca and London, 1990.

Kruger, Steven F. *Dreaming in the Middle Ages*. Cambridge, 1992.

Kubovy, Michael. *The Psychology of Perspective and Renaissance Art*. Cambridge, 1986.

Leclercq, Jean. *The Love of Learning and the Desire for God: A Study of Monastic Culture*, 2nd ed. Trans. Catharine Misrahi. London, 1978.

Leff, Gordon. *William of Ockham*. New York, 1975.

Lewis, C.S. *The Allegory of Love*. Oxford, 1936.

———. *The Discarded Image*. Cambridge, 1964.

Lindberg, David. *Theories of Optics from al-Kindi to Kepler*. Chicago, 1977.

———. 'The Science of Optics.' In his *Studies in the History of Medieval Optics*. London, 1983, I, 338–68.

Lynch, Kathryn L. *The High Medieval Dream Vision*. Stanford, 1988.

Lynch, Lawrence. 'The Doctrine of Divine Ideas and Illumination in Robert Grosseteste, Bishop of Lincoln,' *Medieval Studies* 3 (1941), 161–73.

McEvoy, James. *The Philosophy of Robert Grosseteste*. Oxford, 1982.

McGrade, Arthur Stephen. 'Enjoyment at Oxford after Ockham: Philosophy, Psychology, and the Love of God.' In *From Ockham to Wyclif: Studies in Church History*. Subsidia 5. Ed. Anne Hudson and Michael Wilks. Oxford, 1987, 63–88.

MacIntyre, Alasdair. *After Virtue: A Study in Moral Theory*. London, 1985.

Matthews, Gareth B. 'A Medieval Theory of Vision.' In *Studies in Perception*. Ed. Peter K. Machamer and Robert G. Turnbull. Columbus, 1978, 186–99.

Mazzeo, Joseph Anthony. 'Light Metaphysics, Dante's 'Convivio' and the Letter to Can Grande Della Scala,' *Traditio* 14 (1958), 191–229.

Michaud-Quantin, Pierre. 'Les Champs Semantiques de *Species*. Tradition Latine et Traductions du Grec.' In *Études Sur Le Vocabulaire Philosophique du Moyen Age*. Ed. Pierre Michaud-Quantin et al. Rome, 1970, 113–50.

Miller, James. 'Three Mirrors of Dante's *Paradiso*,' *University of Toronto Quarterly* 46 (1977), 263–79.

Morgan, Joseph. 'Chaucer and the *Bona Matrimonii*,' *Chaucer Review* 4 (1970), 123–41.

Muscatine, Charles. 'Form, Texture, and Meaning in Chaucer's *Knight's Tale*,' *PMLA* 65 (1950), 911–29.

———. 'Locus of Action in Medieval Narrative,' *Romance Philology* 17 (1963), 115–22.

Neuss, Paula. '*Double-Entendre* in *The Miller's Tale*,' *Essays in Criticism* 24 (1974), 325–40.

Newhauser, Richard. 'Augustinian *vitium curiositatis* and its reception.' In *St Augustine and His Influence in the Middle Ages*. Ed. Edward B. King and J.T. Schaefer. Sewanee, 1988, 99–124.

Newman, F.X., ed. *The Meaning of Courtly Love*. Albany, 1968.

North, J.D. *Chaucer's Universe*. Oxford, 1988.

Nolan, Edward Peter. *Now Through A Glass Darkly: Specular Images of Being and Knowing from Virgil to Chaucer*. Ann Arbor, 1991.

Nygren, Anders. *Agape and Eros*. Trans. Philip S. Watson. London, 1953.

Oberman, Heiko. 'The Shape of Late Medieval Thought: The Birthpangs of the Modern Era.' In *The Pursuit of Holiness in Late Medieval and Renaissance Religion*. Ed. Charles Trinkaus with Heiko Oberman. Leiden, 1974, 3–25.

Ogle, M.B. 'The Classical Origin and Tradition of Literary Conceits,' *American Journal of Philology* 34 (1913), 125–52.

Olson, Glending. 'Chaucer, Dante, and the Structure of Fragment VIII (G) of the *Canterbury Tales*,' *Chaucer Review* 16 (1982), 222–36.

Otten, Charlotte F. 'Proserpina: *Libiatrix Suae Gentis*,' *Chaucer Review* 5 (1971), 277–87.

Patterson, Lee. *Negotiating the Past: The Historical Understanding of Medieval Literature*. Madison, 1987.

Peck, Russell. 'Chaucer and the Nominalist Questions,' *Speculum* 53 (1978), 745–60.

Pelikan, Jaroslav. 'The Odyssey of Dionysian Spirituality.' In Pseudo-Dionysius. *The Complete Works*. Trans. Colm Luibheid. London, 1987, 11–24.

Phillips, Heather. 'John Wyclif and the Optics of the Eucharist.' In *From Ockham to Wyclif, Studies in Church History*. Subsidia 5. Ed. Anne Hudson and Michael Wilks. Oxford, 1987, 245–58.

Poirion, Daniel. 'The Imaginary Universe of Guillaume de Machaut.' In *Machaut's World*. Ed. Madeleine Pelner Cosman et al. New York, 1978, 199–206.

Pratt, Robert A. 'Jankyn's Book of Wikked Wyves: Medieval Anti-matrimonial Propaganda in the Universities,' *Annuale Mediaevale* 3 (1962), 5–28.

Robertson, D.W. *A Preface to Chaucer*. Princeton, 1962.

Sage, Athanase. 'La dialectique de l'illumination,' *Recherches Augustiniennes* 2 (1962), 111–23.

Serres, Michel. *Le Parasite*. Paris, 1980.

———. *The Parasite*. Trans. Lawrence R. Schehr. Baltimore, 1982.

Smith, Nathaniel B. and J.T. Snow, ed. *The Expansion and Transformation of Courtly Literature*. Athens, Ga., 1980.

Southern, R.W. *Medieval Humanism and Other Studies*. Oxford, 1970.

———. *Robert Grosseteste: The Growth of an English Mind in Medieval Europe*, 2nd ed. Oxford, 1992.

Spargo, E.M.J. *The Category of the Aesthetic in the Philosophy of St. Bonaventura*. St. Bonaventura, 1953.

Spearing, A.C. *Medieval Dream-Poetry*. Cambridge, 1976.

———. *The Medieval Poet as Voyeur: Looking and Listening in Medieval Love-Narratives*. Cambridge, 1993.

———. 'The Medieval Poet as Voyeur.' In *The Olde Daunce: Love, Friendship, Sex, and Marriage in the Medieval World*. Ed. Robert R. Edwards and Stephen Spector. New York, 1991, 57–86.

Spurgeon, Caroline F.E. *Five Hundred Years of Chaucer Criticism and Allusion 1357–1900*. Vol. 1. Cambridge, 1925.

Stanbury, Sarah. *Seeing the* Gawain-*Poet: Description and the Act of Perception*. Philadelphia, 1991.

Sylla, Edith. 'Medieval Quantifications of Qualities: The 'Merton School,'' *Archive for the History of Exact Sciences* 8 (1971), 9–39.

Tachau, Katherine. *Vision and Certitude in the Age of Ockham: Optics, Epistemology and the Foundation of Semantics 1250–1345*. Leiden, 1988.

Thonnard, François-Joseph. 'La notion de lumière en philosophie augustinienne,' *Recherches Augustiniennes* 2 (1962), 125–75.

Thorndike, Lynn. *A History of Magic and Experimental Science*. Vol. 3. New York, 1934.

Tugwell, Simon. 'Dominican Spirituality, Dominicans.' In *A Dictionary of Christian Spirituality*. Ed. Gordon S. Wakefield. London, 1983, 119–20.

Wack, Mary Frances. *Lovesickness in the Middle Ages: The* Viaticum *and its Commentaries*. Pennsylvania, 1990.

Wasserman, Julian N. 'The Ideal and the Actual: The Philosophical Unity of *Canterbury Tales,* MS. Group III,' *Allegorica* 7 (1982), 65–99.

Williams, Rowan. *The Wound of Knowledge,* 2nd ed. London, 1990.

Wolfson, Harry A. 'The Internal Senses in Latin, Arabic, and Hebrew Philosophical Texts,' *Harvard Theological Review* 28 (1935), 69–113.

Wright, N.T. *The New Testament and the People of God*. London, 1992.

Index